Contents

Mastering Amazon Aurora: Architecting Scalable, Highly Available Cloud Databases on AWS

Part I: Foundations

Chapter 1: Introduction to Amazon Aurora

Amazon Aurora is a fully managed, cloud-native relational database engine that combines the performance and availability of high-end commercial databases with the simplicity and cost-effectiveness of open-source databases. Designed for scalability, durability, and high performance, Aurora is offered in two variants: **Aurora MySQL-Compatible Edition** and **Aurora PostgreSQL-Compatible Edition**, making it easy for developers to migrate existing applications.

What is Aurora?

Amazon Aurora is part of the Amazon Relational Database Service (RDS) family. It provides a robust relational database engine that is compatible with both MySQL and PostgreSQL. Aurora has been architected from the ground up for the cloud, enabling advanced capabilities that go beyond traditional databases running on-premises or even on EC2.

Core Characteristics of Amazon Aurora:

- **Managed Service**: No need to provision, patch, or manage hardware or database software.

- **MySQL and PostgreSQL Compatible**: Run your existing MySQL or PostgreSQL applications with little to no change.

- **High Performance**: Delivers up to 5x the throughput of standard MySQL and 3x that of standard PostgreSQL on the same hardware.

- **Highly Available and Durable**: Six copies of your data are automatically replicated across three Availability Zones (AZs).

- **Auto-scaling Storage**: Storage automatically grows from 10 GB up to 128 TB.

- **Global Databases**: Low-latency global reads and disaster recovery across regions.

- **Pay-as-you-go Pricing**: Only pay for what you use, with on-demand or reserved pricing options.

- **Serverless and Provisioned Options**: Flexibility to use Aurora in a serverless mode (Aurora Serverless v2) or with provisioned instances.

Aurora leverages distributed, fault-tolerant, self-healing storage that auto-scales, and is integrated with AWS services such as IAM, CloudWatch, Secrets Manager, and Lambda for security, observability, and automation.

Key Differentiators from Traditional Databases

Amazon Aurora stands apart from traditional on-premise or cloud-hosted databases due to a combination of architectural innovations, automation, and tight AWS ecosystem integration.

1. Cloud-native Architecture

- Aurora's storage engine decouples compute from storage, allowing independent scaling and automatic failover.

- Distributed storage spans multiple AZs by default, providing fault tolerance without RAID setups or manual replication.

2. Performance and Throughput

- **Aurora MySQL** delivers up to 5x the throughput of standard MySQL.

- **Aurora PostgreSQL** provides up to 3x the performance of standard PostgreSQL.

- Uses a purpose-built log-structured distributed storage engine optimized for high I/O workloads.

3. High Availability and Durability

- Data is replicated six ways across three Availability Zones.

- Automatic failover typically completes in under 30 seconds.

- Support for Multi-AZ deployments and cross-region read replicas.

4. Auto-scaling and Elasticity

- Aurora automatically adjusts storage capacity as your data grows.

- Aurora Serverless v2 provides on-demand autoscaling of compute, ideal for unpredictable or intermittent workloads.

5. Fully Managed and Integrated

- Patching, backups, software updates, failover, and recovery are handled automatically.

- Integrated with AWS services: IAM, KMS, CloudWatch, CloudTrail, and Lambda.

- Supports Blue/Green deployments for seamless updates and zero-downtime testing.

6. Security Built-in

- Data is encrypted in transit and at rest using AWS KMS.

- Supports VPC, IAM-based authentication, and audit logging.

- Offers advanced access control and network isolation.

7. Aurora Global Database

- Cross-region replication with low-latency reads.

- Designed for globally distributed applications.

- Provides up to five read replicas per region with a lag of typically under a second.

8. Cost Optimization

- Pay only for what you use.

- Choice between on-demand and reserved pricing.

- Serverless mode reduces cost for variable workloads.

Use Cases and Customer Success Stories

Aurora is trusted by organizations of all sizes for a wide variety of use cases. Its flexibility and performance make it suitable for both new cloud-native applications and existing enterprise workloads.

Common Use Cases

1. **Web and Mobile Applications**

    o   Use Aurora as a backend for apps with varying workloads and scale requirements.

    o   Integrates easily with APIs, SDKs, and serverless functions.

2. **Enterprise Applications**

    o   Migrate legacy databases to Aurora for better performance and reduced operational overhead.

    o   Run ERP, CRM, and financial systems.

3. **Software as a Service (SaaS)**

    o   Multi-tenant, secure, and scalable backend for SaaS platforms.

    o   Aurora Serverless v2 allows cost savings for customer-based workload patterns.

4. **Analytics and Reporting**

    o   Integrate with Amazon Redshift, S3, and QuickSight for analytical processing.

- Use Zero-ETL integrations for near-real-time data movement to data lakes.

5. Disaster Recovery and High Availability

- Aurora Global Database provides cross-region DR.

- Automated failover ensures business continuity.

6. AI and Machine Learning

- Run inferences directly within SQL queries using **Aurora ML** integrated with Amazon SageMaker.

- Feature engineering and real-time model predictions.

Customer Success Stories

1. Expedia Group

- Migrated from self-managed MySQL databases to Aurora MySQL.

- Reduced failover time from minutes to seconds.

- Gained scalability and eliminated the need for manual database sharding.

2. Samsung Electronics

- Uses Aurora PostgreSQL for their global content management system.

- Benefited from Aurora's high performance and global replication features.

- Achieved latency under 1 second between regions.

3. Blackboard

- Migrated its learning management system to Aurora PostgreSQL.

- Realized better performance with fewer resources.

- Increased uptime and reduced maintenance costs.

4. Dow Jones

- Runs real-time analytics workloads using Aurora with Zero-ETL integration to Redshift.

- Enabled real-time business insights while reducing data pipeline complexity.

5. Zynga

- Scaled Aurora Serverless v2 to handle dynamic gaming workloads.

- Saved costs by automatically scaling down during low-traffic periods.

Best Practices and Tips

- **Choose the right instance type** based on your workload (e.g., memory-optimized vs. general purpose).

- **Use Aurora Serverless v2** for applications with spiky or intermittent workloads.

- **Enable Performance Insights** for SQL tuning and monitoring.

- **Leverage Aurora Global Database** for read scaling and low-latency DR across regions.

- **Use IAM database authentication** to eliminate hardcoded credentials.

- **Automate backups and patching** to ensure compliance and reduce administrative burden.

Summary

Amazon Aurora redefines the expectations of what a relational database can achieve in the cloud. By fusing the scalability and availability of modern distributed systems with the familiarity of SQL-based engines, it empowers organizations to innovate faster while lowering costs and complexity. Whether you're building new microservices or migrating legacy enterprise apps, Aurora is designed to meet the needs of demanding production workloads at scale.

Chapter 2. Aurora vs Traditional RDS and Other Databases

Amazon Aurora is a fully managed relational database engine offered by Amazon Web Services (AWS), designed for high performance and availability. While it is compatible with both MySQL and PostgreSQL, Aurora brings a fundamentally different architecture that provides significant benefits over traditional RDS offerings and other database systems.

In this chapter, we'll walk through detailed, structured comparisons between Aurora and:

- Traditional Amazon RDS MySQL/PostgreSQL

- NoSQL and analytical engines like DynamoDB and Redshift

- Commercial databases such as Oracle and SQL Server

Each section explores how Aurora differs in architecture, scalability, performance, cost, availability, and operational overhead.

Aurora vs RDS MySQL/PostgreSQL

Architecture and Design

- **Aurora** decouples compute and storage. It uses a distributed and fault-tolerant storage layer that replicates data across multiple Availability Zones (AZs).

- **Traditional RDS MySQL/PostgreSQL** uses attached EBS volumes per instance. Each database instance is tightly coupled with its storage.

Key differences:

- Aurora storage automatically grows in 10GB increments up to 128TB without downtime.

- RDS storage must be manually provisioned, and resizing typically involves downtime.

Performance

- **Aurora** delivers up to 5x the throughput of standard MySQL and up to 3x for PostgreSQL due to:

  - Optimized query processing

  - Faster commit and recovery paths

  - Low-latency quorum-based writes across AZs

- **RDS MySQL/PostgreSQL** performance depends on EBS IOPS and engine configuration, and may have more variable performance under load.

Benchmarks (Typical AWS-provided figures):

- Aurora MySQL: 70–80% of transactions are completed in less than 1ms.

- RDS MySQL/PostgreSQL has higher latencies for comparable workloads.

Availability and Durability

- Aurora automatically replicates every 10GB of your data six ways across three AZs.

- With **RDS**, Multi-AZ deployments maintain one standby replica in another AZ for failover.

Aurora Advantages:

- No need for crash recovery or failover delays— Aurora's distributed storage can promote a new writer within ~30 seconds.

- Survivable page cache and auto-repair of storage segments.

Replication

- **Aurora Replicas** (reader nodes) support high-speed replication (under 100ms lag typically) and auto-scaling.

- **RDS Read Replicas** use asynchronous replication, which may experience higher lag.

Aurora Supports:

- Up to 15 reader nodes

- Cross-region replication

- Global databases with <1s replication lag

Cost and Licensing

- Aurora uses a **pay-as-you-go** pricing model with separate billing for compute and I/O.

- RDS offers similar pricing but is less efficient in storage use and I/O.

Aurora Cost Optimizations:

- Serverless v2 offers fine-grained autoscaling based on load.

- Intelligent tiering of backups and snapshots.

Manageability and Operations

- **Aurora** has enhanced automation, including:

  - Zero-downtime patching (ZDP)

- Blue/Green deployments

- Performance Insights and Advanced Monitoring

- RDS requires more manual handling for upgrades and may have longer patch windows.

Use Cases Where Aurora Outperforms

- Applications requiring high availability across AZs

- SaaS platforms with unpredictable workloads

- Multi-tenant architectures needing fast cloning and scalability

---

Aurora vs DynamoDB and Redshift

Aurora vs DynamoDB

Category	Aurora	DynamoDB
Model	Relational	NoSQL (key-value/document)
Consistency	Strong (ACID)	Eventual/strong (configurable)
Schema	Strict schemas with SQL	Schema-less

Query Language	SQL (PostgreSQL/MySQL dialect)	PartiQL or native API
Performance	Optimized for relational workloads	Sub-millisecond for key-value lookups
Scalability	Vertical & read-replica scaling	Horizontal scaling with global tables
Transactions	Full multi-statement SQL transactions	ACID transactions supported but limited
Use Case Fit	OLTP applications needing joins, foreign keys	Real-time apps, IoT, serverless apps

Key Considerations:

- DynamoDB is ideal for **high-scale, low-latency lookups**, not complex joins or reporting.

- Aurora supports **relational integrity**, ideal for ERP, CRM, and financial systems.

Trade-offs:

- Aurora gives better analytics and relational querying.

- DynamoDB simplifies scaling but can be more costly and complex when using features like DAX or Global Tables.

Aurora vs Redshift

Category	Aurora	Redshift
Engine Type	OLTP	OLAP (columnar storage)
Workload Focus	Transactional workloads	Analytical workloads
Query Types	Row-level updates, high concurrency	Complex aggregations, joins over large datasets
Scaling	Instance-based + Aurora Replicas	Massively parallel processing (MPP)
Data Storage	Row-oriented	Columnar-oriented
Integrations	Aurora ML, Lambda, App services	BI tools, Data Lake, ML
Concurrency Scaling	Reader endpoints, Serverless	Dedicated concurrency scaling

Key Differences:

- Use **Aurora** for operational systems like e-commerce apps.

- Use **Redshift** for **data warehouses**, reporting, and dashboarding.

Tip: With Aurora Zero-ETL integration, Redshift can now consume data from Aurora in near real-time—enabling hybrid transactional-analytical processing.

Aurora vs Commercial Databases (Oracle, SQL Server)

Architecture and Ecosystem

- Aurora is **cloud-native** with a distributed storage layer, automatic backups, and no need for complex licensing.

- Oracle and SQL Server are **monolithic** and originally designed for on-premises, though they can run on AWS via RDS or EC2.

Comparison Overview:

Category	Aurora	Oracle	SQL Server
Deployment	Fully managed on AWS	Managed via RDS or EC2	Managed via RDS or EC2
Storage	Auto-scaling, fault-tolerant	Manually provisioned	Manually provisioned

Licensing	Open source or Aurora-proprietary	Expensive, per-core or named user	Per-core or CAL-based
HA Options	Multi-AZ, Global DB, Replicas	Data Guard, RAC (complex)	Always On (enterprise)
Backup/Restore	Continuous, point-in-time	RMAN, more complex	Native tools or third-party
Security	IAM, KMS, SSL, Audit	Advanced but complex	Integrated with AD, TDE

Migration and Compatibility

- **Aurora MySQL/PostgreSQL** can be used as drop-in replacements for applications written for MySQL or PostgreSQL.

- For Oracle/SQL Server migrations, AWS provides **Database Migration Service (DMS)** and **Schema Conversion Tool (SCT)**.

Aurora Migration Benefits:

- Lower cost

- No licensing lock-in

- Integrated monitoring and management

- Simpler high availability and failover

Limitations to Consider:

- Aurora doesn't support Oracle-specific features like PL/SQL packages, RAC, or proprietary data types.

- SQL Server features like CLR, SSRS, or SQL Agent jobs may need re-architecture.

Real-World Migration Scenarios

- **Oracle to Aurora PostgreSQL**: Suitable for enterprise workloads seeking to modernize and reduce cost. Common in fintech and logistics.

- **SQL Server to Aurora MySQL**: Used in retail and content management platforms where licensing costs and scalability become constraints.

Summary of Key Differentiators

Feature	Aurora	RDS	DynamoDB	Redshift	Oracle / SQL Server
Architecture	Cloud-native	Traditional VM	Serverless NoSQL	MPP warehouse	Monolithic legacy
Storage	Auto-scaling, multi-AZ	Fixed EBS	SSD partitions	Managed columnar	Manual
Performance	High throughput	Moderate	Fast (key-value)	High (analytics)	Variable
Pricing	Usage-based	Usage-based	On-demand / reserved	Reserved / concurrent	License-based
Schema	Relational	Relational	Schema-less	Columnar relational	Relational
Language	SQL	SQL	API / PartiQL	SQL (BI)	SQL / PL/SQL / T-SQL
Scaling	Vert. + horiz.	Vertical	Horizontal	Horizontal	Vertical

Best For	Modern apps, HA	Simple apps	IoT, mobile, gaming	Dashboards, analytics	Enterprise legacy workloads

---

Best Practices for Choosing Aurora Over Alternatives

- **Choose Aurora** when:

    - You require managed, highly available SQL databases.

    - You want to avoid vendor lock-in from Oracle or SQL Server.

    - You need global distribution and fast read performance.

    - You prefer open standards and lower TCO.

- **Stick with RDS or Others** when:

    - You have lightweight or legacy applications with minimal change tolerance.

    - You need advanced features only available in Oracle or SQL Server.

    - You're building analytics-heavy workloads better suited for Redshift.

Final Thoughts

Amazon Aurora fills a strategic position in the AWS database ecosystem. It bridges the gap between traditional RDS databases and purpose-built engines like DynamoDB and Redshift. Aurora is especially powerful for organizations looking to modernize legacy applications, reduce licensing costs, and build scalable, cloud-native architectures.

Whether you're an architect planning a migration or a developer building a high-performance app, Aurora's blend of managed operations, high throughput, and seamless integrations make it a compelling choice over traditional RDS and other database engines.

Chapter 3. Aurora Architecture Overview

Storage Engine and Distributed Log Architecture

Amazon Aurora's architecture was built from the ground up to take advantage of the elasticity, scalability, and reliability of the cloud. One of its most distinctive features is the **separation of compute and storage**, enabled by a highly distributed storage engine designed to deliver fault-tolerant, low-latency access to data.

Architecture Principles

Aurora's core architectural principles revolve around the following:

- **Separation of concerns**: Compute and storage functions are separated to allow independent scaling and recovery.

- **Distributed logging**: Aurora logs every change to durable distributed storage, minimizing write latency and enabling faster crash recovery.

- **Quorum-based writes**: Writes are committed using a quorum protocol to ensure consistency and availability.

- **Optimized reads**: Read replicas and reader endpoints allow horizontal read scaling with low replication lag.

Distributed Storage Engine

Aurora's storage engine is built on a **highly distributed, log-structured design**. It manages a **shared cluster volume** across multiple Availability Zones (AZs), which is one of the reasons behind Aurora's high availability and durability.

Key characteristics:

- **6-way replication**: Every 10GB data segment (called a protection group) is replicated across **three AZs** with **two copies per AZ**.

- **Segmented and sharded storage**: The cluster volume is divided into hundreds of 10GB protection groups that can independently be written to, read from, or recovered.

- **Quorum-based writes**: To write data, Aurora only needs a quorum of four out of six storage nodes to acknowledge the change, providing high availability without sacrificing write performance.

- **Redo logging and no double writes**: Traditional databases write to the transaction log and then to the data file. Aurora only writes the redo log to storage, reducing I/O and write amplification.

Distributed Log-Based Replication

Instead of traditional page-based replication, Aurora employs **redo log shipping**, which provides several performance and recovery advantages:

- Replicas apply redo logs rather than full page changes.

- Enables **faster failover and crash recovery**, as the redo logs are already present in the storage layer.

- Reduces replication lag and I/O overhead.

Aurora's log-based architecture directly contributes to its **fast recovery times** (often under 30 seconds), which is significantly faster than traditional RDS engines.

Separation of Compute and Storage

A major innovation in Aurora is the complete **decoupling of compute and storage layers**, allowing for independent scaling, high availability, and improved performance.

Compute Layer

- Consists of **DB instances** (writers and readers).

- Responsible for query processing, execution plans, and in-memory operations like buffer cache and query caches.

- Aurora MySQL and Aurora PostgreSQL instances run a **modified version** of their respective engines, designed to offload storage operations to the Aurora storage layer.

Storage Layer

- Manages all persistent data and implements a distributed, log-structured storage format.

- Handles redo log generation, log application, crash recovery, and replication behind the scenes.

- Designed to be **stateless** with **built-in fault tolerance** through multi-AZ replication.

Benefits of Decoupling

- **Independent scaling**: You can scale the compute independently from storage.

- **Resilience**: Compute failure doesn't require full data recovery; simply attach a new instance to the existing storage.

- **Fast failover**: Since the state is persisted in distributed storage, switching to a new compute instance is fast and seamless.

- **Storage elasticity**: Aurora automatically grows storage in 10GB increments, up to 128TiB, with no downtime or provisioning required.

Example Use Case: Resilience During Failures

If a writer node crashes:

- A new writer can be promoted or created in under a minute.

- The new node mounts the same storage volume and resumes operations almost immediately.

- Reader nodes continue to serve queries (if appropriately configured) without interruption.

Read/Write Paths and I/O Optimization

Aurora has re-engineered the traditional I/O paths to optimize both reads and writes, focusing on minimizing latency and improving throughput.

Write Path Optimization

In traditional databases, the write path includes writing both the redo log and the data pages, often resulting in double writes and potential consistency issues during failures. Aurora handles this differently:

- **Only redo logs are sent to the storage layer**. Aurora does not flush full pages during transactions.

- The **redo logs are written to the distributed storage**, which then replays these logs to construct pages.

- This approach significantly **reduces write latency** and **eliminates the double-write problem**.

Write Path Steps:

1. Transaction begins on compute node.

2. Redo log records are generated.

3. Redo logs are sent to the distributed storage engine.

4. Once **quorum of 4/6 nodes** confirm receipt, the transaction is acknowledged as committed.

5. The transaction can be safely forgotten by compute, as storage ensures durability.

Read Path Optimization

Reads in Aurora are also highly optimized, especially in clusters with multiple reader instances.

- **Buffer cache** is maintained independently on each reader and writer node.

- If a page is not in local cache, the compute node reads from **storage nodes**, which serve pages reconstructed from the redo logs.

- **Cluster Cache Management (CCM)** in Aurora PostgreSQL improves cache warm-up during failovers by tracking hot pages and synchronizing them across nodes.

Read Path Enhancements:

- **Parallelized I/O**: Compute nodes can request pages from multiple storage nodes in parallel.

- **Replica Lag Minimization**: Since replicas apply logs, not full pages, they can stay much closer to the writer.

- **Reader endpoint**: Load-balanced endpoint that intelligently routes reads to the least-loaded replica.

Zero Page Cache Recovery

When a DB instance restarts, traditional databases take time to warm the buffer pool. Aurora avoids this by:

- Reconstructing pages directly from redo logs, bypassing the need to read entire tablespaces.

- **Fast, on-demand cache warm-up**, especially useful during failovers or scaling events.

I/O Reduction Techniques in Aurora

Aurora uses several techniques to reduce I/O overhead and improve efficiency:

- **Log-only writes**: Instead of flushing full data pages, Aurora persists only redo logs.

- **Background page construction**: Storage nodes apply redo logs to reconstruct pages only when needed.

- **No WAL archiving or full-page writes**: Unlike traditional PostgreSQL or MySQL configurations.

- **Copy-on-write for snapshots**: Aurora snapshots use storage-level metadata without copying entire volumes.

High Availability and Durability

The storage engine is built to ensure both **data durability and high availability**, even in the face of multiple component failures.

Key mechanisms:

- **Quorum-based replication**: 6 copies of data across 3 AZs, only 4 required to complete writes.

- **Survivable page cache**: Cache survives failovers and reboots using techniques like CCM.

- **No reliance on RAID or EBS**: Aurora uses its own purpose-built storage infrastructure.

- **Fault-tolerant design**: Automatic failure detection, self-healing storage segments.

Automatic Repair and Healing

- **Storage Auto-Repair**: Aurora continuously monitors segments and replaces failed nodes.

- **No human intervention**: Failed protection groups are automatically reconstructed from the quorum.

Performance and Scalability

Aurora's design directly impacts its ability to scale for demanding workloads.

Read Scalability

- Up to **15 Aurora Replicas** per cluster.

- Each replica has its own cache, reducing load on the writer.

- **Fast replication** via log shipping, often with sub-second lag.

Write Scalability

- **Aurora Serverless v2** enables fine-grained compute autoscaling with millisecond granularity.

- Multi-writer support (Aurora MySQL only) for scaling writes horizontally (with caveats).

- Optimized for **low-latency commits** and high throughput with consistent performance.

Best Practices

To take full advantage of Aurora's architecture:

- **Use Aurora Replicas** for scaling reads.

- Use the **reader endpoint** to load-balance traffic.

- Enable **Cluster Cache Management** on PostgreSQL clusters for faster failovers.

- For high availability, deploy in **Multi-AZ** with appropriate instance class matching.

- Use **Performance Insights** to analyze bottlenecks and understand DB load behavior.

- Leverage **Aurora Global Databases** for multi-region resilience and low-latency reads.

Limitations and Considerations

While Aurora's architecture provides many advantages, it also introduces some trade-offs:

- **Multi-writer mode (Aurora MySQL)** has conflict resolution limitations; not suitable for all workloads.

- **Replication lag** can still occur under heavy load, although typically lower than traditional engines.

- **Log-based storage** may result in increased latency for certain types of read-after-write workloads (e.g., analytics-heavy).

- Aurora PostgreSQL lacks some features like logical decoding (though improvements are ongoing).

Summary

Amazon Aurora's architectural innovations—separation of compute and storage, a distributed log-based storage engine, and optimized read/write paths—make it a powerful choice for modern cloud-native applications. With fault-tolerant design, near-instantaneous failovers, and elastic scalability, Aurora fundamentally redefines what's possible with relational databases in the cloud.

These features collectively enable:

- Greater fault isolation

- Faster crash recovery

- Linear read scalability

- Simplified operational management

Aurora continues to evolve, especially with advancements like Serverless v2 and Zero-ETL integrations, making it a foundational choice for scalable, resilient, and performance-sensitive workloads.

Chapter 4. Aurora DB Engines: MySQL and PostgreSQL Compatibility

Amazon Aurora offers two major database engine types— **Aurora MySQL-Compatible Edition** and **Aurora PostgreSQL-Compatible Edition**—each engineered to combine the speed and reliability of high-end commercial databases with the simplicity and cost-effectiveness of open-source engines. This chapter explores the version compatibility, feature gaps and enhancements between the two engines, and practical considerations for choosing the right one based on your application needs.

Version Compatibility

Version compatibility is a critical aspect when evaluating Aurora's compatibility with MySQL and PostgreSQL. Aurora maintains **wire compatibility**, which means applications that connect to MySQL or PostgreSQL can generally connect to Aurora without modification.

Aurora MySQL-Compatible Versions

Aurora MySQL supports selected versions of **MySQL 5.6, 5.7, and 8.0**:

- **Aurora MySQL v1** is compatible with MySQL 5.6.

- **Aurora MySQL v2** aligns with MySQL 5.7.

- **Aurora MySQL v3** is compatible with MySQL 8.0.

Support is maintained with minor version upgrades, and AWS manages the maintenance updates, patches, and underlying infrastructure. However, not every MySQL feature or plugin is available in Aurora, and in some cases, the behavior is slightly different due to Aurora's unique architecture (e.g., the distributed storage layer).

Aurora PostgreSQL-Compatible Versions

Aurora PostgreSQL tracks **major community PostgreSQL versions**, including:

- PostgreSQL 11.x

- PostgreSQL 12.x

- PostgreSQL 13.x

- PostgreSQL 14.x

- PostgreSQL 15.x (latest supported as of early 2025)

AWS generally releases Aurora PostgreSQL versions after thorough compatibility and performance testing, which introduces a delay behind upstream PostgreSQL releases. Despite this, Aurora PostgreSQL aims for **full API and feature-level compatibility** with the core PostgreSQL engine.

Maintenance and Upgrades

- **Automatic Minor Version Updates:** You can enable automatic patching for minor updates.

- **Major Version Upgrades:** Must be initiated manually and may require testing application compatibility.

Compatibility Summary

Feature	Aurora MySQL	Aurora PostgreSQL
Core Engine Version	MySQL 5.6, 5.7, 8.0	PostgreSQL 11 through 15
Version Numbering	Follows Aurora-specific versioning	Follows PostgreSQL versioning
Wire Compatibility	Yes	Yes
Driver Support	MySQL clients & drivers	PostgreSQL clients & drivers
Plugin Compatibility	Limited	Limited
Upgrade Mechanism	In-place (minor), snapshot+restore (major)	Same

Feature Gaps and Enhancements

Aurora introduces a range of enhancements beyond what the community editions provide, but each engine also comes with certain limitations compared to its open-source base.

Aurora MySQL Enhancements

- **Faster crash recovery:** Due to the decoupling of compute and storage.

- **Parallel query execution** (Aurora MySQL 2.10+).

- **Aurora Global Databases**: Multi-region replication.

- **Backtrack:** "Undo" feature that rewinds your DB cluster without using backups.

- **Advanced monitoring**: Integration with Performance Insights and CloudWatch.

- **Zero-ETL Integration with Amazon Redshift**.

- **Aurora Machine Learning (Aurora ML)** for in-database inference.

- **Custom endpoints** to load balance read/write traffic.

Aurora PostgreSQL Enhancements

- **Aurora Parallel Query**: Pushes SQL predicates to the storage layer for analytics acceleration.

- **Aurora Machine Learning (Aurora ML)**.

- **Aurora Global Databases**.

- **PostgreSQL Extensions**: Support for `pg_stat_statements`, `pg_cron`, `PostGIS`, `hll`, and more.

- **Zero-ETL Integration** for real-time analytics.

- **Cluster Cache Management (CCM)** to reduce failover impact.

- **Logical replication** support.

Feature Gaps Compared to Open Source Engines

While Aurora is designed to be highly compatible, there are **feature gaps**:

- **Aurora MySQL:**

  - Does not support MySQL plugins such as `Audit`, `InnoDB Full-Text` search (partially supported), or custom storage engines.

  - Some system tables and status variables differ or are unavailable.

- **Aurora PostgreSQL:**

  - Not all PostgreSQL extensions are supported; installation of new C-language extensions is not allowed.

- ○ Write-Ahead Logging (WAL) is handled differently due to Aurora's distributed storage model.

Comparison Table: Key Enhancements and Gaps

Capability	Aurora MySQL	Aurora PostgreSQL
Parallel Query	Yes	Yes
Global Database	Yes	Yes
Machine Learning (Aurora ML)	Yes	Yes
Backtrack	Yes	No
Logical Replication	Limited	Yes
Extension Support	Limited	Rich ecosystem supported
Custom Engine Plugins	Not supported	Not supported

Full-Text Search	Basic	With `tsvector`, `GIN`, etc.

Choosing Between MySQL and PostgreSQL

The choice between Aurora MySQL and Aurora PostgreSQL depends on **application requirements, existing technology stack, and performance needs.**

When to Choose Aurora MySQL

You might prefer Aurora MySQL if:

- You're migrating from an existing MySQL or MariaDB environment.

- Your team has MySQL expertise and operational tooling.

- Your application uses MySQL-specific syntax or functions.

- You need Aurora's **Backtrack** feature to easily "rewind" your database.

- Your application is latency-sensitive and benefits from Aurora MySQL's **faster failover** and **low read replica lag**.

When to Choose Aurora PostgreSQL

Aurora PostgreSQL is typically better suited if:

- You require **advanced SQL** features (window functions, recursive queries, CTEs).

- Your application leverages PostgreSQL-specific extensions such as `PostGIS` or `pg_partman`.

- You are building analytical or geospatial applications.

- You need **full logical replication** or **fine-grained role management**.

- You're migrating from an Oracle database, since PostgreSQL has similar features and extensions (e.g., procedural languages like PL/pgSQL).

Performance & Scalability Considerations

Criteria	Aurora MySQL	Aurora PostgreSQL
Read Replica Lag	Lower (typically sub-10ms)	Slightly higher (~100ms typical)
Parallel Query Support	Yes	Yes
Storage Engine	Aurora custom engine	Aurora custom engine
In-Place Backups	Yes	Yes

Cross-Region Replication	Yes	Yes

Developer Experience & Ecosystem

- **Aurora MySQL** benefits from a huge developer community, many ORM tools (e.g., Prisma, Sequelize), and wide industry adoption.

- **Aurora PostgreSQL** offers a rich extension system, better standards compliance (e.g., SQL:2011), and features like JSONB, powerful indexing strategies, and foreign data wrappers.

Best Practices and Recommendations

For Solution Architects

- Use **Aurora Global Databases** with either engine to support low-latency reads in multiple AWS Regions.

- Leverage **RDS Proxy** to manage connections efficiently at scale.

- Integrate **CloudWatch and Performance Insights** to monitor query latency and DB load.

For Developers

- Validate app-level compatibility before switching engines.

- Use **parameter groups** to fine-tune database behavior.

- Enable **Performance Insights** for detailed query analysis.

For AI & Data Engineers

- Use **Aurora ML** to bring SageMaker models into your Aurora queries.

- Combine Aurora PostgreSQL with **PostGIS** for geospatial ML pipelines.

- Explore **Zero-ETL integrations** to feed Aurora data directly into Amazon Redshift or other analytics pipelines.

Final Thoughts

Amazon Aurora gives you the flexibility to choose the engine that best suits your application and organizational needs, without sacrificing performance or scalability. Aurora MySQL offers familiarity and exceptional performance for traditional web applications, while Aurora PostgreSQL unlocks powerful analytical and extensibility features ideal for modern, complex workloads. The key is to align your choice with your team's expertise, workload patterns, and future scaling requirements.

    💡 **Tip:** When in doubt, benchmark both engines using a representative workload in a dev/test environment using Amazon Aurora's performance insights, before finalizing your architecture.

Chapter 5. Understanding the Shared Responsibility Model

Amazon Web Services (AWS) operates under a **Shared Responsibility Model**, which defines the distinct security and operational obligations of AWS and its customers. This model is especially important when deploying managed services like **Amazon Aurora**, where AWS handles much of the infrastructure management, but customers must still secure and manage their data and configurations properly.

This chapter explores the Shared Responsibility Model in the context of Amazon Aurora, diving into AWS's and the customer's responsibilities, and the implications this division has for **compliance**, **auditing**, and **operational best practices**.

AWS Responsibilities

Under the Shared Responsibility Model, AWS is responsible for **security "of" the cloud**. This includes managing the global infrastructure and foundational services that run AWS offerings, including Amazon Aurora. Key areas of AWS responsibility include:

Physical and Environmental Security

- Data center security, including access controls, surveillance, and physical barriers.

- Power redundancy, cooling systems, and fire prevention.

- Network connectivity between AWS Regions and Availability Zones.

Infrastructure Management

- **Hardware management**: AWS handles the provisioning, maintenance, and decommissioning of servers, storage, and networking equipment.

- **Virtualization layer**: For Aurora, AWS is responsible for securing the hypervisor and host operating system.

- **Patch management**: AWS applies patches to the underlying infrastructure and managed database engines for Aurora, ensuring critical vulnerabilities are addressed.

Amazon Aurora-Specific Security Controls

AWS handles several built-in Aurora controls:

- **Encryption at rest** using AWS Key Management Service (KMS).

- **Network isolation** via Virtual Private Cloud (VPC).

- **Automatic backups**, snapshots, and **failover mechanisms**.

- **Automatic software updates** and security patches for Aurora database engines.

- Enforcement of **AWS Identity and Access Management (IAM)** for RDS-level access.

Availability and Durability

AWS ensures high availability and durability through:

- Multi-AZ deployments and replication strategies.

- Aurora's distributed and self-healing **cluster volume storage**.

- Aurora global databases for cross-region resilience.

Customer Responsibilities

While AWS manages the infrastructure, customers are responsible for **security "in" the cloud**—that is, what they do with the Aurora service. This includes:

Data Management

- **Data classification**: Understanding the sensitivity and regulatory requirements of the data stored in Aurora.

- **Data integrity**: Ensuring that application and user operations don't corrupt or compromise data.

- **Backup strategy**: Although Aurora supports automatic backups, customers must define appropriate **backup retention policies** and verify recoverability.

Identity and Access Management (IAM)

- Define **IAM roles and policies** that control who can manage Aurora clusters and instances.

- Manage **database-level users and privileges** (e.g., using PostgreSQL or MySQL authentication systems).

- Implement **multi-factor authentication (MFA)** and least-privilege access principles.

Database Configuration

- Set secure **parameter group settings** (e.g., disallowing remote root login or enabling SSL).

- Configure **encryption settings** for client connections (e.g., enforcing SSL/TLS).

- Manage **application-level security**, such as input validation and access control.

Networking and Firewalls

- Configure **security groups**, **network ACLs**, and **VPC subnets** to isolate database access.

- Ensure **Aurora endpoints** are only accessible to trusted applications or users.

- Use **Amazon RDS Proxy** or **Secrets Manager** to manage secure and scalable connectivity.

Monitoring and Logging

- Enable and review **Amazon CloudWatch** metrics for Aurora performance.

- Use **AWS CloudTrail** to log and audit API calls.

- Turn on **Performance Insights** for real-time query analysis and bottleneck detection.

Compliance Configuration

- Manage **auditing settings** (e.g., PostgreSQL's `pgaudit`, MySQL's audit plugin).

- Encrypt **data in transit** using SSL and enforce connection-level encryption.

- Conduct **periodic vulnerability assessments** and **penetration tests** (with AWS approval).

Implications for Compliance and Auditing

Understanding the shared responsibility model is critical for maintaining **compliance with regulatory frameworks** such as **HIPAA**, **PCI DSS**, **GDPR**, **SOC 2**, and more. Here's how the responsibilities divide in the context of compliance:

AWS's Role in Compliance

AWS provides:

- **Compliance certifications and attestations**: Including ISO 27001, SOC 1/2/3, PCI DSS, FedRAMP, and more.

- **Security documentation and whitepapers**: For auditors and assessors.

- **Service-level agreements (SLAs)** and **business associate agreements (BAAs)** where applicable.

- **Service infrastructure compliance**: AWS ensures that services like Aurora are deployed and maintained in accordance with AWS-level security controls.

Customers can access AWS compliance documentation through the **AWS Artifact** service.

Customer's Role in Compliance

Customers are responsible for:

- Ensuring **data handling** practices meet regulatory requirements.

- Configuring **Aurora and VPC settings** in compliance with internal or external policies.

- Implementing **database encryption, auditing**, and **access control**.

- Maintaining and proving **data governance**, including data retention, deletion, and subject rights management (GDPR).

- Conducting and documenting **security assessments**, **risk analyses**, and **audits** on application and database usage.

Best Practices for Compliance

- **Enable encryption**: Use Aurora's support for at-rest and in-transit encryption.

- **Log everything**: Use CloudTrail and Aurora's native logging to retain audit trails.

- **Restrict access**: Use IAM roles, security groups, and database users with strict permissions.

- **Validate configurations**: Use **AWS Config** rules to verify compliance continuously.

- **Document procedures**: Maintain clear SOPs for database operations and incident response.

Real-World Scenario: PCI DSS with Aurora

To meet **PCI DSS** requirements while using Aurora:

- Ensure all Aurora clusters use **encryption at rest** with KMS-managed keys.

- Use **SSL/TLS** for all client connections to secure data in transit.

- Enable **CloudTrail** logging and integrate with a SIEM solution for log retention.

- Implement **least-privilege IAM roles** and **rotate credentials** regularly.

- Use **database auditing tools** (like PostgreSQL `pgaudit`) to log access to cardholder data.

Trade-offs and Considerations

Understanding the shared responsibility model helps balance **security**, **performance**, and **usability**, but it also introduces some nuanced trade-offs:

- **Flexibility vs. Complexity**: While AWS automates infrastructure management, customers must still understand configurations deeply to avoid missteps.

- **Security Responsibility**: Misconfigured IAM roles or open security groups can expose Aurora databases to risk—AWS won't catch this for you.

- **Customization Limits**: Aurora, as a managed service, limits certain administrative privileges.

Customers may need to adjust traditional security models.

- **Audit Complexity**: Aligning Aurora configurations with compliance audits requires cross-team collaboration between security, engineering, and DevOps.

Summary

The Shared Responsibility Model is not just a conceptual framework—it's a practical guideline for operational and security success in the cloud. In the context of Amazon Aurora:

- **AWS** handles the infrastructure and service-level security.

- **Customers** are responsible for configurations, access control, and data management.

To ensure robust security and regulatory compliance, both parties must clearly understand and fulfill their respective roles. Applying best practices to your Aurora deployments—and documenting them—is key to building secure, reliable, and compliant database systems in AWS.

Chapter 6. Regions, Availability Zones, and Global Reach

Introduction

Amazon Aurora is designed as a highly available, fault-tolerant, and globally scalable database engine that leverages the AWS cloud infrastructure. A core architectural principle of Aurora is its deep integration with AWS Regions and Availability Zones (AZs), enabling deployments that can achieve low-latency performance, rapid failover, and global reach.

In this chapter, we explore the deployment models of Aurora in relation to Regions and AZs, examine how these configurations impact latency, replication, and high availability (HA), and outline the limitations and capabilities specific to Region-based architecture.

Regions and Availability Zones in Aurora

What Are AWS Regions and AZs?

- **Region**: A geographical area containing multiple isolated locations known as Availability Zones.

- **Availability Zone (AZ)**: One or more discrete data centers with redundant power, networking, and connectivity in an AWS Region.

Aurora uses AZs to distribute compute and storage resources to maximize availability and minimize the impact of outages.

Aurora's Use of AZs

Aurora is architected for HA by automatically replicating data across multiple AZs in a Region. This replication is **synchronous** for primary-write operations and **asynchronous** for read-only replicas, balancing consistency and performance.

- Each Aurora cluster spans multiple AZs by default.

- A primary instance (writer) resides in one AZ.

- One or more read replicas (readers) can be deployed in the same or different AZs.

Aurora Deployment Models

1. Single-Region Multi-AZ Deployment

This is the most common and default deployment model:

- **Primary writer** in one AZ.

- **Aurora Replicas** in one or more other AZs.

- **Cluster volume** is replicated six ways across three AZs for durability.

Use cases:

- Standard production applications

- Latency-sensitive workloads within a single Region

Benefits:

- Automated failover

- Low-latency replication

- Cost-effective compared to multi-Region

2. Aurora Global Databases (Multi-Region)

Aurora Global Databases are designed for globally distributed applications that need fast read performance in multiple Regions and disaster recovery from Region-wide outages.

- **Primary Region**: Accepts all writes.

- **Secondary Regions**: Accept read-only replicas.

- **Replication** is asynchronous using Aurora storage-level replication, typically under one second lag.

Use cases:

- Global web applications

- Regulatory or geographic data locality

- Disaster recovery across Regions

Key features:

- Up to 5 secondary Regions

- Up to 16 read replicas per Region

- Fast cross-Region failover (~1 minute)

3. Serverless v2 in Multi-AZ

Aurora Serverless v2 offers on-demand auto-scaling in fine-grained increments while retaining Multi-AZ HA.

- Runs in one AZ but can span AZs for failover.

- **Cold starts** are not an issue in v2 due to warm pools and rapid scale-up.

Best suited for:

- Variable workloads

- Development and test environments

- Applications requiring cost efficiency with occasional spikes

Impact on Latency, Replication, and High Availability

Latency Considerations

1. **Within a Region**

   ○ Reads from Aurora Replicas are **low-latency**, typically sub-millisecond within the same AZ.

   ○ **Network latency** across AZs in a Region is minimal, typically 1–2 milliseconds.

2. **Cross-Region**

   ○ Read latency depends on inter-Region distance—generally 30ms to 150ms.

   ○ **Write latency** is not affected since only the primary Region accepts writes in Aurora Global Databases.

   ○ Use **local read replicas** in each Region to optimize for latency.

Replication Types

1. **Synchronous Replication**

   ○ Occurs within the primary Region.

- Maintains durability by writing each data block six times across three AZs.

- Ensures **zero data loss** during instance failover.

2. **Asynchronous Replication**

- Used for Aurora Replicas in the same Region and for Aurora Global Databases.

- Global replication is **storage-level** and highly optimized.

- Near-real-time lag (~1s), suitable for global read scaling and disaster recovery.

High Availability Strategies

Aurora enhances availability using:

- **Automatic failover** to a healthy replica in the event of a failure.

- **Monitoring via Amazon RDS Events and CloudWatch** to trigger alerts and automation.

- **Aurora Replica promotion** within seconds to minimize downtime.

If deployed across Regions:

- **Failover to another Region** is a manual step or can be automated using custom scripts and Amazon Route 53.

- Aurora Global Databases reduce downtime during Region failures from hours to minutes.

Region-Based Limitations and Capabilities

Aurora Global Database Constraints

While Aurora Global Databases offer powerful cross-Region capabilities, they have several limitations:

- **Only one writer Region at a time**: Applications requiring multi-Region writes must implement custom conflict resolution.

- **Replication lag visibility**: Requires monitoring functions such as `aurora_global_db_status()` and `aurora_global_db_instance_status()`.

- **Failover is manual** unless scripted.

- **Aurora Serverless is not yet supported** in Global Databases (as of 2025).

Supported DB Engines and Versions

Global Database support varies by engine and version:

- **Aurora MySQL**: Supported for MySQL 5.7-compatible and 8.0-compatible versions.

- **Aurora PostgreSQL**: Supported from PostgreSQL 11.9+, 12.4+, 13.4+, and later.

Check compatibility before creating global clusters.

Region and Instance Type Restrictions

Not all instance classes are supported for Performance Insights or Global Databases. For example:

- `db.t2`, `db.t3`, and `db.t4g.micro/small` are **not supported** for Performance Insights.

- Global clusters **require supported instance types**, typically general-purpose or memory-optimized classes like `db.r6g` or `db.r5`.

Monitoring and Optimizing for Multi-AZ and Multi-Region

Key Metrics

Use the following CloudWatch metrics and Aurora functions:

- **Replica lag**: `AuroraReplicaLag`, `aurora_replica_status()`

- **Replication throughput**:
  `LogStreamSpeedInKibPerSecond`

- **Durability lag** (Global):
  `aurora_global_db_status()`

- **Visible lag**:
  `aurora_global_db_instance_status()`

Best Practices

1. **Distribute read workloads**

   - Place read replicas close to users geographically.

   - Use **reader endpoints** to load balance across replicas.

2. **Automate failover**

   - Implement Route 53 health checks and Lambda functions to promote a secondary Region.

   - Use Aurora failover APIs where supported.

3. **Plan for Region-specific quotas**

   - Limits on instances, IOPS, storage, and networking can vary.

- Pre-provision resources in secondary Regions to reduce RTO.

4. **Use Global Databases for Disaster Recovery**

   - For business-critical applications, use Global Databases to maintain data integrity across Regions.

   - Regularly test failover procedures.

Example Architecture Patterns

Pattern 1: Multi-AZ for High Availability

- Aurora cluster in **us-east-1** with primary in **AZ-a**

- 2 Aurora Replicas in **AZ-b** and **AZ-c**

- Automatic failover enabled

- Performance Insights used for monitoring

Result: High durability, low failover time (~30s), optimized read scaling

Pattern 2: Global Read-Optimized Deployment

- Writer in **us-west-2**

- Reader Regions in **eu-central-1** and **ap-southeast-1**

- Users routed to nearest reader via Route 53

- Lag monitored with `aurora_global_db_status()`

Result: Low read latency for global users, centralized write control

Pattern 3: Global DR Deployment

- Primary Region: **eu-west-1**

- Secondary Region: **us-east-2**

- Warm standbys pre-provisioned

- Failover drill automated with Lambda + CLI

Result: Business continuity in case of primary Region outage

Configuration Notes

Enabling Global Databases

Steps to create a Global Database:

1. Create a new Aurora DB cluster in the primary Region.

2. In the console, select **"Add Region"**.

3. Choose secondary Region(s) and instance class.

4. Aurora replicates the cluster volume; no manual snapshot copy needed.

Use CLI or RDS API for infrastructure-as-code support.

Reader Endpoint Strategy

Use **reader endpoints** and **custom endpoints** to:

- Balance reads across AZs

- Separate analytics from application workloads

- Scale read traffic without overloading the writer

Cost Considerations

- Cross-Region replication incurs **data transfer costs**.

- Running multiple clusters across Regions increases **compute and storage costs**.

- Use **Reserved Instances** and **Compute Savings Plans** for long-term cost optimization.

Trade-Offs and Limitations

Feature	Benefit	Limitation
Global Database	DR and global reads	No multi-Region writes, added complexity
Multi-AZ	Fast failover, built-in HA	Higher cost than single-AZ
Aurora Serverless v2	Auto-scaling, cost-effective	Not available in Global Databases
Custom Endpoints	Query routing flexibility	Manual management needed
Reader Scaling	Improves read throughput	Asynchronous; potential stale reads

Conclusion

Regions and Availability Zones are fundamental to how Aurora delivers high availability, fault tolerance, and global scalability. By understanding Aurora's deployment models—ranging from Multi-AZ to Global Databases—you can design systems that meet stringent SLAs and support geographically distributed users.

Properly architected Aurora deployments ensure low-latency access, high durability, and rapid recovery. Yet, these benefits must be weighed against operational complexity and cost. Ultimately, Aurora's regional and global deployment capabilities make it a robust choice for cloud-native, mission-critical databases.

Chapter 7. Aurora Versioning and Upgrade Strategy

Amazon Aurora's versioning and upgrade strategy is central to ensuring high availability, security, and performance for production workloads. This chapter will explore the architecture and best practices around versioning, the distinction between major and minor versions, the mechanisms for automatic versus manual upgrades, and the role of RDS Extended Support in maintaining legacy applications.

Overview of Aurora Versioning

Aurora versioning aligns with its MySQL- and PostgreSQL-compatible engines. Each Aurora cluster is associated with a specific engine version that reflects the core engine compatibility (MySQL 5.7, 8.0 or PostgreSQL 12, 13, 14, etc.), plus Aurora-specific enhancements for performance, availability, and security.

Aurora applies versioning through:

- **Engine version numbers**: Reflecting the underlying database engine compatibility.

- **Aurora enhancements**: Additional features layered on top of the open-source engine (e.g., Aurora Parallel Query, Global Databases).

- **Cluster-level version control**: Each Aurora cluster operates on a specific version, distinct from the instance level.

Versioning is crucial because not all features or behaviors are backward-compatible. Aurora uses semantic versioning principles to manage compatibility.

Major vs Minor Versioning

Major Versions

A **major version** upgrade represents a shift in the underlying database engine, such as moving from MySQL 5.7 to 8.0 or PostgreSQL 12 to 13. These changes often include:

- Schema or syntax changes

- Deprecated features

- New core features that affect query execution, planner behavior, and performance

- Incompatibilities that may require application changes

Examples of major upgrades:

- Aurora MySQL: 5.7 → 8.0

- Aurora PostgreSQL: 12 → 13

Considerations for major upgrades:

- Major version upgrades **require downtime** and **manual intervention**.

- They are **not performed automatically** by AWS.

- Data integrity checks and pre-upgrade testing are strongly advised.

- Often require compatibility testing in a staging environment.

- Schema dumps or `pg_upgrade` equivalent processes may be involved (depending on engine).

Minor Versions

A **minor version** upgrade delivers improvements to performance, bug fixes, or new Aurora features while maintaining compatibility with the major version.

Examples of minor upgrades:

- Aurora PostgreSQL 13.4 → 13.9

- Aurora MySQL 5.7.mysql_aurora.2.10.0 → 5.7.mysql_aurora.2.11.1

Characteristics:

- Generally backward-compatible.

- Require **less application validation** than major upgrades.

- Can be **applied automatically or manually**, based on your configuration.

Automatic vs Manual Upgrades

Aurora provides flexibility in managing upgrades, with both automatic and manual options depending on operational and compliance requirements.

Automatic Minor Version Upgrades

Aurora can automatically apply **minor version upgrades** during the **maintenance window** when:

- The option is enabled on the cluster (`Auto minor version upgrade = true`)

- The new version is deemed stable and compatible by AWS

- You haven't explicitly pinned your engine version

How it works:

- Applied during the configured maintenance window.

- Does **not cause failover** unless required (typically in single-instance setups).

- Notifies users via RDS Events and the AWS Console before and after the upgrade.

Use cases:

- Environments that want to stay updated with the latest security and performance patches.

- Dev/test environments or production environments with validated rollback plans.

Manual Upgrades

Manual upgrades offer more control and are suitable when:

- You want to test new versions before applying them.

- You have strict change management or compliance requirements.

- You are performing **major version upgrades**.

How to initiate:

- Through AWS Console, AWS CLI, or RDS API.

- Requires a **DB cluster modification operation**.

- The upgrade process typically involves **rebooting instances** (for minor upgrades) or **complete replacement of the engine binaries** (for major).

Best practices:

- Enable backups and snapshots before upgrades.

- Validate the application against the new version in a staging environment.

- Monitor the cluster during and after the upgrade for anomalies.

Managing Upgrade Behavior

To control upgrade behavior:

- Use **DB cluster parameter groups** to manage settings across instances.

- Use **engine version pinning** to avoid unexpected upgrades.

- Regularly monitor for **deprecation notices** and **supported version lists**.

Aurora Version Support Lifecycle

AWS maintains an Aurora **version support lifecycle**, which determines how long each engine version receives updates and support. When versions approach end-of-life (EOL), AWS may:

- Notify customers via email, AWS Console, or RDS Events.

- Offer options to upgrade to newer versions.

- Begin charging for **RDS Extended Support** if users choose to remain on unsupported versions.

Extended Support

What Is RDS Extended Support?

RDS Extended Support is a paid feature that allows customers to continue using Aurora versions that have reached end-of-standard-support (EoSS). It is available for select Aurora MySQL and PostgreSQL engine versions.

Purpose:

- To provide critical security and bug fixes for legacy workloads.

- To give teams more time to refactor and test application compatibility.

Key Features:

- Continues to receive essential updates (e.g., CVE patches, stability improvements).

- Applies **only to versions explicitly enrolled** in the extended support program.

- Managed and delivered by AWS — no changes needed in your application logic.

Pricing

Extended support incurs an additional cost:

- **Charged per vCPU per hour**, in addition to standard Aurora instance pricing.

- **Applies only after the standard support window ends**.

- Customers can **opt-in or out** through the AWS Console or CLI.

Identifying Versions Under Extended Support

To find versions in extended support:

- Use the `aws rds describe-db-engine-versions` CLI command.

- Look for versions marked with `"Supports RDS Extended Support": true`.

Limitations

- Extended support only applies to certain Aurora MySQL and PostgreSQL versions.

- No feature enhancements are provided — only critical patches.

- Not a substitute for keeping databases up to date with actively supported versions.

Best Practices for Versioning and Upgrades

1. **Track version deprecations**:

    o Subscribe to RDS announcements or use AWS Config rules.

2. **Use staging environments**:

    o Test upgrades in isolated environments before rolling out to production.

3. **Leverage snapshots**:

    o Take a snapshot before upgrades to enable rollback if needed.

4. **Set maintenance windows** wisely:

- Choose low-traffic periods to minimize impact of automatic upgrades.

5. **Enable auto minor version upgrades** in non-critical environments:

    - Keeps you current without manual overhead.

6. **Use parameter groups** to pin versions:

    - Prevent automatic engine upgrades for clusters that require strict version control.

Real-World Upgrade Scenarios

Example 1: Production Read Scaling Cluster

- Engine: Aurora MySQL 5.7

- Setup: Multi-AZ, 4 readers, auto minor version upgrades disabled

- Upgrade Plan:

    - Test minor version (2.11.0 → 2.11.1) in staging

    - Snapshot cluster

    - Upgrade readers first, then writer

- o Monitor read replica lag and query performance

Example 2: Compliance-Driven Application

- Engine: Aurora PostgreSQL 12

- Requirement: Stay on a tested version beyond AWS EoSS

- Action:

  - o Enroll in RDS Extended Support

  - o Budget for per-vCPU support cost

  - o Plan for gradual transition to PostgreSQL 14 after validation

---

Tools for Managing Upgrades

AWS CLI:

```
aws rds modify-db-cluster \

  --db-cluster-identifier my-cluster \

  --engine-version 13.9 \

  --apply-immediately
```

-
- **AWS Management Console**:

    - Navigate to **Databases > Modify**

    - Select desired engine version

    - Choose when to apply the upgrade

- **RDS Events & CloudWatch**:

    - Monitor RDS-EVENT-0079 for successful upgrades

    - Track performance with Performance Insights post-upgrade

---

Summary

Versioning and upgrade strategy in Amazon Aurora is not just a technical necessity but a critical component of a robust operational model. By understanding the distinctions between major and minor upgrades, leveraging automatic processes wisely, and planning for extended support when needed, organizations can ensure continuity, compliance, and performance.

> **Pro Tip**: Use blue/green deployments in Aurora (where available) to test new versions in production-like conditions with zero downtime.

Part II: Designing Aurora for Scale

Chapter 8. Aurora DB Cluster Design Patterns

Single-region Designs

Amazon Aurora offers a range of design patterns tailored for high performance, availability, and fault tolerance within a single AWS Region. These patterns are foundational for workloads that require high availability and read scalability but do not need cross-Region disaster recovery or active-active configurations.

Overview

A single-region Aurora deployment consists of a **DB cluster**, which includes:

- A **primary instance** (also known as the writer)

- **Aurora Replicas** (readers) for scaling read workloads and improving failover times

- A **shared cluster volume** distributed across three Availability Zones (AZs)

Aurora separates compute and storage, allowing automatic failover and high durability without the complexity of traditional replication architectures.

Basic Design Pattern: 1 Writer + 0 Readers

This is the simplest Aurora pattern:

- **Use Case:** Development, testing, or workloads with low traffic

- **Components:**

  - One DB instance (writer)

  - Shared Aurora cluster volume

- **Availability:** Relying solely on the writer means failover requires a manual or automated promotion of a new instance, which introduces some downtime

Enhanced Read and Availability: 1 Writer + N Readers

This is a common production-grade pattern:

- **Use Case:** High-read applications (e.g., reporting, dashboards)

- **Components:**

  - One writer DB instance

  - One or more reader DB instances (Aurora Replicas)

- **Benefits:**

  - Distributes read workloads across replicas

- Readers can be promoted during failover

- Replicas in different AZs provide zonal fault tolerance

Best Practices:

- Use **Reader Endpoint** for load balancing across replicas

- Use **Cluster Endpoint** for read/write operations (automatically points to writer)

- Configure **failover priority** (tiered model) to control which replica becomes the writer in case of failure

- Place replicas in different AZs to ensure fault tolerance

Reader Auto Scaling Pattern

To handle variable workloads (e.g., ecommerce peaks), Aurora supports reader **Auto Scaling**.

- **Auto Scaling Policy:**

  - Triggers scale-out when average CPU or connections exceed thresholds

  - Scales in when load reduces

- **Infrastructure:**

- A minimum and maximum number of replicas is configured

- **Trade-offs:**

  - Scale-in may introduce temporary latency during decommissioning

  - Cold-start time for replicas may affect scale-out responsiveness

Multi-tier Read Architecture

For very high throughput applications, some designs introduce a multi-tier approach:

- **High-throughput consumers** (e.g., BI dashboards, ML model scoring) connect to dedicated read replicas

- **General consumers** use the shared reader endpoint

- **Design Considerations:**

  - Match replica class size to workload type

  - Use custom endpoints to direct traffic to specific replicas

---

Multi-AZ Replication

Aurora inherently replicates storage across three Availability Zones in a single Region. This architecture ensures high availability even if a full AZ goes down.

Aurora vs. Traditional Multi-AZ in RDS

Feature	Aurora	Traditional RDS Multi-AZ
Storage replication	6-way across 3 AZs	2-way synchronous
Failover	Fast failover (typically under 30s)	Slower due to synchronous nature
Replica type	Aurora Replicas (reader)	No readable replicas
Read scaling	Yes	No
Write scalability	Limited to one writer (except multi-master)	One writer

How Aurora Achieves Multi-AZ Availability

Aurora's **shared storage layer** automatically:

- Writes to 6 copies (2 per AZ)

- Tolerates loss of up to 2 copies or 1 AZ

- Uses quorum-based writes (4/6) for consistency

Failover Mechanism

- **Trigger:** Instance crash, host failure, network partition, or AZ outage

- **Mechanism:**

  - Aurora automatically promotes the highest-priority replica in a different AZ to be the new writer

  - DNS of the **Cluster Endpoint** is updated to point to the new writer

- **Recovery time:** Typically under 30 seconds

Best Practices:

- Distribute replicas across **multiple AZs**

- Use **lower-tier failover priorities** for non-critical replicas

- Monitor using **Amazon RDS Events** and **CloudWatch Alarms**

- Test failover periodically to validate application resilience

Monitoring Multi-AZ Health

Key metrics and tools:

- `aurora_replica_status()` – Returns lag, transaction replay latency, and other replica metrics

- **RDS Performance Insights** – Visualize DB load per instance

- **CloudWatch Alarms** – Monitor CPU, disk queue depth, connections

Cost Considerations

- Aurora charges per instance and storage consumed

- You only pay for compute instances and **I/O operations**, not per AZ storage replication

---

Multi-master Considerations (MySQL only)

Aurora MySQL (not PostgreSQL) supports **multi-master clusters** for active-active workloads. This design enables multiple writers in the same Region.

Overview

In a **multi-master cluster**, you can have **two writer instances** that can both perform read/write operations simultaneously. These are backed by a **single shared storage volume**, providing high throughput and availability.

Use Cases:

- Write-heavy workloads distributed across multiple services or microservices

- Applications requiring **high write availability** without relying on failover

- Reduced impact during writer node failures

Architecture Diagram (Conceptual)

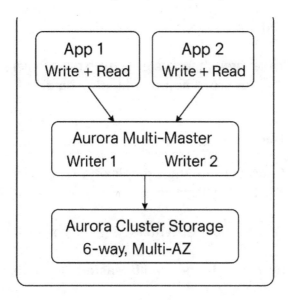

Write Conflict Management

Aurora multi-master provides **session-level consistency** and supports **conflict detection**:

- **Write conflict detection** is handled automatically at the storage layer

- When two writers try to update the same row:

    - Aurora uses **first-commit-wins** semantics

    - The conflicting transaction gets a **deadlock error**

Latency and Throughput

- Latency is low due to Aurora's high-speed network and quorum-based replication

- Write throughput scales up with more writers **only if** writes are to **non-overlapping data**

Trade-offs and Limitations

- **Conflict Handling Complexity:** Applications must handle retry logic

- **Max Number of Writers:** 2 (as of now)

- **No Cross-Region Multi-Master:** Only within the same Region

- **Aurora Serverless is not compatible** with multi-master

Best Practices

- Design **data partitioning schemes** to avoid write conflicts

- Use **idempotent writes** where possible

- Monitor `Deadlocks`, `Rollback` rates via Performance Insights

- Combine with **RDS Proxy** for efficient connection pooling

Monitoring Multi-Master Clusters

Use the following tools:

- `SHOW ENGINE INNODB STATUS` – for deadlock detection

- CloudWatch metrics like:

  o `Deadlocks`

  o `DDL Statements`

  o `ReplicaLag`

- Aurora's **Performance Insights** with `top SQL` and `waits`

Summary Comparison of Design Patterns

Design Pattern	Read Scaling	Write Scaling	AZ Resilience	Failover Time	Complexity

Single Writer	☑	✗	☑	~30s	Low
Multi-AZ Replication	☑	✗	☑☑☑	~30s	Moderate
Multi-master (MySQL)	☑☑	☑☑	☑☑☑	~5s	High

Tips for Choosing a Pattern

- Use **Single Writer + Replicas** for most production systems

- Choose **Multi-Master** only when you need true write availability from multiple apps

- Always use **Multi-AZ** for fault tolerance

- Evaluate **Aurora Global Databases** if cross-region HA is needed (covered in a separate chapter)

Example Scenarios

To bring the discussed design patterns into real-world perspective, here are common deployment scenarios that map directly to Aurora's capabilities:

📊 Scenario 1: High-Read, Low-Write Analytics Platform

- **Pattern**: 1 Writer + 3 Readers (in different AZs)
- **Why**: Scales read traffic efficiently and ensures fast failover via zonal redundancy. Ideal for dashboards and reporting tools.

⚡ Scenario 2: API Service with Low Latency SLAs

- **Pattern**: Aurora Multi-Master
- **Why**: Two active writers provide high write availability and reduce failover time to near-zero. Suited for latency-sensitive systems.

🛒 Scenario 3: OLTP Web App in a Single Region

- **Pattern**: 1 Writer + 2 Readers with Auto Scaling
- **Why**: Dynamically handles traffic spikes while maintaining high availability. Recommended for ecommerce and transactional workloads.

Chapter 9. High Availability and Fault Tolerance

Amazon Aurora is engineered to deliver high availability and fault tolerance as core features. It does so through a combination of innovative storage architecture, automated failover mechanisms, distributed replication, and durable design principles. This chapter explores three key mechanisms used in Aurora to ensure these capabilities: **Replica Promotion, Auto-Failover**, and **Quorum-Based Durability**.

Replica Promotion

Replica promotion in Aurora enables a fast transition of a replica DB instance into the writer role in the event of a failure. This feature is central to achieving high availability and minimizing downtime in both single-region and multi-region deployments.

What is Replica Promotion?

Replica promotion refers to the process by which a **read replica**—also known as an **Aurora Replica**—is elevated to become the **writer instance** (primary DB instance) when the existing writer becomes unavailable due to a failure or maintenance.

How It Works

Aurora maintains a pool of replicas (up to 15) that continuously apply changes from the primary using a highly efficient and low-latency replication mechanism. When a failover is triggered, Aurora:

1. **Monitors Health** – Through Amazon RDS health monitoring and instance-level metrics.

2. **Selects a Candidate** – Based on replica lag, priority tier, and instance health.

3. **Promotes the Replica** – The chosen replica is converted into the new writer.

4. **Reconfigures Endpoints** – The cluster endpoint automatically points to the new writer.

Replica Promotion Criteria

Replica promotion uses a combination of **promotion tiers** and **replica lag** to determine the best candidate. Each replica is assigned a **failover priority tier** (0–15), where **lower numbers mean higher promotion priority**.

- If multiple replicas share the same priority, the one with the **least replica lag** is selected.

- If no Aurora Replica is available, the system will need manual intervention.

Real-World Use Cases

- **Planned maintenance**: When upgrading the writer DB instance, a replica can be promoted to minimize downtime.

- **Disaster recovery**: In the event of hardware or availability zone failure, replica promotion maintains service continuity.

- **Blue/Green deployments**: Promotion can facilitate switchover to a new environment post-validation.

Best Practices

- **Distribute replicas across multiple AZs** to ensure failover capability even if an AZ fails.

- **Monitor replica lag** and keep at least one low-lag replica.

- **Set proper failover priorities** aligned with your recovery time objectives (RTO).

Auto-Failover

Auto-failover is Aurora's ability to automatically detect failures and transition service to a healthy replica or newly promoted writer instance without administrative intervention.

What is Auto-Failover?

Auto-failover refers to the **automated detection and recovery process** triggered when the current writer DB instance becomes unavailable. This mechanism minimizes downtime and maximizes availability.

Failure Detection Triggers

Aurora continuously monitors for the following failure conditions:

- Loss of heartbeat between writer and the storage subsystem

- Writer instance crash or power failure

- Network partition between writer and other nodes

- Unresponsive health checks (using Amazon RDS monitoring)

Auto-Failover Flow

1. **Failure Detection** – Aurora detects failure through internal health checks.

2. **Election of New Writer** – Uses promotion tiers and replica health.

3. **Failover Action** – Reassigns the cluster endpoint to the new writer.

4. **Client Reconnection** – Applications reconnect using the same endpoint with minimal disruption.

Failover Time

- Aurora typically completes failover in **less than 30 seconds**, though this may vary based on the complexity of the workload and instance size.

Considerations for Aurora Global Databases

- In a **global database**, Aurora performs **cross-Region failovers** by promoting a secondary cluster in another Region.

- This failover is **not automatic** and must be initiated manually unless orchestrated via external tools or scripts.

Monitoring and Alerts

You can monitor failover events using:

- **Amazon CloudWatch Alarms**

- **RDS Events**

- **Aurora performance insights**

- **Enhanced Monitoring**

Best Practices for Auto-Failover

- **Use Multi-AZ deployments** with replicas in different zones.

- **Test failover scenarios** regularly using the `failover-db-cluster` CLI or AWS Console.

- **Gracefully handle connection interruptions** in your application drivers or ORM.

Trade-offs

- Auto-failover may cause **short interruptions** while DNS propagation and endpoint updates complete.

- It is **not suitable** for environments requiring hard real-time guarantees unless combined with application-level retries and caching strategies.

Quorum-Based Durability

Aurora's storage subsystem is built on a distributed, fault-tolerant model that ensures data consistency and durability using **quorum-based write acknowledgment**.

What is Quorum-Based Durability?

Quorum-based durability refers to the requirement that a write is only acknowledged when a **majority (quorum) of storage nodes** confirms receipt. Aurora uses this mechanism to maintain **data integrity and consistency** even during partial infrastructure failures.

How Aurora Storage Works

- Aurora's storage volume is **quorum-replicated** across **6 storage nodes** distributed across 3 **Availability Zones (AZs)**.

- Each write operation must be acknowledged by **at least 4 out of 6 nodes** to be considered durable.

This model is similar to consensus algorithms (like Paxos or Raft) but optimized for high-throughput, low-latency database operations.

Benefits

- **Fault tolerance**: Can survive the loss of up to 2 storage nodes or an entire AZ.

- **Strong durability**: Complies with ACID properties without synchronous replication between DB instances.

- **Scalability**: Decouples compute and storage, allowing both to scale independently.

Read and Write Path

- **Writes**: A commit is sent from the writer DB instance to all 6 nodes. Once 4 acknowledge, the transaction is confirmed.

- **Reads**: Data is read from the nearest in-sync copy, usually local to the AZ hosting the reader.

Durability During Failures

Aurora's design allows it to maintain operation during:

- **Single-node failure**: Remaining 5 nodes still maintain quorum.

- **AZ failure**: As long as 4 nodes across other AZs are available, operations continue.

- **Node replacement**: Aurora automatically rebalances and heals the storage layer.

Storage Auto-Repair

Aurora uses **background healing processes** to replace failed nodes and copy data from healthy ones. This process is invisible to the application and ensures the quorum is always maintained.

Best Practices for Leveraging Quorum Durability

- **Enable cross-AZ placement of instances** to maximize read/write availability.

- **Monitor storage health** using CloudWatch metrics such as `VolumeWriteIOPS` and `VolumeReadIOPS`.

- **Use DB cluster endpoints** (writer, reader, and custom) for intelligent routing.

Limitations

- **Latency impact**: Quorum writes may introduce slight latency under high load or degraded storage conditions.

- **Write consistency model**: Aurora uses read-after-write consistency for the writer, but eventual consistency for replicas unless explicitly synchronized.

Summary: Building Fault-Tolerant Aurora Architectures

To build resilient Aurora environments, combine these features into a layered high-availability strategy:

- Use **Aurora Replicas** with proper failover priorities.

- Enable **Auto-Failover** and regularly simulate failure events.

- Rely on **Quorum-Based Durability** for data protection at the storage level.

- Consider **Aurora Global Databases** for cross-region disaster recovery.

- Implement **monitoring and alerting** across metrics such as failover events, replica lag, and storage I/O.

Tip: Validating HA Architecture

Use this checklist to validate that your Aurora setup is highly available and fault-tolerant:

- At least one Aurora Replica exists in a different AZ than the writer

- Failover priority tiers are correctly configured

- Auto-failover has been tested in staging

- CloudWatch alerts are set for `ReplicaLag`, `CPUUtilization`, `VolumeWriteIOPS`

- Backups and snapshots are configured with appropriate retention

Chapter 10. Aurora Global Databases

Architecture and Replication Process

Amazon Aurora Global Databases are designed for globally distributed applications that require low-latency reads and disaster recovery capabilities across AWS Regions. They build upon the high-performance, distributed architecture of Amazon Aurora and extend its capabilities to provide multi-Region replication with minimal performance impact and high availability.

Overview of Aurora Global Database Architecture

An **Aurora Global Database** consists of:

- **Primary DB Cluster** – Located in a single AWS Region and handles both read and write workloads.

- **Secondary DB Clusters** – Located in other AWS Regions. These are read-only replicas that asynchronously replicate changes from the primary cluster.

Key architectural components include:

- **Aurora Storage Engine** – Storage is decoupled from compute. Aurora uses a distributed, log-structured storage system that writes changes to a quorum of storage nodes across three Availability Zones (AZs) in a Region.

- **Cross-region Replication** – Aurora uses dedicated infrastructure for fast, reliable storage-level replication. Writes from the primary are replicated to secondary clusters using Aurora's specialized network layer, minimizing impact on primary workloads.

- **Aurora Replicas** – Each cluster can contain one or more replicas for load balancing and high availability. The primary Region can support both read and write replicas, while secondary Regions support read-only replicas.

Replication Flow

1. **Write at the Primary**:

    ○ Applications send write transactions to the primary writer instance.

    ○ Aurora records the log sequence numbers (LSNs) and writes changes to durable storage.

2. **Cross-region Storage-level Replication**:

    ○ Changes are asynchronously pushed from the primary cluster's storage volume to the secondary Regions' volumes.

    ○ Replication occurs at the storage layer (not SQL-based), which significantly reduces lag.

3. **Secondary Cluster Behavior**:

- Secondary clusters apply the replicated changes and maintain read-only replicas that can serve low-latency reads for applications in the local Region.

4. **Monitoring and Health Checks**:

   - Amazon RDS constantly monitors replication health and synchrony.

   - Functions like `aurora_global_db_status()` and `aurora_global_db_instance_status()` provide fine-grained replication metrics.

Benefits of Aurora Global Databases

- **Low-latency Global Reads**: Applications can serve users worldwide with local read replicas.

- **Disaster Recovery**: In case of Region failure, failover to a secondary Region can be performed quickly.

- **Reduced Application Complexity**: Aurora handles replication and synchronization, reducing the need for custom data movement.

Cross-Region Failover

Cross-region failover allows you to promote a secondary cluster in another Region to be the new primary in the event of a failure or planned switchover.

How Cross-Region Failover Works

- **Manual Process**: Currently, cross-region failover must be initiated manually via the AWS Management Console, AWS CLI, or RDS API.

- **Promotion Steps**:

    o Choose a secondary Region to promote.

    o AWS promotes the secondary cluster, making it writable.

    o DNS endpoints are updated to reflect the change.

    o Other Regions can now replicate from the new primary.

- **Replication Direction Reversal**:

    o After failover, the previous primary Region becomes a read replica (if desired).

    o Storage replication flow is reversed to support the new primary.

Considerations for Cross-Region Failover

- **Lag and Data Loss**: As replication is asynchronous, some transactions may not have been replicated before the failover. This is where RPO (Recovery Point Objective) becomes critical.

- **Application Reconnection**: Applications must be designed to reconnect to the new writer endpoint post-failover.

- **Manual Step Only**: Currently, there is no automatic failover for cross-region Aurora Global Databases.

Best Practices for Cross-Region Failover

- Monitor lag using `aurora_global_db_status()` and `aurora_global_db_instance_status()` to determine best candidate for failover.

- Use Amazon Route 53 or custom logic to reroute application traffic during failover.

- Regularly test failover processes in staging environments.

RPO/RTO Strategies

Understanding RPO (Recovery Point Objective) and RTO (Recovery Time Objective) is critical when designing for high availability and disaster recovery with Aurora Global Databases.

Recovery Point Objective (RPO)

- **Definition**: Maximum acceptable amount of data loss measured in time.

- **Aurora Global Database Context**:

    o RPO is typically under a second due to fast replication at the storage layer.

    o Measured using `durability_lag_in_msec` from the `aurora_global_db_status()` function.

Example query to check durability lag:

```
SELECT * FROM
aurora_global_db_status();
```

Key output fields:

- `durability_lag_in_msec` – Milliseconds of potential data loss.

- `rpo_lag_in_msec` – Time between a commit on the primary and its durability on the secondary.

Tip: You can build dashboards using CloudWatch to monitor these metrics.

Recovery Time Objective (RTO)

- **Definition**: Maximum acceptable time to restore service after a failure.

- **Aurora Global Database Context**:

    o RTO depends on how quickly you can initiate and complete a failover.

    o Typically ranges from a few minutes to under 10 minutes.

Factors that affect RTO:

- Time to detect a failure.

- Time to promote a secondary cluster.

- DNS propagation or routing switch time.

Best Practices to Minimize RTO:

- Automate failover detection and trigger using Lambda or custom monitoring tools.

- Use low-TTL settings for DNS endpoints to reduce propagation time.

- Pre-test application failover logic regularly.

Monitoring Global Database Performance

To manage RPO and RTO effectively, continuous monitoring is essential.

Key Monitoring Tools

- **Amazon CloudWatch** – Use for tracking metrics like:

    - Replication lag

    - CPU and memory utilization

- **Aurora Built-in Functions**:

    - `aurora_global_db_status()` – For durability and RPO lag

    - `aurora_global_db_instance_status()` – For replica-level visibility lag

Sample Queries

Check current replica lag per instance:

```
SELECT server_id, aws_region,
visibility_lag_in_msec

FROM
aurora_global_db_instance_status();
```

Check average RPO across secondary clusters:

```
SELECT aws_region,
round(avg(rpo_lag_in_msec),2) as
avg_rpo

FROM aurora_global_db_status()

WHERE durability_lag_in_msec != -1

GROUP BY aws_region;
```

Use Cases for Aurora Global Databases

- **Global E-Commerce Platforms**:

  - Provide local read access in customer Regions for faster shopping experience.

- **Global SaaS Platforms**:

  - Improve reliability and performance for international clients.

- **Disaster Recovery and Regulatory Compliance**:

- Meet business continuity goals and compliance requirements like GDPR or HIPAA with data replication across geopolitical boundaries.

Trade-Offs and Limitations

While Aurora Global Databases provide powerful capabilities, they are not without limitations:

- **Write Latency**:

  - Writes are only allowed in the primary Region.

  - Applications needing multi-Region write capability must implement custom conflict resolution.

- **Asynchronous Replication**:

  - Data loss is possible during failover due to inherent lag.

  - Not suitable for applications requiring zero data loss.

- **Manual Failover Only**:

  - Lack of automatic cross-region failover requires planning and tooling for robust disaster recovery.

Best Practices Summary

- Enable **detailed monitoring** and log collection in all Regions.

- Use **short DNS TTLs** for quick re-routing after failover.

- Design applications for **read-local/write-global** architecture.

- Regularly **test and simulate failovers** to ensure RTO objectives are met.

- Continuously **track replication lag** with built-in SQL functions.

- Use **AWS CloudFormation** or Infrastructure as Code (IaC) to standardize deployment and configuration across Regions.

Conclusion

Aurora Global Databases enable mission-critical applications to scale globally with high availability, low-latency reads, and robust disaster recovery capabilities. By understanding the architecture, replication mechanics, and recovery strategies, architects and engineers can design resilient, performant systems that meet modern SLAs and compliance needs.

Tip: Always evaluate your RPO/RTO requirements, infrastructure automation, and monitoring maturity before deploying Aurora Global Databases in production.

Chapter 11. Replication Models: Intra-Region and Cross-Region

Replication in Amazon Aurora is a foundational capability that enhances scalability, high availability, disaster recovery, and performance. Aurora supports a variety of replication models tailored to different use cases, including **intra-region replication** within the same AWS Region and **cross-region replication** across different AWS Regions. This chapter provides an in-depth look at Aurora's replication mechanisms, focusing on Aurora Replicas, binlog-based replication, and the differences between asynchronous and semi-synchronous replication modes.

Aurora Replicas vs Read Replicas

Amazon Aurora supports two types of replicas, each suited to different scenarios and workloads:

Aurora Replicas

Aurora Replicas are native to Aurora and offer high-performance, low-latency replication using the Aurora storage engine. These are the recommended replication method within an Aurora cluster.

Key Characteristics:

- Share the same distributed storage volume as the primary instance.

- Typically have a replication lag of **less than 100 milliseconds**.

- Can be promoted to become the primary instance in the event of a failure.

- Up to **15 Aurora Replicas** can be created within the same region.

- Do **not use binlog-based replication**, making them faster and more efficient.

Use Cases:

- Read scaling for high-throughput applications.

- High availability and failover support.

- Application workloads with read-heavy traffic.

Benefits:

- Near real-time consistency.

- Seamless integration with cluster endpoint management.

- Minimal replication lag and automatic failover support.

Read Replicas (Binlog-Based)

Aurora also supports **binlog-based replication** for use cases such as cross-region replication or replicating from an external MySQL-compatible source.

Key Characteristics:

- Rely on **MySQL binary logs (binlogs)** for data replication.

- Higher replication lag (typically **seconds to minutes**).

- Commonly used for **cross-region replication** or integration with external systems.

- Support read-only workloads but are less performant than Aurora Replicas.

Use Cases:

- Disaster recovery across regions.

- Geographically distributed applications with local read access.

- Migration from MySQL to Aurora.

Limitations:

- Higher replication lag due to network latency and binlog processing.

- Cannot be used for high availability/failover within a region.

- Requires manual promotion and reconfiguration during failover.

Binlog-Based Replication

Binary log (binlog) replication is a standard method used in MySQL and Aurora MySQL to replicate changes from one database to another. Aurora supports **binlog-based replication** for scenarios involving **external MySQL databases** or **Aurora-to-Aurora replication** in **cross-region** or **inter-cluster** configurations.

How It Works:

- The **source** database writes changes to the **binary log**.

- The **replica** reads the binary log entries and applies them to its local database.

- This method replicates **row-based**, **statement-based**, or **mixed-format** binlogs.

Aurora Usage:

- Aurora **MySQL-Compatible Edition** supports binlog replication to other Aurora MySQL clusters, RDS MySQL, or external MySQL databases.

- Binlog replication is **asynchronous** by default, but can be configured to simulate semi-synchronous behavior.

- **Aurora PostgreSQL** does **not** use binlog replication; it uses native PostgreSQL streaming replication methods.

Enabling Binlog Replication in Aurora:

- Enable `binlog_format` parameter (typically `ROW`) in the DB parameter group.

- Enable `binlog_row_image` (commonly `FULL`).

- Use stored procedures like `mysql.rds_set_external_master` to configure replication targets.

Limitations:

- Binlogs increase write latency and storage costs.

- Increased complexity compared to Aurora Replicas.

- Not suitable for low-latency read scaling within the same region.

Asynchronous vs Semi-Synchronous Replication

Replication in Aurora, like in traditional MySQL/PostgreSQL, can follow **asynchronous** or **semi-synchronous** models, depending on the setup.

Asynchronous Replication

Definition: Changes are sent from the primary to the replica **without waiting** for acknowledgment. This improves write performance but introduces the possibility of data loss during a failover.

Characteristics:

- Default mode for both Aurora Replicas and binlog-based replication.

- Write operations return to the client as soon as they are committed on the primary.

- Replica may lag behind the primary (depending on replication method).

- Used for performance optimization and loosely coupled replicas.

Implications:

- Risk of data loss if the primary fails before changes reach the replica.

- Suitable for read scaling and analytical workloads.

Semi-Synchronous Replication

Definition: The primary waits for **at least one replica** to acknowledge receipt of the transaction log before confirming the write to the client. This reduces the risk of data loss at the cost of increased write latency.

Aurora Implementation:

- Aurora uses an **enhanced semi-synchronous** model internally for Aurora Replicas.

- Even though replication is technically asynchronous, Aurora's storage layer replicates data across AZs before acknowledging the commit.

Characteristics:

- Aurora Replicas receive log records directly from the writer node.

- Failover targets (Aurora Replicas) are near-synchronously updated due to shared storage.

- Aurora does not expose semi-sync settings directly as MySQL does; it manages consistency through its distributed engine.

Benefits:

- Low risk of data loss.

- Ideal for mission-critical applications that prioritize durability.

Intra-Region vs Cross-Region Replication

Intra-Region Replication

This refers to replication within the same AWS Region using Aurora Replicas.

Features:

- Uses shared storage for high-speed replication.

- Low latency (typically < 10 ms).

- Supports failover and automatic promotion.

- Ideal for high availability and horizontal read scaling.

Topology Example:

pg

```
Aurora Cluster (us-east-1)

    ├──── Writer (instance-1)

    ├──── Aurora Replica 1 (instance-2)

    └──── Aurora Replica 2 (instance-3)
```

Cross-Region Replication

This model uses either **Aurora Global Database** or **binlog-based replication** to replicate across different AWS Regions.

Aurora Global Database:

- Designed for **low-latency global reads** and **disaster recovery**.

- Up to five secondary regions.

- Replication lag typically < 1 second.

- Reader nodes in remote regions can serve read traffic.

- Failover involves promoting a secondary region manually.

Binlog-Based Replication:

- Alternative for Aurora MySQL where Global Database is not used.

- Uses binary logs to stream changes to external or remote databases.

- Higher latency (seconds to minutes).

Cross-Region Considerations:

- Additional cost for cross-region replication.

- AWS Regions should be selected for lowest possible latency.

- Use Global Database for mission-critical, low-latency applications.

- Use binlog replication for integration with non-Aurora systems or custom DR strategies.

Summary

Replication in Amazon Aurora is robust, flexible, and tailored to meet a wide range of application requirements. Aurora Replicas provide low-latency, high-performance replication within a Region, while binlog-based replication and Aurora Global Database offer powerful cross-region replication capabilities. Understanding the trade-offs between asynchronous and semi-synchronous replication helps ensure the right architecture is in place for availability, performance, and durability.

Quick Comparison Table

Feature	Aurora Replicas	Binlog-Based Read Replicas
Replication Type	Storage-based	Binary log-based
Latency	< 100 ms	Seconds to minutes
High Availability	Yes	No
Cross-Region Support	No (unless Global DB)	Yes
Failover Target	Yes	No

Storage	Shared with writer	Independent
Promotion Support	Immediate	Manual
Max Replicas	15	5

Chapter 12. Blue/Green Deployment Strategies

Blue/Green deployments provide a powerful and low-risk strategy for updating Amazon Aurora databases. They enable seamless transitions between environments, reducing downtime and mitigating deployment risks such as failed migrations, performance regressions, or application incompatibilities.

In this chapter, we'll explore:

- How Blue/Green deployments work in Aurora

- Step-by-step guidance for creating Blue/Green environments

- How to perform a safe and reliable switchover

- Validating metrics, performing health checks, and using automation tools

---

Overview of Blue/Green Deployment in Aurora

What is Blue/Green Deployment?

A **Blue/Green deployment** is a deployment strategy where two separate environments run side-by-side:

- **Blue environment**: The current production environment handling live traffic.

- **Green environment**: The clone of the production environment where changes (schema, configuration, or version upgrades) are safely tested before going live.

Once the green environment is validated, traffic is switched over to it with minimal downtime and near-zero risk.

Aurora Support for Blue/Green Deployment

As of recent AWS updates, Aurora supports native **Blue/Green Deployments** for:

- Aurora MySQL-Compatible Edition (v5.7 and v8.0)

- Aurora PostgreSQL-Compatible Edition (v13.4+)

Aurora Blue/Green Deployments are tightly integrated with:

- Amazon RDS Console

- AWS CLI

- AWS SDKs

- AWS CloudFormation

The system handles provisioning, syncing, and switching between environments with safety checks and automated orchestration.

Creating Blue/Green Environments

Step 1: Preparing the Blue (Production) Environment

Before creating a Green environment:

- Ensure your Aurora cluster is stable.

- Apply monitoring tools like **Amazon CloudWatch**, **Performance Insights**, or **Enhanced Monitoring**.

- Review parameter groups and custom configurations.

- Ensure that the Aurora cluster is running a supported engine version for Blue/Green deployments.

Step 2: Initiating the Green Environment

In the RDS Console:

1. Navigate to your **Aurora cluster**.

2. Select **Actions > Create Blue/Green Deployment**.

3. The system will automatically:

   - Clone the entire cluster (writer and readers).

   - Keep replication active between Blue and Green environments.

○ Preserve security groups, DB parameters, IAM roles, and endpoint structure.

Important Notes:

- The Green environment is launched in the same Region.

- It shares the same storage backend, minimizing clone time and cost.

- Changes can be safely made to the Green environment before switchover.

Step 3: Applying Changes in the Green Environment

You can now make controlled changes to the Green environment without affecting production:

- **Schema changes**: Alter tables, indexes, stored procedures.

- **Parameter changes**: Modify DB cluster and instance parameter groups.

- **Version upgrades**: Upgrade Aurora engine versions.

- **Extensions or features**: Enable Aurora ML, IAM auth, or SSL changes.

Tip: Use feature flags or controlled testing scripts to validate your application's compatibility with the changes.

Step 4: Verifying the Green Environment

Before initiating switchover:

- Run integration and regression tests.

- Connect non-production workloads (e.g., staging EC2 or Lambda).

- Compare query performance using **Performance Insights** and **Enhanced Monitoring**.

You can use tools such as:

- **AWS X-Ray** for tracing application latency

- **Amazon CloudWatch Logs** for error tracking

- **Database query logs** to validate performance and correctness

---

Performing Switchover

The switchover process shifts traffic from the Blue environment to the Green environment with minimal disruption. Aurora handles this via automated failover mechanisms that re-point the writer and reader endpoints.

Step-by-Step Switchover Process

1. **Initiate the Switchover**:

   - In RDS Console, select the Blue/Green deployment and click **Switch Over**.

   Alternatively, use the AWS CLI:

   ```
   aws rds switch-over-blue-green-
   deployment \

      --blue-green-deployment-id bgd-
   1234567890abcdef0
   ```

   -

2. **Aurora performs the following actions**:

   - Disconnects clients from Blue (minimal downtime).

   - Promotes the Green writer and readers.

   - Updates endpoints (writer and reader endpoints).

   - Ensures replication has zero lag before cutover.

3. **Switchover Duration**:

   - Typically under **1 minute**, depending on connection teardown time and replication lag.

4. **Post-Switchover State**:

   o The Green environment becomes the new
   production environment.

   o The Blue environment is retained
   temporarily (up to 7 days) for rollback if
   needed.

Built-in Safety Mechanisms

- Aurora prevents switchover if:

   o Replication lag exceeds threshold

   o Incompatible parameter group settings exist

   o Engine versions are unsupported or
   mismatched

Tips for Minimizing Downtime

- Use **connection pooling** with RDS Proxy.

- Gracefully drain application traffic before initiating
  the switch.

- Temporarily reduce write traffic or batch workloads.

- Pre-warm caches and connections in the Green environment.

Automated and Manual Control

You can automate switchover using:

- **AWS CloudFormation**

- **AWS CDK**

- **Custom CI/CD pipelines**

Sample CDK snippet (Python):

```python
rds.CfnBlueGreenDeployment(self,
"MyBlueGreen",

blue_green_deployment_name="MyAppBGDep
loyment",

source=db_cluster.cluster_identifier,

target=db_cluster_new.cluster_identifi
er

)
```

Validating Metrics and Health Checks

After or before switchover, validation of metrics ensures performance and functionality meet expectations. This includes checking CPU usage, replica lag, IOPS, and application behavior.

Key Metrics to Monitor

Database-Level Metrics:

- **AuroraReplicaLag** – Lag in replication to reader nodes.

- **CPUUtilization** – Spikes may indicate under-provisioning.

- **FreeableMemory** – Watch for out-of-memory conditions.

- **DatabaseConnections** – Ensure limits aren't exceeded.

Application-Level Metrics:

- **Query performance**: Using Performance Insights

- **Response latency**: Via Application Load Balancer metrics

- **Error rates**: Monitored via CloudWatch Alarms and X-Ray

Replication Health:

- **AuroraGlobalDBReplicaLag** – For global deployments.

- Use `aurora_global_db_instance_status()` for cross-region replication health.

Health Check Automation

Use CloudWatch alarms and Lambda functions to:

- Trigger rollback if health metrics degrade

- Validate success of post-deployment queries

- Notify via Amazon SNS or Slack integrations

Example CloudWatch Alarm:

```
{

    "MetricName": "AuroraReplicaLag",

    "Threshold": 1000,
```

```
    "ComparisonOperator":
"GreaterThanThreshold",

    "EvaluationPeriods": 1

}
```

Post-Switchover Validation Steps

1. **Connect to the new Green endpoints**.

   Run health-check scripts or queries:

```
SELECT now(), version();
```

2.
3. Validate read/write capability.

4. Confirm application sessions are stable.

5. Inspect CloudWatch dashboards and logs.

Rollback and Cleanup

Automatic Rollback Scenarios

Aurora cancels the switchover if:

- Replication is not in sync

- Parameter conflicts exist

- Health checks fail

Manual Rollback (if needed)

To roll back to the Blue environment:

1. Use the **revert** option in the RDS Console (only within 7 days).

2. Ensure no destructive schema changes were applied after the switch.

3. Update application endpoints accordingly.

Deleting the Blue Environment

After confirming that the Green environment is healthy:

1. Delete the old Blue deployment via RDS Console or AWS CLI.

2. Consider exporting logs or snapshots for audit.

CLI Example:

```
aws rds delete-blue-green-deployment \
```

```
--blue-green-deployment-id bgd-
0987654321abcdef
```

Best Practices for Blue/Green Deployments

- **Always test schema changes in isolated Green environment**.

- **Use parameter group snapshots** before switching.

- **Monitor replica lag** constantly during the deployment.

- **Stagger changes** (schema, version, parameters) to isolate failures.

- **Use Aurora Global Database** for cross-region Blue/Green if DR is required.

- **Pre-warm connections and cache** in the Green cluster.

Limitations and Considerations

- Not all Aurora versions support Blue/Green. Ensure compatibility.

- Serverless v2 is not supported in current Blue/Green deployments.

- Backups are not automatically enabled for the Green environment—configure post-switch.

- Active write traffic during schema changes may cause replication conflicts.

- Aurora charges apply for both Blue and Green environments during overlap period.

Real-World Use Cases

1. Version Upgrade Testing

Upgrade Aurora MySQL 5.7 to 8.0 in the Green environment. Validate all application features and queries, then switch over.

2. Regional Expansion

Clone a US-East production environment to a new region using Aurora Global DB and perform Blue/Green deployment for phased rollout.

3. Compliance Validations

Apply audit-trigger-based logging only in the Green environment and validate logging behavior before switching.

Conclusion

Blue/Green deployments in Amazon Aurora are a best-in-class strategy for zero-downtime updates, safe testing, and rollback assurance. By separating environments and introducing automation, teams can confidently release schema changes, patches, and upgrades without disrupting production workloads.

From high-availability web apps to mission-critical financial systems, Blue/Green deployment empowers development teams with agility, safety, and observability.

Chapter 13. Aurora Cloning and Volume Copying

Use Cases for Cloning

Aurora's **volume cloning feature** enables fast, space-efficient creation of a new database that is a near-exact copy of an existing Aurora DB cluster. Rather than physically duplicating the entire dataset, Aurora uses a **copy-on-write** mechanism, which significantly reduces both the time and storage overhead required to create clones.

What Is Cloning in Aurora?

Aurora cloning creates a new DB cluster that shares the same storage volume as the source cluster. Pages are only duplicated if they are modified in the clone or the source after the cloning operation.

This behavior offers:

- **Fast provisioning**: Clones can be created in minutes, regardless of database size.

- **Minimal storage cost**: Data is not duplicated unless it changes (copy-on-write).

- **Isolation**: Clone behaves like an independent cluster and can be used for independent testing, development, or experimentation.

Primary Use Cases

1. **Testing and Development**

    o Developers can create clones from production databases to test application features, schema changes, or new queries without impacting production workloads.

    o Ideal for testing code against real-world data patterns.

2. **Performance Tuning**

    o Use a clone to benchmark different indexing strategies, query structures, or configurations.

    o Fine-tune parameters using realistic datasets.

3. **Data Validation and ETL Testing**

    o Safely validate ETL pipelines, schema migrations, or data anonymization processes.

    o Prevent contamination of source environments during testing.

4. **Troubleshooting and Debugging**

    o Investigate database issues using a clone of the live environment.

o   Reproduce production scenarios in a sandboxed environment.

5. **Training and Demos**

   o   Use realistic datasets to provide training environments for internal teams or demos for stakeholders.

   o   Each trainee can receive their own isolated clone.

6. **Backup Validation**

   o   Validate that backups and snapshots are functional by restoring and comparing behavior with production environments.

Example: Safe Schema Migration

You could clone a production Aurora PostgreSQL database and apply schema changes to the clone. If migration scripts succeed and application queries behave as expected, then you can safely apply the changes to the original cluster or use the clone in production after promoting it.

Cross-Account and Cross-VPC Cloning

Aurora supports **cloning across AWS accounts and VPCs,** but this requires a deeper understanding of how snapshots and encryption keys work in Aurora.

Cross-VPC Cloning

When cloning between DB clusters in different VPCs:

- **Same AWS account** is typically used.

- **Snapshots** are used to transfer the data reference across VPCs.

- You must ensure **network connectivity** between VPCs if the clone will access external resources (e.g., via VPC peering or Transit Gateway).

Steps for Cross-VPC Cloning:

1. Take a manual **DB cluster snapshot** of the source cluster.

2. Ensure the snapshot is **shared** with the target VPC environment (via account-level or region-level access).

3. Use the AWS Console or CLI to **create a new cluster from the shared snapshot** in the desired VPC.

4. Configure connectivity (subnets, security groups, routing).

Cross-Account Cloning

This use case allows you to **share Aurora DB clusters across AWS accounts** securely. It requires attention to

snapshot sharing, encryption key policies, and IAM permissions.

Prerequisites:

- The source snapshot must be **manual** (automated snapshots can't be shared).

- If the snapshot is **encrypted**, you must share the AWS KMS key used to encrypt it with the destination account.

- The source account must **explicitly grant snapshot access** to the destination account using AWS CLI, SDK, or console.

High-Level Workflow:

1. **Create a manual snapshot** in the source account.

2. **Share the snapshot** with the destination AWS account.

3. If the snapshot is encrypted:

    - Modify the **KMS key policy** to allow access to the destination account.

    - Share the **KMS key ID** with the destination user.

4. The destination account can now **restore the snapshot** to create a new Aurora cluster.

CLI Example for Cross-Account Sharing

In the source account:

```
aws rds modify-db-cluster-snapshot-
attribute \

    --db-cluster-snapshot-identifier
my-prod-snapshot \

    --attribute-name restore \

    --values-to-add 123456789012
```

If encrypted, also update the KMS key policy to grant usage to the target account.

In the target account:

```
aws rds restore-db-cluster-from-
snapshot \

    --db-cluster-identifier my-cloned-
cluster \

    --snapshot-identifier
arn:aws:rds:region:123456789012:cluste
r-snapshot:my-prod-snapshot \
```

```
--engine aurora-mysql \

--kms-key-id your-kms-key-id
```

Considerations for Network Configuration

- Ensure the **subnet group and VPC** in the target account are compatible with the cluster configuration.

- Use **appropriate security groups** to allow application traffic.

Common Use Case: Secure Analytics Environment

Data teams often need to analyze production data without having access to production environments. Using cross-account cloning, an analytics team can operate on a secure, sandboxed copy of data.

Security and Limitations

While Aurora cloning offers speed and efficiency, it also introduces some **important security and operational considerations**.

Data Access and IAM Policies

- Aurora cloning respects the **IAM permissions** of the user/account performing the operation.

- Snapshot sharing and KMS access **must be explicitly granted** to allow cloning across accounts or VPCs.

- Users cloning encrypted clusters must have `kms:Decrypt` permission on the key used to encrypt the snapshot.

Encryption Considerations

- If your Aurora cluster uses **encryption**, clones will also be encrypted using the same key unless you specify a new one.

- You can clone to a different KMS key, but the new key must be accessible in the destination region/account.

- Unencrypted clusters cannot be cloned into encrypted clusters unless a snapshot-based restore is used with a specified key.

Limitations and Constraints

1. **Clone Scope**:

   - Clones include **all databases** in the cluster.

   - You cannot clone a single schema or table—granularity is at the cluster level.

2. **Availability**:

- Cloning is supported only for **Aurora MySQL and Aurora PostgreSQL**.

- Must be performed within **same AWS Region**, unless using snapshot export/import for cross-region purposes.

3. **Cluster Type**:

- Only **provisioned clusters** can be cloned.

- Aurora Serverless v1 and v2 clusters **cannot be used as clone sources or targets**.

4. **Lifecycle Dependency**:

- Since clones share the storage volume, deleting the source cluster can impact clone behavior if copy-on-write pages are still being used.

- However, if the source cluster is deleted after the clone has written to most of its own data pages, the clone remains unaffected.

5. **Performance Impacts**:

- Initial clones have minimal storage impact, but performance may degrade if both source and clone heavily modify the same data.

- ○ Clone storage usage grows with divergence from the source dataset.

Monitoring and Auditing

- Use **AWS CloudTrail** to audit clone creation events, especially across accounts.

- Monitor clone performance using **Amazon CloudWatch** metrics and **Performance Insights**.

Tips for Secure Operations

- **Tag all snapshots and clones** for cost and access control.

- **Rotate KMS keys** periodically and validate access.

- Use **resource-level permissions** to restrict who can perform clone operations.

Summary

Aurora cloning and volume copying provide a powerful mechanism for creating space-efficient, fast, and flexible copies of your databases. These capabilities are especially valuable for:

- Isolated testing environments

- Development and staging setups

- Data science and analytics use

- Training and educational purposes

- Disaster recovery drills

By leveraging **copy-on-write storage**, **snapshot sharing**, and **IAM/KMS permissions**, you can securely perform cross-VPC and cross-account clones with minimal administrative overhead.

While cloning offers many benefits, it's essential to understand its **security implications, limitations, and lifecycle dependencies**. When used strategically, cloning can accelerate development cycles, enhance data governance, and reduce risk across environments.

Chapter 14. Aurora Serverless: v1 vs v2

Amazon Aurora Serverless is an **on-demand, autoscaling configuration** of Amazon Aurora. It enables databases to scale up or down seamlessly based on your application's needs, without requiring manual provisioning or instance sizing. Aurora Serverless is ideal for applications with **infrequent, unpredictable, or variable workloads**, such as dev/test environments, SaaS applications with variable usage, or infrequently used APIs.

Aurora Serverless comes in two major versions—**v1 and v2**—each with significantly different capabilities. This chapter explores their **auto-scaling behavior**, **session management**, and **pricing models**, while identifying key differences, limitations, and use cases for each.

Auto-Scaling Behavior

Auto-scaling is the defining feature of Aurora Serverless. It allows the database to adapt compute capacity based on application load. However, **Aurora Serverless v1** and **v2** differ substantially in how they implement and manage this auto-scaling.

Aurora Serverless v1 Auto-Scaling

Aurora Serverless v1 uses a **capacity unit-based model** (Aurora Capacity Units - ACUs), ranging from **1 to 256 ACUs**. Each ACU is roughly equivalent to a specific amount of compute and memory.

- **Scaling Triggers:**

    - Automatically scales based on CPU utilization, connections, and active sessions.

    - Capacity is adjusted in *doubling/halving steps* (e.g., $2 \rightarrow 4 \rightarrow 8$ ACUs), which can cause latency during transitions.

- **Cold Start Penalty:**

- If the database has been idle and is paused, the first connection triggers a **cold start**, adding noticeable latency (typically several seconds).

- **Scale Timing:**

  - Scaling can take **30 to 60 seconds**.

  - Scaling is **disruptive**, i.e., existing connections may be dropped during scaling events.

- **Pause/Resume:**

  - Supports automatic pausing after a configurable idle timeout (5 minutes to 1 day).

  - Good for infrequently used databases, but **not suitable for real-time apps** due to cold start latency.

Aurora Serverless v2 Auto-Scaling

Aurora Serverless v2 introduces **fine-grained, millisecond-level autoscaling**. It offers **instantaneous scaling** without dropping connections or impacting performance.

- **Granular Scaling:**

- Scales in **0.5 ACU increments**, from **0.5 ACUs to 128 ACUs** (as of 2025).

- Capacity is allocated dynamically to match the workload in real time.

- **No Cold Start:**

  - The database remains "warm" even when idle. It doesn't pause, so there is no cold start delay.

- **Seamless Scaling:**

  - Scaling is *non-disruptive*. Ongoing queries and connections remain uninterrupted.

- **Concurrency & Workload Spikes:**

  - Can handle large spikes in connections or query concurrency (e.g., thousands of connections).

  - Ideal for unpredictable or highly variable workloads (e.g., web apps, microservices).

Summary Comparison: Auto-Scaling

Feature	Aurora Serverless v1	Aurora Serverless v2
Scaling Unit	1–256 ACUs (doubling steps)	0.5–128 ACUs (fine-grained)
Cold Start	Yes	No
Scale Latency	30–60 seconds	Millisecond-level

Connection Disruption	Possible during scale-up/down	No
Pause/Resume	Supported	Not applicable
Scale-to-Zero	Yes	No
Use Case Fit	Infrequent workloads	High-concurrency, real-time

---

Session Management

Session management differs significantly between v1 and v2, impacting application connection strategies, compatibility with connection pooling, and user experience during scale events.

Aurora Serverless v1 Session Management

- **Stateless Scaling:**

  - Connections may be **dropped or reset** during scaling operations or resume from pause.

- **Connection Handling:**

  - Applications must be resilient to dropped connections.

  - Does **not support RDS Proxy**, which complicates session management.

- **Idle Session Behavior:**

- o After a pause, existing sessions are terminated.

- o Application must reconnect on resume, which may result in errors or delays.

- **Best Practice:**

  - o Use retry logic and exponential backoff in clients to handle disconnects.

  - o Keep idle timeouts configured appropriately to avoid unwanted pauses.

Aurora Serverless v2 Session Management

- **Stateful Scaling:**

  - o Maintains **persistent, uninterrupted sessions** during scaling.

- **RDS Proxy Support:**

  - o Fully supports **Amazon RDS Proxy**, improving connection management and app resiliency.

- **High Connection Volume:**

  - o Scales to handle **thousands of concurrent connections**.

- Connections are pooled and reused efficiently across compute capacity.

- **Seamless User Experience:**

    - Applications do not need special logic to handle scaling events.

    - Ideal for low-latency, always-available workloads.

Summary Comparison: Session Management

Feature	Aurora Serverless v1	Aurora Serverless v2
Connection Persistence	Not guaranteed	Guaranteed
RDS Proxy Integration	Not supported	Supported
Scaling Disruption	Disruptive	Non-disruptive
Session-aware Scaling	No	Yes
Idle Session Handling	Sessions dropped after pause	Sessions preserved

Pricing Model and Limitations

Aurora Serverless pricing is based on **consumed compute and storage** resources. However, the pricing model and limitations differ between v1 and v2.

Aurora Serverless v1 Pricing

- **Billed per second** based on ACUs consumed while the database is active.

- Supports **scale-to-zero**, making it **cost-efficient for infrequent workloads**.

- Paused time is **not billed**, except for storage and I/O.

- No support for **reserved capacity discounts** or instance-based pricing.

Limitations

- Limited **regional availability**.

- Not supported for **global databases** or **cross-Region replicas**.

- Does not support many enterprise features:

  - Aurora Global Databases

  - Backtrack

  - Performance Insights (limited)

- **Scaling granularity is coarse**, leading to over-provisioning.

Aurora Serverless v2 Pricing

- **Billed per second** based on actual ACUs used.

- No scale-to-zero, but can **scale down to 0.5 ACU**, which is low-cost for idle periods.

- Supports **enterprise features**:

  - Aurora Global Databases

  - Performance Insights

  - RDS Proxy

  - Blue/Green Deployments

- Compatible with **Aurora I/O-Optimized** and **provisioned storage tiers**.

Cost Optimization Tips

- Use **I/O-Optimized** if your workload is I/O heavy to reduce IOPS costs.

- Combine with **Auto Scaling read replicas** for analytics or high-volume reads.

- Monitor usage via **CloudWatch metrics** and use **cost allocation tags**.

Summary Comparison: Pricing and Limitations

Feature	Aurora Serverless v1	Aurora Serverless v2
Pricing Unit	Per-second ACUs	Per-second ACUs
Scale-to-Zero	Yes	No
Min Billing Unit	1 ACU	0.5 ACU
Enterprise Features	Limited	Full support

Global Database Support	No	Yes
Performance Insights	Limited	Full support
RDS Proxy	No	Yes
Availability	Limited Regions	Broad availability

Best Use Cases

Aurora Serverless v1

- **Infrequent or intermittent workloads**:

    o Internal dashboards

    o Scheduled reporting

    o Developer testing environments

- **Cost-sensitive scenarios**:

    o Lightweight web apps with occasional traffic

    o Development or staging environments

Aurora Serverless v2

- **Modern, cloud-native applications**:

    o Web applications

    o APIs

- Serverless backends

- **High concurrency, real-time workloads**:

  - SaaS multi-tenant apps

  - Event-driven microservices

  - Data pipelines using Aurora ML or Zero-ETL

Migration and Compatibility Notes

Migrating from v1 to v2

- Aurora Serverless v1 and v2 are **not interchangeable**.

- You cannot **upgrade in-place**; migration involves:

  - Creating a new Aurora Serverless v2 cluster

  - Exporting and importing data via snapshot or dump

  - Reconfiguring application endpoints

Feature Compatibility

Capability	v1 Supported	v2 Supported
IAM Authentication	Yes	Yes
SSL/TLS Encryption	Yes	Yes
Backtrack	No	Yes

Cross-Region Replication	No	Yes
Zero-ETL to Redshift	No	Yes
Aurora ML	No	Yes
Blue/Green Deployments	No	Yes

Final Thoughts

Aurora Serverless v1 introduced the concept of truly dynamic, on-demand relational databases. However, it came with limitations that made it suitable only for certain workloads.

Aurora Serverless v2, on the other hand, brings **enterprise-grade performance, seamless scalability, and full feature compatibility** with Aurora's capabilities. For most production applications today—especially those needing high concurrency, low latency, or integration with ML and analytics—**Aurora Serverless v2 is the preferred choice**.

> 💡 **Tip:** Always evaluate Aurora Serverless v2 over v1 unless you explicitly need scale-to-zero behavior for dev/test workloads. The operational and performance advantages of v2 far outweigh the cold start benefits of v1.

Part III: Infrastructure and Setup

Chapter 15. Instance Classes and Hardware Specifications

When deploying Amazon Aurora, selecting the right **instance class** is one of the most crucial decisions that affects **performance**, **cost-efficiency**, and **scalability** of your database workload. Aurora supports a wide range of instance classes optimized for different use cases—from dev/test environments to high-performance, production-grade enterprise applications.

This chapter provides a deep dive into Aurora instance classes, including a comprehensive overview of instance types, detailed memory and CPU considerations, and best practices to help you choose the right instance class for your workload.

Instance Types Overview

Aurora runs on **Amazon EC2 instances** behind the scenes, grouped into families based on hardware capabilities and use cases. Each **instance class** within a family defines a combination of **vCPUs**, **RAM**, **network throughput**, and **storage performance**. These instances power Aurora **primary instances** (writers) and **replica instances** (readers).

Key Aurora-Compatible Instance Families

Here's an overview of the most common EC2 instance families supported by Amazon Aurora:

- **General Purpose (Burstable)**

  - **T3** and **T4g**

  - Use CPU credits to burst above baseline

  - Ideal for dev/test or low-throughput workloads

  - Limited by performance ceiling and not ideal for production

- **General Purpose**

  - **M5, M6g**

  - Balanced CPU and memory

  - Good default choice for mixed workloads

  - Suitable for OLTP applications and mid-size data processing

- **Memory Optimized**

  - **R5, R6g**

  - Higher RAM-to-vCPU ratio

  - Optimized for in-memory databases and high-read workloads

- Excellent for analytical queries, caching, or large dataset processing

- **Compute Optimized**

  - **C5**, **C6g**

  - High CPU-to-memory ratio

  - Suitable for CPU-bound workloads such as analytics or simulations

- **Graviton-Based Instances (ARM)**

  - **T4g**, **M6g**, **R6g**, **C6g**

  - Cost-effective and energy-efficient

  - Require ARM-compatible applications

Aurora Serverless Instance Classes

Aurora Serverless v2 supports **automatic scaling** of compute capacity based on demand using **Aurora Capacity Units (ACUs)**. ACUs scale up or down in fine-grained increments (0.5 ACU steps), making it ideal for variable or unpredictable workloads.

Memory and CPU Considerations

Your Aurora database's performance will depend heavily on the **memory capacity, vCPU availability**, and **throughput** provided by the selected instance class.

vCPU Considerations

- **vCPUs** are virtual cores available for query processing, background operations, and replication.

- More vCPUs enable:

    - Higher **concurrency**

    - Faster **parallel query execution**

    - Reduced **latency** for heavy workloads

- **CPU-bound applications** like real-time analytics may require compute-optimized or higher-tier general-purpose classes.

Memory Considerations

- Memory impacts:

    - Query execution, sorting, joins

    - Size of **buffer/cache pools**

    - **In-memory data structures** (e.g., for JSON operations, hash joins)

- Memory-optimized classes are ideal when:

- Running **large joins or aggregations**

- Minimizing **disk I/O** by caching large datasets in memory

- Supporting **in-memory workloads** (e.g., AI feature engineering)

Network and Storage IOPS

- Aurora's storage is **decoupled and distributed**, but instance type still impacts:

  - **Network throughput to the storage layer**

  - **Replication speed** for Aurora Replicas

- Larger instance classes typically have higher **bandwidth** and **IOPS quotas**

Aurora Serverless Considerations

- Aurora Serverless v2 allocates **vCPUs and memory automatically**

- Provisioning scales **between 0.5 to 128 ACUs**, where 1 ACU ~ 2GB RAM + fraction of vCPU

- Trade-off: May have **slightly higher latency** on scaling events compared to provisioned

Best Practices for Instance Class Selection

Choosing the optimal instance class requires balancing **performance**, **scalability**, and **cost**. Below are best practices for selecting Aurora instance types for different use cases.

1. Analyze Workload Characteristics

Start by profiling your workload:

- Is it **read-heavy**, **write-intensive**, or **balanced**?

- Does it involve **complex queries**, **joins**, or **in-memory computation**?

- How important is **latency**, **throughput**, and **bursting ability**?

Based on this, choose:

Workload Type	Recommended Instance Family
Development / Testing	T3, T4g
General Purpose OLTP	M5, M6g
Read-Heavy / In-Memory	R5, R6g
CPU-Intensive Analytics	C5, C6g
Variable Demand	Aurora Serverless v2

2. Use Aurora Serverless v2 for Variable Workloads

- Ideal for unpredictable workloads or microservices architectures

173

- Avoids overprovisioning and reduces idle compute costs

- Automatically handles scale-up during peak loads

- Use **provisioned Aurora** for steady-state, predictable workloads

3. Consider Graviton-Based Instances for Cost Efficiency

- Graviton2/3 (ARM) instances (e.g., M6g, R6g) offer:

  - **Up to 40% better price/performance** over x86

  - Support for Aurora MySQL and Aurora PostgreSQL

- Ensure application is **ARM-compatible**

4. Test with Performance Insights

- Use **Performance Insights** to evaluate CPU usage, wait events, and bottlenecks

- Monitor for metrics like:

  - High average **active sessions (AAS)**

  - Queries waiting on **CPU or I/O**

- Consider scaling up if CPU consistently exceeds **Max vCPU** threshold

5. Align Aurora Replicas with Writer Instance Class

- For consistent performance across read replicas, use **same class and size** as the writer

- Avoid having weaker replicas if read query performance is critical

6. Monitor and Adjust

- Set up **CloudWatch alarms** for CPU, memory, throughput

- Periodically reevaluate instance sizing as application evolves

- Use **Auto Scaling** with Aurora Replicas to handle read surges

7. Use Reserved Instances for Cost Optimization

- If workloads are stable and long-term, buy **Reserved Instances** to save up to 65%

- Applies to **provisioned Aurora** instances only

- Combine with **Savings Plans** for broader EC2/RDS coverage

Example Use Cases and Instance Recommendations

OLTP for SaaS Platform

- **Workload**: Balanced reads/writes, high concurrency

- **Instance class**: M6g.large or M6g.xlarge (Graviton)

- **Aurora version**: MySQL or PostgreSQL

- **Why**: Balanced compute/memory, cost-effective with predictable load

Analytical Reporting App

- **Workload**: Complex read queries, large data scans

- **Instance class**: R6g.2xlarge

- **Aurora version**: PostgreSQL (for advanced SQL features)

- **Why**: High memory to cache data, faster joins/aggregations

Event-Driven Architecture

- **Workload**: Spiky, unpredictable demand

- **Instance class**: Aurora Serverless v2 (1–64 ACUs)

- **Aurora version**: MySQL

- **Why**: Scales with event load, cost savings during idle

High-Performance API Backend

- **Workload**: High QPS, low latency requirement

- **Instance class**: C6g.xlarge

- **Aurora version**: MySQL or PostgreSQL

- **Why**: Compute-optimized for rapid request handling

Summary

Choosing the right instance class for Amazon Aurora is essential to achieving the **right balance between cost and performance**. Aurora offers flexibility with a wide range of **provisioned instances** and **serverless compute**, allowing you to tailor deployments to your workload patterns.

Key takeaways:

- Understand your **workload** before selecting an instance class.

- Use **Performance Insights** to guide ongoing optimization.

- Match **replica instances** to writer for performance parity.

- Leverage **Aurora Serverless v2** and **Graviton instances** for efficiency.

- Periodically revisit instance choices as **usage and applications evolve**.

By applying these strategies and understanding the technical implications of each instance type, you can ensure your Aurora database remains **high-performing, scalable, and cost-efficient**.

Chapter 16. Configuring Storage and Auto-Scaling

Introduction

Amazon Aurora is designed with a decoupled storage and compute architecture that enables near-infinite storage scalability, high availability, and fault tolerance. Unlike traditional databases where storage must be pre-allocated, Aurora uses a distributed storage engine that **automatically expands and contracts** the underlying volume as needed. This capability simplifies provisioning, eliminates the need for manual resizing, and enhances performance through Aurora's high-performance I/O subsystem.

In this chapter, we examine how Aurora's storage auto-expansion works, how to monitor and manage storage thresholds, and explore the IOPS behavior in different Aurora configurations.

Aurora Storage Architecture

Cluster Volume Design

Aurora clusters use a **cluster volume** architecture:

- **Shared across all DB instances** in a cluster (writer and readers)

- **Distributed across six storage nodes** in three Availability Zones (AZs)

179

- Fault-tolerant to the loss of up to two copies of data without affecting write availability

Aurora's storage engine is **log-structured**, meaning it stores only changes (redo log records), which improves write efficiency and allows for features like backtracking and snapshots without full-volume copies.

Storage Auto-Expansion

How Storage Scaling Works

Aurora storage grows automatically in **10 GB increments**, based on demand. There's no downtime or performance degradation during scaling. The process is **fully managed**, requiring no user intervention or configuration.

Key characteristics:

- **Minimum size**: 10 GB (starting volume)

- **Maximum size**:

    - Aurora MySQL: Up to **128 TiB**

    - Aurora PostgreSQL: Up to **128 TiB**

- **Scale-up only**: Storage does not shrink when data is deleted, although logical reclamation of space is possible using VACUUM or OPTIMIZE TABLE.

Triggers for Scaling

Aurora triggers volume expansion automatically when:

- Data or logs written approach current allocated storage

- Backups, snapshots, or logs accumulate (e.g., during long-running transactions or heavy writes)

Scaling is **predictive**, based on internal heuristics and storage pressure.

Storage Efficiency

Aurora's log-based storage minimizes disk usage:

- For updates, only changes are logged, not full page writes

- For deleted rows, space is not immediately reclaimed but becomes available for reuse

- Compression is applied in storage layers to reduce I/O overhead and storage footprint

---

Monitoring Limits and Alerts

Storage Monitoring Tools

Aurora provides several ways to monitor storage usage and thresholds:

1. **Amazon CloudWatch Metrics**

   - `VolumeBytesUsed`: Current size of data in bytes

   - `VolumeWriteIOPS` and `VolumeReadIOPS`: IOPS usage

   - `FreeStorageSpace`: Deprecated for Aurora (use VolumeBytesUsed instead)

2. **Performance Insights**

   - IOPS impact from SQL queries

   - Identify write-heavy transactions contributing to volume expansion

3. **Aurora DB Events**

   - RDS event subscriptions can notify you when storage usage grows rapidly or exceeds thresholds

4. **SQL Functions (Aurora PostgreSQL)**

   - Use `aurora_stat_file` or `pg_stat_database` for file-level usage statistics

   - Use `pg_stat_user_tables` to identify bloated or large tables

Setting Storage Alerts

To proactively monitor growth:

- Set CloudWatch Alarms on:

    - `VolumeBytesUsed` threshold (e.g., alert when >90% of known usage baseline)

    - `WriteIOPS` spikes indicating bulk imports or log growth

Best Practice: Tag large data loads or ETL pipelines and correlate them with storage metrics to anticipate changes.

Managing Growth and Controlling Storage

Preventing Uncontrolled Expansion

Though Aurora auto-scales, it's still important to manage storage wisely:

- **Identify long-running or uncommitted transactions**: They prevent log truncation and consume storage.

- **Monitor binary logs** (Aurora MySQL): Excessive binlogs can accumulate and grow the volume.

- **Archive infrequently accessed data**: Use tiered storage patterns (e.g., move old data to S3).

Vacuuming and Reclamation (PostgreSQL)

For Aurora PostgreSQL:

- Use `VACUUM` and `ANALYZE` to:

    - Reclaim storage from dead rows

    - Update planner statistics

- Monitor `pg_stat_user_tables.dead_tup` for bloat

OPTIMIZE TABLE (MySQL)

For Aurora MySQL:

- Use `OPTIMIZE TABLE` on tables with frequent updates or deletes to reclaim storage

- Avoid running on large tables during peak times due to temporary I/O and CPU load

---

IOPS Characteristics and Performance Behavior

Aurora I/O Subsystem

Aurora uses a **highly parallel, distributed log-based storage engine**. IOPS behavior is influenced by:

- Volume of concurrent writes

- Read patterns (random vs. sequential)

- Page cache hit ratios

- Network transfer and replication overhead (within and across AZs)

Key Aurora I/O principles:

- Writes are **appended logs** sent to six replicas (two per AZ)

- Reads served from **local cache** where possible; misses go to storage nodes

- Read replicas have their own buffer caches to reduce I/O

Baseline vs. Burst IOPS

Unlike provisioned IOPS in RDS, Aurora uses **shared, burstable IOPS**:

- Baseline IOPS: Determined by workload and storage volume

- Burst capacity: Aurora storage automatically adjusts throughput based on demand

- For sustained high IOPS needs, larger instance classes (e.g., `db.r6g.4xlarge+`) provide more network bandwidth and throughput

Aurora does **not charge separately for IOPS**, unlike RDS or EBS volumes.

Read vs. Write IOPS

I/O Type	Description	Optimization Strategy
Write IOPS	Triggered by INSERTs, UPDATEs, DELETEs, WAL	Batch writes, monitor transactions
Read IOPS	Cache misses, cold starts, complex queries	Use replicas, warm cache, optimize plans
Log Writes	Background writes for replication, crash logs	Reduce checkpoint frequency, batch ops
Metadata IOPS	Schema changes, index rebuilds	Schedule off-peak, use maintenance mode

Performance and Storage Sizing Recommendations

Choosing Instance Classes

Aurora storage scales independently, but I/O throughput benefits from larger instances:

- **Memory-rich instances** improve caching and reduce read IOPS

- **Graviton2/3-based instances** (db.r6g) offer better price/performance for I/O-heavy workloads

Planning for Growth

- Use historical data from CloudWatch to forecast storage usage

- Consider:

    ○ Dataset growth rate

    ○ Snapshot retention policies

    ○ Binary log accumulation

    ○ Schema evolution (e.g., adding indexes)

Tip: Aurora charges for actual storage used (GB/month), not provisioned capacity.

Real-World Examples

Case 1: Analytics Workload

- Writes large datasets daily (~500 GB/day)

- Experiences spikes in write IOPS and storage

- Mitigation:

    ○ Load data into staging tables

    ○ Run `OPTIMIZE TABLE` nightly

- Use Aurora Replica for BI queries to offload reads

Case 2: Multi-Tenant SaaS

- High transactional volume

- Encountered rapid storage growth due to long-lived transactions

- Resolution:

  - Improved app logic to avoid uncommitted writes

  - Added alerting on transaction age and log usage

  - Enabled Performance Insights to trace bloated queries

Case 3: Aurora PostgreSQL CDC System

- Uses logical replication with `wal2json`

- Disk usage increased due to retained WAL segments

- Actions:

  - Adjusted `wal_keep_segments`

- o Increased vacuum frequency

- o Monitored replication slot lag

Summary of Key Metrics

Metric	Description	Tool
`VolumeBytesUsed`	Total storage consumed	CloudWatch
`VolumeWriteIOPS`	Write operations per second	CloudWatch, Perf Insights
`aurora_replica_status()`	Read replica lag and read LSN	SQL function (PostgreSQL)
`pg_stat_user_tables`	Table bloat and row churn	PostgreSQL internal view
`pg_stat_activity`	Transaction age	PostgreSQL internal view
`SHOW ENGINE INNODB STATUS`	Buffer pool stats (Aurora MySQL)	SQL

Best Practices

For Storage Management

- Enable **automatic monitoring** of storage usage via CloudWatch alarms

- Periodically analyze **long-running transactions**

- Clean up obsolete tables or unused indexes

- **Partition large tables** to reduce index and vacuum overhead

For Performance Optimization

- Use **Aurora Replicas** to offload reads and reporting

- Scale instance size to match I/O demand

- Tune memory buffers (e.g., `innodb_buffer_pool_size`, `shared_buffers`)

- Use **parallel query** for large analytics workloads (Aurora PostgreSQL)

For Cost Efficiency

- Archive cold data to **Amazon S3**

- Enable **snapshot export to S3** for long-term backups

- Use **Reserved Instances** to reduce compute cost

- Monitor and trim **excessive binlog or WAL retention**

Conclusion

Amazon Aurora's storage architecture eliminates the need for manual provisioning, offering dynamic, transparent storage scaling. By leveraging log-based replication, multi-AZ durability, and intelligent I/O distribution, Aurora ensures high performance and availability at massive scale.

Understanding how storage growth is triggered, how IOPS behave under various workloads, and how to monitor these characteristics is essential for optimizing performance and cost. With the right monitoring and tuning practices, Aurora can support diverse workloads—from OLTP to analytics—without the typical limitations of legacy RDBMS storage subsystems.

Chapter 17. Cluster Endpoints and Networking

Amazon Aurora provides a flexible and highly available connection model through multiple endpoint types, each tailored for specific roles in an Aurora DB cluster. These endpoints simplify application connectivity, facilitate load distribution, support fault tolerance, and allow dynamic scaling without hardcoding host addresses.

This chapter provides an in-depth exploration of Aurora's networking and endpoint system, focusing on **Writer**, **Reader**, **Custom**, and **Cluster endpoints**, as well as **DNS-based failover** mechanisms and **query routing strategies**.

Understanding Aurora's Endpoint Architecture

Aurora abstracts physical database instances behind logical endpoints. Each endpoint resolves to a **Network Load Balancer (NLB)**-style DNS name, allowing Aurora to dynamically map application traffic to the appropriate DB instance, depending on the type of endpoint.

Aurora endpoint design delivers:

- **Seamless failover** via DNS

- **Dynamic scaling** support

- **Simplified client configuration**

- **Workload-specific routing**

Writer, Reader, Custom, and Cluster Endpoints

Aurora provides several endpoint types. Each plays a distinct role in ensuring performance, high availability, and flexibility for read and write workloads.

Writer Endpoint

- **Purpose**: Directs traffic to the **primary (writer)** instance in the cluster.

- **Use case**: All **write operations**, **DML/DDL** queries, and transactions requiring consistency.

- **Behavior during failover**:

    - If the writer fails, the endpoint is **remapped via DNS** to the newly promoted writer.

    - This DNS change can take up to **30 seconds** to propagate, depending on the client and TTL settings.

Example:

pg

```
mydb-cluster.cluster-ABCDEFGHIJKL.us-
east-1.rds.amazonaws.com
```

Reader Endpoint

- **Purpose**: Distributes traffic **across Aurora Replicas**.

- **Use case**: Read scaling, reporting, analytics, read-only queries.

- **Load balancing**: Routes traffic **randomly** to available replicas (round-robin at DNS level).

- **Failover behavior**: Continues routing to other readers if one fails.

Benefits:

- Ideal for **horizontal scaling** of reads.

- Application logic can remain simple — connect to one endpoint, let Aurora balance the load.

Example:

pg

```
mydb-cluster.cluster-ro-
ABCDEFGHIJKL.us-east-
1.rds.amazonaws.com
```

Custom Endpoints

- **Purpose**: Offers granular control by targeting **a subset of Aurora Replicas**.

- **Use case**:

  - Routing to high-memory or optimized read-only replicas.

  - Isolating workloads (e.g., BI tools, batch jobs).

  - Controlling query routing manually.

How it works:

- You define a custom endpoint and **associate specific replica instances**.

- Aurora maintains the mapping and uses DNS to route to those instances.

Example:

```
analytics-endpoint.mydb-cluster-
custom.us-east-1.rds.amazonaws.com
```

Cluster Endpoint

- **Alias**: Also called the **primary cluster endpoint**.

- **Purpose**: Used interchangeably with the **writer endpoint** in Aurora documentation.

- **Behavior**:

  - Always points to the current writer.

  - Ensures application writes go to the right place even after failover.

How DNS Failover and Routing Work in Aurora

Aurora's endpoint system relies on **Amazon Route 53** to dynamically resolve endpoints. Here's how failover and DNS routing work under the hood.

DNS Behavior

- Each Aurora endpoint resolves to **IP addresses of healthy DB instances** based on its type.

- Aurora updates DNS records during failovers or scaling events.

- The TTL is low (typically **30 seconds**) to ensure quick updates, but client DNS caching may delay resolution.

DNS Failover Mechanics

During a failover:

- Aurora **promotes a new writer instance**.

- The **cluster endpoint DNS** record is updated to point to the new writer.

- **Reader endpoints** continue to function, excluding the failed instance.

Client-side considerations:

- Ensure that your database drivers and clients **respect TTL** and re-resolve DNS frequently.

- Use **retry logic** in your connection layers to recover from short failures.

Multi-AZ and Cross-AZ Resiliency

- Aurora automatically deploys **instances across Availability Zones (AZs)**.

- Endpoints resolve to **instances in multiple AZs** (when replicas exist).

- Aurora detects instance or AZ failures and shifts DNS mappings to healthy targets.

Endpoint-Based Query Routing

Aurora's endpoint architecture enables you to **separate workloads** at the network level — a key design pattern for performance and scalability.

Use Case: Application Workload Separation

You can configure your application to send:

- **OLTP traffic (writes + reads)** to the **cluster endpoint**

- **Reporting traffic** to a **custom endpoint with analytics-optimized readers**

- **Ad-hoc BI queries** to a **dedicated reader endpoint**

This design avoids overloading the writer and preserves write throughput while scaling reads.

Query Routing Patterns

1. **Writer-focused**:

   - Use the **cluster endpoint** for all transactions when strict consistency is required.

2. **Read scaling**:

   - Use the **reader endpoint** for read-only workloads.

- The application doesn't need to track replica health — Aurora handles it.

3. **Custom workload isolation**:

   - Create **custom endpoints** mapped to specific reader instances.

   - Tag high-memory or high-throughput instances for analytics workloads.

4. **Failover-safe**:

   - Ensure your connection layer handles brief disconnections during failover.

   - Use **connection pools** that can refresh DNS mappings (e.g., HikariCP with TTL refresh).

Configuring and Managing Endpoints

You can manage endpoints using:

- **AWS Management Console**

- **AWS CLI**

- **RDS API**

Creating Custom Endpoints (via CLI)

```
aws rds create-db-cluster-endpoint \

  --db-cluster-identifier mydb-cluster
\

  --db-cluster-endpoint-type READER \

  --db-cluster-endpoint-identifier
analytics-endpoint \

  --static-members replica1 replica2 \

  --excluded-members replica3
```

Viewing Endpoints

```
aws rds describe-db-cluster-endpoints
\

  --db-cluster-identifier mydb-cluster
```

Best Practices for Endpoint Usage

- **Use reader endpoints** for non-critical reads to distribute load.

- **Isolate batch or reporting workloads** using custom endpoints.

- **Design for failover**: Ensure your apps retry failed connections gracefully.

- **Refresh DNS**: Use libraries that respect TTL and re-resolve endpoints frequently.

- **Monitor**: Track which endpoints are being used and evaluate query performance by endpoint.

Real-World Example Architectures

Example 1: Microservice-Based E-Commerce App

- **Cluster endpoint**: Used by transactional services (checkout, cart).

- **Reader endpoint**: Used by product search and recommendations.

- **Custom endpoint**: Dedicated for order history analytics via Athena Federated Queries.

Example 2: Financial Data Platform

- **Custom endpoint**: Routes traffic to a high-performance read replica for Tableau dashboards.

- **Reader endpoint**: Used by internal services for price history lookups.

- **Cluster endpoint**: Handles secure transactions and updates.

Summary

Aurora's cluster endpoint system is more than just a connection string — it's a powerful abstraction layer that supports dynamic scaling, failover resilience, and workload-aware routing. By leveraging the full set of endpoint types, you can build robust, high-performance applications without tightly coupling to specific infrastructure.

Endpoint Type	Role	DNS Mapping	Use Case
Writer (Cluster)	Write + read	Writer only	Transactional apps
Reader	Read-only	Any healthy reader	Read scaling
Custom	Custom read-only	Specific replicas	Analytics, isolation, load shaping

Tip: Avoid hardcoding IPs. Always use Aurora's endpoints for connectivity. Use IAM roles, Secrets Manager, or Parameter Store for managing credentials securely.

Chapter 18. Aurora Provisioning with CloudFormation

Provisioning Amazon Aurora using **AWS CloudFormation** enables infrastructure as code (IaC), allowing repeatable, consistent, and scalable deployments of database resources. In this chapter, we'll dive into how CloudFormation templates can be used to provision Aurora clusters, instances, and associated components. We'll explore sample templates, define parameters and resource dependencies, and wrap up with best practices for building modular and reusable infrastructure stacks.

Sample Templates

CloudFormation templates for Aurora deployments can vary in complexity depending on the desired architecture. Here, we explore common patterns through practical examples.

Basic Aurora Cluster (Aurora MySQL/PostgreSQL Compatible)

This basic template provisions:

- A VPC

- Subnet groups

- A DB cluster (Aurora MySQL-compatible or PostgreSQL-compatible)

- A single DB instance (writer)

```
AWSTemplateFormatVersion: '2010-09-09'

Description: Aurora MySQL DB Cluster
with one writer instance


Resources:

  DBSubnetGroup:

    Type: AWS::RDS::DBSubnetGroup

    Properties:

      DBSubnetGroupDescription: Aurora
subnet group

      SubnetIds:

        - subnet-abc123

        - subnet-def456


  DBCluster:

    Type: AWS::RDS::DBCluster
```

```yaml
    Properties:

      Engine: aurora-mysql

      DBClusterIdentifier:
MyAuroraCluster

      MasterUsername: !Ref DBUsername

      MasterUserPassword: !Ref
DBPassword

      VpcSecurityGroupIds:

        - sg-0123456789abcdef0

      DBSubnetGroupName: !Ref
DBSubnetGroup


  DBInstance:

    Type: AWS::RDS::DBInstance

    Properties:

      DBInstanceClass: db.r6g.large

      Engine: aurora-mysql

      DBClusterIdentifier: !Ref
DBCluster
```

```
        PubliclyAccessible: false

        DBSubnetGroupName: !Ref
DBSubnetGroup


    Parameters:

      DBUsername:

        Type: String

        Default: admin

        NoEcho: false


      DBPassword:

        Type: String

        NoEcho: true

        MinLength: 8
```

Aurora Cluster with Replicas and Custom Parameter Group

This variant introduces:

- Aurora Replicas (readers)

- A custom DB cluster parameter group

- Instance-level parameter groups for fine-grained control

```
DBParameterGroup:

  Type: AWS::RDS::DBParameterGroup

  Properties:

    Description: Aurora MySQL
parameter group

    Family: aurora-mysql5.7

    Parameters:

      slow_query_log: 1

      long_query_time: 2


ReaderInstance:

  Type: AWS::RDS::DBInstance

  Properties:
```

```
DBInstanceClass: db.r6g.large

Engine: aurora-mysql

DBClusterIdentifier: !Ref
DBCluster

PubliclyAccessible: false
```

Serverless Aurora (v2) Template

```
ServerlessCluster:

  Type: AWS::RDS::DBCluster

  Properties:

    Engine: aurora-postgresql

    EngineMode: provisioned

    DBClusterIdentifier:
AuroraServerlessV2

    ServerlessV2ScalingConfiguration:

      MinCapacity: 0.5

      MaxCapacity: 8
```

Note: Aurora Serverless v2 is "provisioned" in CloudFormation with `ServerlessV2ScalingConfiguration`.

Parameters and Resource Dependencies

Provisioning Aurora involves tightly coupled resources with specific ordering requirements. CloudFormation handles dependencies automatically using the `Ref` and `DependsOn` constructs, but understanding these relationships helps avoid common pitfalls.

Key Resource Dependencies

1. **DBSubnetGroup**

    - Must exist before the DB cluster or DB instance is created

    - Must include subnets in at least two AZs for high availability

2. **DBCluster**

    - Depends on DBSubnetGroup and optionally on parameter groups

    - Writer instance must refer to it via `DBClusterIdentifier`

3. **DBInstance**

- Refers to a specific cluster and subnet group

- Must match the engine of the cluster (e.g., aurora-mysql)

4. **Security Groups**

- Must be defined and referenced before DB resources are launched

Parameters in CloudFormation Templates

Parameters allow reusable and flexible templates:

```
Parameters:

  DBInstanceClass:

    Type: String

    Default: db.r6g.large

    AllowedValues:

      - db.t3.medium

      - db.r6g.large

      - db.r6g.xlarge
```

```
    Description: Aurora DB instance
size


  DBEngine:

    Type: String

    Default: aurora-postgresql

    AllowedValues:

      - aurora-mysql

      - aurora-postgresql


  DBClusterIdentifier:

    Type: String

    Default: MyAuroraCluster
```

Outputs

CloudFormation outputs are useful for referencing resource properties in higher-level stacks:

```
Outputs:
```

```
ClusterEndpoint:

    Description: Writer endpoint

    Value: !GetAtt
DBCluster.Endpoint.Address


ReaderEndpoint:

    Description: Load-balanced read
endpoint

    Value: !GetAtt
DBCluster.ReaderEndpoint
```

Best Practices for Modular Deployments

When designing production-ready CloudFormation stacks, modularity, reusability, and maintainability are critical. Below are best practices for building scalable and flexible Aurora deployments.

1. Use Nested Stacks or StackSets

- **Nested Stacks:** Break infrastructure into reusable logical units

- Example: VPC Stack, Aurora Stack, Monitoring Stack

- **StackSets:** Use for multi-account or multi-Region deployments

2. Parameterize Everything That Might Change

- DB instance classes, engine versions, VPC IDs, subnets, etc.

- Allows reuse in dev/staging/prod environments

3. Use Mappings for Region-specific Configurations

Example:

```
Mappings:

  RegionMap:

    us-east-1:

      DBFamily: aurora-mysql5.7

    us-west-2:

      DBFamily: aurora-mysql5.7
```

Then reference as:

```
Family: !FindInMap [RegionMap, !Ref
"AWS::Region", DBFamily]
```

4. Avoid Hardcoding Sensitive Values

- Use `NoEcho: true` for passwords

- Leverage AWS Secrets Manager and Systems Manager Parameter Store to securely inject secrets

5. Add Resource Tags

```
Tags:

    - Key: Environment

      Value: Production

    - Key: Application

      Value: InventoryService
```

Tags help with:

- Cost allocation

- IAM access controls

- Automation and monitoring

6. Include Deletion Policies

Prevent accidental deletion of databases:

```
DeletionPolicy: Snapshot
```

Or retain resources:

```
DeletionPolicy: Retain
```

7. Enable CloudWatch Logs and Monitoring Options

Within the cluster:

```
EnableCloudwatchLogsExports:

    - audit

    - error

    - general
```

```
- slowquery
```

Set `PerformanceInsightsEnabled: true` to use Aurora's native monitoring capabilities.

8. Use Conditions for Optional Resources

```
Conditions:

  CreateReadReplica: !Equals [!Ref
CreateReplicas, "true"]


Resources:

  ReaderInstance:

    Type: AWS::RDS::DBInstance

    Condition: CreateReadReplica
```

This allows toggling features such as replicas or monitoring agents with a simple flag.

9. Test with Change Sets

Before deploying changes, always run a **Change Set** to validate the impact:

```
aws cloudformation create-change-set \

  --stack-name MyStack \

  --template-body file://template.yaml
\

  --parameters file://params.json \

  --change-set-name preview
```

Example: Modular Aurora Stack Structure

Stack 1: Networking

- VPC

- Subnets

- Security Groups

Stack 2: Aurora DB Cluster

- Parameterized engine (MySQL/PostgreSQL)

- Cluster and instances

- IAM roles (if needed)

Stack 3: Monitoring and Logging

- CloudWatch Alarms

- Log groups

- Performance Insights

Stack 4: Application Integration

- Lambda triggers

- Secrets Manager secrets

- RDS Proxy

These stacks can be deployed independently or together using nested stacks or CDK constructs.

Real-World Deployment Tips

- Align DB parameter group with engine version (e.g., `aurora-mysql8.0`)

- Use instance-level `DBParameterGroup` if tuning session-specific behavior

- Use `DependsOn` to control provisioning order if implicit references are missing

- Apply backtracking or snapshot configurations if your application needs time travel or rapid recovery

- Manage state drift using **CloudFormation Drift Detection**

Troubleshooting Common CloudFormation Aurora Issues

Symptom	Likely Cause	Fix
DB cluster creation stuck at CREATE_IN_PROGRESS	Invalid subnet group or missing AZs	Ensure at least 2 subnets in different AZs
Password field exposed in logs	`NoEcho` not set to `true`	Use `NoEcho: true` in parameter definition
Replicas not launching	Missing `DBClusterIdentifier` reference	Ensure replica points to `!Ref DBCluster`
Cannot delete stack	Missing deletion policy or dependency	Add `DeletionPolicy: Snapshot` or delete manually

Chapter 19. Setting Up Development Environments

A productive development environment for Amazon Aurora typically involves integrating compute instances, database clusters, networking configurations, and tooling. This chapter walks you through a complete setup that includes:

- **Provisioning EC2 instances for development**

- **Creating and configuring Aurora clusters**

- **Networking with VPCs, subnets, and security groups**

- **Connecting from popular development tools like DBeaver and** `psql`

This guide is especially useful for developers, data engineers, and cloud architects preparing to build and test applications locally or in cloud-based dev/test environments.

EC2 + Aurora Setup Walkthrough

Overview

To simulate real-world application-to-database interaction, you can set up an **Amazon EC2 instance** to connect with an **Aurora DB cluster**. This setup helps you:

- Test application connections and credentials

- Benchmark query performance

- Run integration or unit tests

- Explore Aurora features with client-side tools

Architecture

The high-level architecture includes:

- An **EC2 instance** in a public or private subnet

- An **Aurora cluster** (MySQL or PostgreSQL compatible) in a private subnet

- **Security groups** to allow EC2-to-Aurora traffic

- Optional: Bastion host or SSM Session Manager for secure access

Step-by-Step Setup

Step 1: Create a VPC

1. Go to **VPC Dashboard** in AWS.

2. Choose **Create VPC → VPC only**.

3. Define:

   - VPC name (e.g., dev-vpc)

   - IPv4 CIDR block (e.g., 10.0.0.0/16)

4. Click **Create VPC**.

Step 2: Create Subnets

Create two subnets:

- **Public subnet** for the EC2 instance

- **Private subnet** for Aurora

Example:

- `dev-public-subnet` → `10.0.1.0/24`

- `dev-private-subnet` → `10.0.2.0/24`

Associate them with your VPC.

Step 3: Internet Gateway and Routing

1. Attach an **Internet Gateway** to the VPC.

2. Update the **Route Table** of the public subnet to allow `0.0.0.0/0` through the Internet Gateway.

3. Leave the private subnet route table unchanged (no direct internet access).

Step 4: Create Security Groups

- **Aurora SG**:

    - Allow inbound on port 3306 (MySQL) or 5432 (PostgreSQL)

- Restrict source to your EC2 security group or CIDR (e.g., `10.0.1.0/24`)

- **EC2 SG**:

  - Allow SSH inbound from your IP (e.g., `203.0.113.0/32`)

  - Allow outbound to Aurora's port

Step 5: Launch Aurora DB Cluster

1. Go to **Amazon RDS > Databases > Create database**

2. Choose either:

   - **Aurora MySQL-Compatible Edition**

   - **Aurora PostgreSQL-Compatible Edition**

3. DB Cluster Settings:

   - Choose **Provisioned** (not Serverless for dev simplicity)

   - Assign to **dev-private-subnet**

   - Choose the **Aurora SG** created earlier

   - Set DB instance class (e.g., `db.t3.medium`)

4. Set initial credentials and enable Performance Insights if desired.

5. Click **Create Database**.

🔒 **Tip:** Ensure the Aurora cluster is not publicly accessible for dev environments unless behind a bastion.

Step 6: Launch EC2 Instance

1. Choose **Amazon Linux 2** or **Ubuntu** AMI

2. Place the instance in the **dev-public-subnet**

3. Associate the **EC2 SG**

4. Enable:

   - Key pair for SSH access

   - IAM role (optional) for SSM Session Manager

Install required dev tools (e.g., `psql`, `mysql-client`, DBeaver dependencies) using `yum` or `apt`.

VPC, Subnet, and Security Group Configuration

Aurora is tightly integrated into your VPC. Understanding how VPC components work together is critical for establishing and securing your development environment.

Key Components

- **VPC** – Isolated network environment where your EC2 and Aurora resources live

- **Subnets** – Segments of the VPC spread across AZs

- **Route Tables** – Define how traffic flows within the VPC and externally

- **Security Groups** – Act as virtual firewalls for EC2 and Aurora

- **Network ACLs (optional)** – Add stateless packet filtering rules

Configuration Guidelines

Subnet Group for Aurora

Aurora requires a **DB Subnet Group**, which must include **at least two subnets** in different AZs for high availability. When creating your DB cluster:

- Choose your **private subnets**

- Tag them appropriately (e.g., `Environment=Dev`)

Security Group Rules

Aurora Security Group (assigned to DB instances):

- Inbound:

    - Type: Custom TCP

    - Port: 3306 (MySQL) or 5432 (PostgreSQL)

    - Source: EC2 security group ID or CIDR range

- Outbound:

    - Default (allow all) or limit to internal VPC CIDR

EC2 Security Group:

- Inbound:

    - SSH from your laptop IP or corporate IP range

- Outbound:

    - Aurora DB port to the private subnet CIDR

Testing Connectivity

From EC2:

```
telnet <aurora-endpoint> 3306  # MySQL
```

```
telnet <aurora-endpoint> 5432    #
PostgreSQL
```

If connection fails:

- Verify NACLs and SGs

- Ensure Aurora is in a **"available"** state

- Check DNS resolution inside EC2 using `dig` or `nslookup`

Connecting from Dev Tools (DBeaver, psql, etc.)

Once the infrastructure is in place, developers can connect using familiar client tools to run queries, manage schema, and test applications.

DBeaver Setup

DBeaver is a universal SQL client with rich GUI features.

1. **Install DBeaver** (Community Edition or Pro)

2. Add a new connection:

   ○ Choose **Aurora MySQL** or **Aurora PostgreSQL**

- Enter:

  - Hostname: Aurora cluster endpoint

  - Port: 3306 or 5432

  - Database: `defaultdb` or custom name

  - Username/password from RDS setup

3. Click **Test Connection**

💡 **Tip:** If Aurora is in a private subnet, and DBeaver is on your local machine, connect through:

- A **bastion EC2 host** with port forwarding

- **SSM Session Manager** + port forwarding tunnel (no bastion needed)

Example: SSH Tunnel for Local DBeaver

```
ssh -i ~/.ssh/dev-key.pem ec2-
user@<bastion-ip> -L 5432:<aurora-
endpoint>:5432
```

Then configure DBeaver to connect to `localhost:5432`.

`psql` CLI (for PostgreSQL)

Install PostgreSQL client:

```
sudo yum install postgresql  # Amazon
Linux

# OR

sudo apt install postgresql-client  #
Ubuntu
```

Connect:

```
psql -h <aurora-endpoint> -U myuser -d
mydb -p 5432
```

`mysql` CLI (for Aurora MySQL)

Install MySQL client:

```
sudo yum install mysql

# OR
```

```
sudo apt install mysql-client
```

Connect:

```
mysql -h <aurora-endpoint> -u myuser -
p -P 3306
```

AWS Systems Manager Port Forwarding

Instead of exposing a bastion host, use SSM:

1. Attach AmazonSSMManagedInstanceCore to
   EC2 IAM Role

2. Connect via CLI:

```
aws ssm start-session \

  --target i-0abcdef123456 \

  --document-name AWS-
StartPortForwardingSession \

  --parameters
'{"portNumber":["5432"],"localPortNumb
er":["5432"]}'
```

Then connect locally on `localhost:5432`.

Automating the Setup (Optional)

Use **AWS CloudFormation** or **Terraform** to automate:

- VPC creation

- Subnets and routing

- Security groups

- Aurora cluster setup

- EC2 instance launch

Example CloudFormation snippet for DB subnet group:

```
DBSubnetGroup:

   Type: AWS::RDS::DBSubnetGroup

   Properties:

     DBSubnetGroupDescription: "Subnet
group for Aurora DB"

     SubnetIds:
```

```
      - !Ref PrivateSubnet1

      - !Ref PrivateSubnet2
```

Best Practices for Development Environments

- **Isolate environments**: Use separate VPCs or subnets for dev, test, and prod.

- **Use IAM roles for access control**: Avoid hardcoding credentials.

- **Clean up resources**: Use TTL tags or scheduled jobs to terminate idle dev resources.

- **Monitor costs**: Use cost allocation tags and budgets for dev environments.

- **Test failover and scaling scenarios** periodically.

Troubleshooting Tips

Issue	Possible Cause	Resolution
Timeout connecting from EC2	Wrong security group	Allow EC2 SG in Aurora SG
DBeaver can't connect	Private subnet without tunnel	Use SSH tunnel or SSM

DNS not resolving Aurora endpoint	Missing DNS hostnames on subnet	Enable DNS support in VPC
`psql` or `mysql` CLI errors	Wrong port, user, or credentials	Double-check inputs and RDS logs
EC2 not accessible via SSH	Public IP not assigned or SG blocked	Check subnet settings and SSH rules

Part IV: Security and Access Control

Chapter 20. IAM Database Authentication

Introduction

IAM Database Authentication for Amazon Aurora allows you to authenticate to your DB clusters using AWS Identity and Access Management (IAM) credentials instead of database-specific usernames and passwords. This feature provides centralized, temporary, and secure access control for applications, improving your security posture and aligning with AWS best practices for identity and access management.

This chapter covers the setup process for IAM authentication, its integration with AWS Security Token Service (STS), and practical usage in serverless and containerized environments such as AWS Lambda and Amazon ECS.

Setup Process

Overview

IAM database authentication allows Amazon Aurora MySQL and Aurora PostgreSQL users to:

- Connect to Aurora using an **IAM token** generated through AWS STS.

- Avoid the need to store static database credentials in application code.

- Integrate access control with IAM policies, roles, and permissions.

Supported engines:

- **Aurora MySQL-compatible editions** (versions ≥ 5.6.10a)

- **Aurora PostgreSQL-compatible editions** (versions ≥ 10.7)

Step-by-Step Setup

1. Enable IAM DB Authentication on the Aurora Cluster

To enable IAM authentication:

- Go to the **RDS Console**.

- Select your Aurora DB cluster.

- Choose **Modify**.

- Under **Database authentication**, enable the checkbox for **IAM DB authentication**.

- Apply changes immediately or during the next maintenance window.

You can also use the AWS CLI:

```
aws rds modify-db-cluster \
    --db-cluster-identifier my-cluster \
    --enable-iam-database-authentication \
    --apply-immediately
```

⚠ **Note**: This enables IAM auth at the cluster level. You must also grant individual users access.

2. Create an IAM Role or User with RDS Permissions

To allow IAM users or roles to generate database tokens:

- Attach the following policy:

```
{
    "Version": "2012-10-17",
```

```
"Statement": [

  {

    "Effect": "Allow",

    "Action": "rds-db:connect",

    "Resource": "arn:aws:rds-db:us-
east-1:123456789012:dbuser:db-
XYZ123/db_user"

  }

]

}
```

You can also scope this to a specific database, user, or role.

3. Create a Database User that Maps to IAM

The database user must match the IAM user or role name (depending on integration method).

For Aurora MySQL:

```
CREATE USER 'db_user'@'%' IDENTIFIED
WITH AWSAuthenticationPlugin AS 'RDS';
```

For Aurora PostgreSQL:

```
CREATE ROLE db_user WITH LOGIN;
```

The PostgreSQL user does **not** need to reference an authentication plugin but must exist in the DB.

4. Grant Appropriate Privileges to the DB User

Use standard SQL GRANT statements to assign roles and permissions.

Example for MySQL:

```
GRANT SELECT, INSERT ON mydb.* TO
'db_user'@'%';
```

Example for PostgreSQL:

```
GRANT CONNECT ON DATABASE mydb TO
db_user;
```

```
GRANT USAGE ON SCHEMA public TO
db_user;
```

5. Generate IAM Authentication Token

Tokens are generated using the AWS SDK, CLI, or RDS library. They are valid for **15 minutes**.

Example (AWS CLI):

```
aws rds generate-db-auth-token \

  --hostname my-cluster.cluster-
xyz.us-east-1.rds.amazonaws.com \

  --port 3306 \

  --region us-east-1 \

  --username db_user
```

6. Connect Using the Token

You can now use the token in place of a password in your connection string.

For MySQL:

```
mysql -h my-cluster.cluster-xyz.us-
east-1.rds.amazonaws.com \

  -u db_user \

  --enable-cleartext-plugin \

  -p'<IAM_TOKEN>'
```

For PostgreSQL:

```
psql "host=my-cluster.cluster-xyz.us-
east-1.rds.amazonaws.com port=5432
dbname=mydb user=db_user
sslmode=require password=<IAM_TOKEN>"
```

🔒 Always ensure connections use SSL/TLS
to protect IAM tokens in transit.

Integrating with STS

Role of AWS Security Token Service (STS)

STS is the backbone of IAM authentication. It enables
temporary, time-limited credential generation. When IAM
database authentication is used:

- STS issues a signed token that represents the user.

- The token is valid for **15 minutes**.

- Aurora validates the token by verifying the signature and ensuring the IAM entity has permission via `rds-db:connect`.

Use Cases for STS Integration

- **Cross-account access**: Assume a role in a different account that has database access.

- **Short-lived access**: Great for CI/CD pipelines, ephemeral containers, or serverless functions.

- **Centralized access management**: Consolidate access rules through IAM roles rather than DB-specific accounts.

How STS Works with Aurora

1. IAM user or role requests an auth token.

2. AWS STS issues a signed request.

3. The application sends the token to Aurora during DB connection.

4. Aurora verifies:

- Token validity.

- IAM permissions via `rds-db:connect`.

Fine-grained Access Control via IAM

You can grant token-based DB access only for specific users or services by writing precise IAM policies:

```
{

  "Effect": "Allow",

  "Action": "rds-db:connect",

  "Resource": [

    "arn:aws:rds-db:us-east-
1:123456789012:dbuser:db-
XYZ123/db_user"

  ]

}
```

Note: You can scope this down further by conditionally allowing access only during business hours or from specific IP ranges using IAM condition keys.

Use in Lambda and Containers

IAM database authentication integrates especially well in modern, serverless and container-based architectures where secrets management can be challenging.

Using IAM Auth with AWS Lambda

Why Use IAM Auth in Lambda?

- Avoid hardcoding secrets or managing Secrets Manager.

- Use Lambda execution role to assume identity.

- Automatically refreshes token on every invocation.

Steps to Integrate

1. **Enable IAM Auth** on your Aurora cluster and create corresponding DB user.

2. **Attach IAM policy** to the Lambda execution role:

```
{

  "Effect": "Allow",

  "Action": "rds-db:connect",
```

```
    "Resource": "arn:aws:rds-db:us-east-
1:123456789012:dbuser:db-
XYZ123/db_user"

}
```

3. **Generate token in your Lambda code**: Example using Python:

```python
import boto3

import pymysql


def lambda_handler(event, context):

    rds_client = boto3.client('rds')

    token =
rds_client.generate_db_auth_token(

        DBHostname='my-
cluster.cluster-xyz.us-east-
1.rds.amazonaws.com',

        Port=3306,

        DBUsername='db_user',
```

```python
    Region='us-east-1'
)


conn = pymysql.connect(
    host='my-cluster.cluster-xyz.us-east-1.rds.amazonaws.com',
    user='db_user',
    passwd=token,
    port=3306,
    ssl={'ssl': True}
)


with conn.cursor() as cursor:
    cursor.execute("SELECT NOW();")
    result = cursor.fetchone()
    print(result)
```

Considerations

- Ensure Lambda has network access (VPC) to the Aurora DB cluster.

- Use **connection pooling** or **RDS Proxy** for better performance (IAM auth is compatible with RDS Proxy).

Using IAM Auth in Containers (e.g., ECS/Fargate, EKS)

Benefits

- Avoid storing secrets in environment variables.

- Use IAM roles for tasks (ECS) or service accounts (EKS).

- Scales seamlessly with ephemeral infrastructure.

Integration Steps

1. **Enable IAM auth and DB user** as before.

2. **Create IAM Role for Task (ECS)** or **Service Account (EKS)** with `rds-db:connect` permission.

3. **Generate token at runtime** in your container app: Example using AWS SDK (Node.js):

```
const signer = new AWS.RDS.Signer({
```

```
    region: 'us-east-1',

    hostname: 'my-cluster.cluster-
xyz.us-east-1.rds.amazonaws.com',

    port: 3306,

    username: 'db_user'
});


const token = signer.getAuthToken({});
```

4. **Use the token to connect** using any supported
   database client.

Using with Sidecar or Proxy

You can also centralize token generation in a sidecar
container or through a custom proxy that injects tokens on
behalf of the application.

Best Practices

- **Use IAM for ephemeral workloads**: Lambda,
  containers, CI/CD jobs.

- **Use RDS Proxy with IAM auth** to minimize connection overhead.

- **Use AWS Secrets Manager** for hybrid setups (IAM + password rotation).

- **Monitor auth activity** via **CloudTrail**.

- **Audit permissions** using IAM Access Analyzer and policy simulators.

Limitations and Considerations

- Token lifespan is 15 minutes; applications must manage expiration.

- Not all DB clients support IAM tokens natively.

- Aurora Serverless v1 does **not support IAM authentication**.

- Aurora MySQL requires the `--enable-cleartext-plugin` for CLI access.

- IAM users/roles must be mapped to DB users manually.

Conclusion

IAM Database Authentication for Amazon Aurora significantly enhances your security model by eliminating the need for stored passwords, enabling temporary access tokens, and tightly integrating with AWS IAM and STS. It's particularly effective in modern, scalable architectures like Lambda and containers, offering a seamless way to authenticate to Aurora securely and programmatically.

By following best practices and deeply integrating IAM auth into your development and deployment pipelines, you can maintain a robust, passwordless security posture that scales with your infrastructure and organizational needs.

> ☑ Next Step: Combine IAM authentication with **Aurora auditing** and **CloudTrail logging** to get full visibility into DB access patterns.

Chapter 21. SSL/TLS and Encrypted Connections

Securing data in transit is a foundational aspect of database security, especially for cloud-native, internet-facing, or compliance-driven workloads. Amazon Aurora provides robust support for **SSL/TLS encryption**, enabling secure client connections to Aurora MySQL and Aurora PostgreSQL clusters. This chapter explores the mechanisms Aurora provides to enforce encrypted connections, how to verify their use, and the performance trade-offs to consider.

Enabling SSL in Aurora

Amazon Aurora supports **SSL (Secure Sockets Layer)** and **TLS (Transport Layer Security)** protocols to encrypt data in transit between clients and the database. Encryption ensures that sensitive information such as authentication credentials, queries, and result sets cannot be intercepted or tampered with by unauthorized actors.

SSL Support Overview

- **Aurora MySQL-Compatible Edition** supports SSL using the **X.509 certificate** chain, similar to standard MySQL.

- **Aurora PostgreSQL-Compatible Edition** uses native PostgreSQL **SSL support** with TLS for encrypted communications.

- Aurora automatically provisions and installs **AWS-signed certificates** on each DB instance.

- Clients can validate server certificates using **Amazon RDS root certificates**.

Steps to Enable SSL:

SSL is **enabled by default** in Aurora. However, to enforce or use it at the client level, several configuration steps are required.

Aurora MySQL

1. **Get the RDS Root Certificate**

   ○ Download from: RDS SSL Certificates

2. **Enable SSL in Client Connection**

   Use command-line options:

```
mysql -h your-cluster-endpoint \

    -u your-username \

    --password \

    --ssl-ca=path_to_rds-combined-
ca-bundle.pem \

    --ssl-mode=REQUIRED
```

- o

3. **Require SSL at the User Level (Optional)**

Enforce SSL using:

```
GRANT ALL PRIVILEGES ON dbname.* TO
'ssl_user'@'%' REQUIRE SSL;
```

- o

4. **Verify Connection**

Run:

```
SHOW STATUS LIKE 'Ssl_cipher';
```

- o

Aurora PostgreSQL

1. **Get the RDS Root Certificate**

   - o Same certificate used as with MySQL.

2. **Enable SSL in pgAdmin or psql**

Example psql connection:

```
psql "host=your-cluster-endpoint
port=5432 user=your-username
```

253

```
dbname=your-db sslmode=require
sslrootcert=path_to_rds-combined-ca-
bundle.pem"
```

    o

3. **Modify PostgreSQL Users for SSL Requirement**

    o While PostgreSQL doesn't support a per-user SSL requirement, you can restrict connections using `pg_hba.conf` logic via parameter groups.

4. **Verify SSL Connection**

Run the following query:

```
SELECT ssl_is_used();
```

    o

Enforcing SSL via Parameter Groups

While Aurora does not allow full customization of `pg_hba.conf` (PostgreSQL) or `my.cnf` (MySQL), you can:

- Set `require_secure_transport=ON` in Aurora MySQL parameter groups.

- Configure network-level policies using **security groups**, **IAM**, and **RDS Proxy** to restrict access paths.

Verifying Secure Connections

Ensuring that your applications are using SSL as intended is critical. Aurora provides multiple ways to verify the encryption status of database sessions.

Aurora MySQL

Using SQL:

```
SHOW SESSION STATUS LIKE 'Ssl_cipher';
```

- If SSL is active, it shows the name of the cipher in use.

- If empty, the connection is unencrypted.

Using Performance Insights or CloudTrail:

- SSL usage is not directly visible in Performance Insights.

- For audit-level verification, you can log connection events in **CloudTrail** if using IAM authentication or **Amazon RDS Enhanced Monitoring**.

Aurora PostgreSQL

Check with SQL:

```
SELECT ssl_is_used();  -- Returns true
or false
```

Identify SSL Sessions in pg_stat_ssl:

```
SELECT * FROM pg_stat_ssl WHERE pid =
pg_backend_pid();
```

CloudTrail Auditing:

- Aurora PostgreSQL connection audits via IAM are logged if configured.

- For full compliance, use **Aurora Database Activity Streams** to capture session-level metadata.

Application-Side Logging

To enforce and verify SSL usage:

- Enable **SSL logging** on the client application.

- In middleware such as **JDBC**, **ODBC**, or **Python psycopg2**, ensure that `sslmode=require` or `verify-full` is explicitly set.

Recommended Verification Checklist

Component	Action
DB Client	Ensure SSL/TLS flags and certs are used correctly
DB User	Set `REQUIRE SSL` in MySQL or restrict with policies
SQL Validation	Use `SHOW STATUS` or `ssl_is_used()`
Monitoring	Enable enhanced logging, Database Activity Streams
VPC Security	Allow only encrypted connections through RDS Proxy

Performance Impact

While SSL encryption provides strong security for data in transit, it can introduce some **CPU and latency overhead**. However, Aurora minimizes this impact through efficient implementation and instance-level optimization.

CPU Usage

- SSL encryption consumes **CPU cycles** during handshake and data encryption.

- Aurora instances with **higher vCPU counts** or **dedicated crypto hardware** handle SSL with minimal overhead.

- Enabling **SSL for all clients** on large-scale deployments may require choosing **compute-optimized instances** (e.g., r6g, r5, m6i).

Latency

- Initial connection latency increases due to **SSL handshake negotiation**.

- For persistent connection pools, this is negligible.

- Overhead is more significant in **short-lived or serverless** client connections.

Throughput

- Aurora benchmarks show **2–5% throughput reduction** when SSL is used for all client connections in write-heavy workloads.

- Read workloads experience negligible SSL-related degradation, especially when query result sets are small.

Mitigation Strategies

1. **Connection Pooling**

   - Use connection pools like **pgbouncer** (PostgreSQL) or **ProxySQL** (MySQL) to reduce connection overhead.

2. **Instance Sizing**

   ○ Choose larger instances for SSL-heavy workloads to mitigate CPU strain.

3. **Use RDS Proxy**

   ○ Acts as a secure, pooled intermediary.

   ○ Reduces connection churn and improves SSL session reuse.

4. **Optimize SSL Parameters**

   ○ Configure SSL ciphers for speed vs. strength as needed (available for Aurora MySQL).

   ○ Use stronger encryption only where compliance mandates it (e.g., PCI DSS, HIPAA).

Summary

Amazon Aurora provides robust support for SSL/TLS-encrypted client connections, enabling secure data transit and compliance with industry regulations. SSL is enabled by default, and Aurora makes it easy to configure, enforce, and verify encryption at multiple levels. While there are some performance trade-offs, these can be effectively managed through right-sizing, pooling, and architecture strategies.

Quick Tips

- ☑ Use Amazon's **CA certificates** for validation and secure client trust.

- ☑ Always set `sslmode=require` (or stricter) in your client apps.

- ☑ Monitor `SHOW STATUS`, `ssl_is_used()`, and `pg_stat_ssl` to confirm encrypted sessions.

- ☑ Plan for **modest performance overhead**, especially during peak CPU utilization.

- ☑ Leverage **Aurora Serverless v2 with RDS Proxy** for secure, elastic, and efficient SSL usage.

Chapter 22. KMS Key Management and Encryption at Rest

Data protection is a cornerstone of modern database systems. In Amazon Aurora, encryption at rest is seamlessly integrated using AWS Key Management Service (KMS). Aurora supports both **default AWS-managed keys** and **customer-managed KMS keys**, enabling flexibility in compliance, security control, and access governance.

This chapter provides an in-depth exploration of:

- How Aurora integrates with KMS for encryption at rest

- The differences between default and custom keys

- Key rotation and lifecycle management

- The impact of encryption on operations like snapshot sharing

---

Understanding Encryption at Rest in Aurora

What It Is

Encryption at rest refers to encrypting data while it is stored on persistent media. In Aurora, this includes:

- Database files

- Automated and manual snapshots

- Backups in Amazon S3

- Cluster logs (e.g., audit logs)

- Cluster volume storage

Encryption is applied at the cluster level and persists across the lifecycle of the database. Once an Aurora cluster is created as encrypted, **it cannot be unencrypted**.

How It Works

Aurora uses **AES-256** encryption via the AWS Key Management Service (KMS). Aurora integrates with KMS in the following ways:

- Uses a **KMS key** to generate **data keys**.

- Each data key is encrypted with the KMS key and stored with the data.

- Aurora uses envelope encryption to ensure that the master key is never exposed.

Default vs Custom Keys

Encryption in Aurora can be configured with either **AWS-managed keys** or **customer-managed (CMK)** KMS keys.

Default AWS-Managed Keys

- Automatically created and managed by AWS.

- Named using the pattern: `aws/rds`.

- Rotated automatically by AWS on a periodic schedule.

- Ideal for simplicity and standard compliance needs.

Pros:

- No configuration needed

- Seamless integration

- No cost for key management

Cons:

- No audit control

- No granular IAM permissions

- Limited customization

Customer-Managed KMS Keys (CMK)

You can create and manage your own KMS keys through the AWS KMS console or API. These allow:

- Full control over key policies and IAM access

- Audit logging via CloudTrail

- Optional key rotation settings

- Sharing keys across accounts (for snapshots and replication)

Creating a CMK:

```
aws kms create-key --description
"Aurora Encryption Key"
```

Specifying a CMK when creating a cluster (via CLI):

```
aws rds create-db-cluster \

  --db-cluster-identifier my-
encrypted-cluster \

  --engine aurora-mysql \

  --storage-encrypted \

  --kms-key-id
arn:aws:kms:region:account-id:key/key-
id
```

Best Use Cases for CMK:

- Compliance with data sovereignty or HIPAA/GDPR

- Role-based access control

- Multi-account architectures with shared resources

- Audit-intensive environments

Key Rotation

Key rotation is critical for maintaining cryptographic hygiene and meeting security compliance.

Default Key Rotation (AWS-managed Keys)

- Handled automatically by AWS.

- Key rotation interval is not customizable.

- Aurora clusters automatically start using the new backing key with no manual steps.

- Old data remains encrypted with older keys but accessible using the key's version chain.

Customer-Managed Key Rotation

- You can enable automatic rotation on CMKs via AWS KMS.

- Rotation occurs every 365 days when enabled.

- You can also perform **manual rotation** by re-encrypting resources using a new key.

Enabling auto-rotation:

```
aws kms enable-key-rotation --key-id
<key-id>
```

Rotating Encryption Keys on Aurora Clusters

Aurora does **not support live re-keying** of encrypted clusters. To rotate the CMK used by an Aurora cluster:

1. Create a snapshot of the existing cluster.

2. Copy the snapshot and specify the new CMK.

3. Restore a new cluster from the copied snapshot.

Snapshot copy with new key:

```
aws rds copy-db-cluster-snapshot \

  --source-db-cluster-snapshot-
identifier original-snapshot \

  --target-db-cluster-snapshot-
identifier rekeyed-snapshot \

  --kms-key-id <new-kms-key-arn>
```

Restoring from rekeyed snapshot:

```
aws rds restore-db-cluster-from-
snapshot \

  --db-cluster-identifier new-cluster
\

  --snapshot-identifier rekeyed-
snapshot
```

Important: This process incurs downtime and requires endpoint updates in your application.

Encryption Impact on Snapshot Sharing

Aurora supports snapshot sharing across accounts, but encryption adds important constraints.

Unencrypted Snapshots

- Can be shared directly across AWS accounts.

- Simple and flexible for DR or migration workflows.

Encrypted Snapshots

- Can only be shared **if** the CMK used for encryption is shared with the target AWS account.

- The CMK must allow **cross-account use** via key policy.

Example Key Policy for Cross-Account Snapshot Sharing:

```json
{

  "Sid": "AllowOtherAccount",

  "Effect": "Allow",

  "Principal": {

    "AWS": "arn:aws:iam::123456789012:root"

  },

  "Action": [

    "kms:Decrypt",

    "kms:DescribeKey"

  ],

  "Resource": "*"

}
```

Steps to Share an Encrypted Snapshot

1. Share the KMS key (CMK) with the target account.

   Modify the snapshot's attributes to include the target account.

```
aws rds modify-db-cluster-snapshot-
attribute \

   --db-cluster-snapshot-identifier
snapshot-id \

   --attribute-name restore \

   --values-to-add 123456789012
```

2.
3. Target account can now copy the snapshot using their own CMK if needed.

Snapshot copy with re-encryption in the target account:

```
aws rds copy-db-cluster-snapshot \

   --source-db-cluster-snapshot-
identifier arn:aws:rds:region:account-
id:cluster-snapshot:snapshot-id \
```

```
--target-db-cluster-snapshot-
identifier new-snapshot \

 --kms-key-id target-account-kms-key-
arn
```

Key Takeaways

- You **cannot** directly restore a snapshot encrypted with an unshared CMK.

- Always **pre-plan** CMK sharing when using Aurora snapshots for DR or CI/CD pipelines.

Other Encryption-Related Considerations

Performance Impact

- Aurora uses optimized hardware-based encryption (via AES-NI).

- Minimal performance penalty, generally <1–2% in most workloads.

- Fully transparent to applications.

Logging and Auditing

- All KMS key operations are logged in **AWS CloudTrail**.

- You can audit:

  - Key creation

  - Usage patterns

  - Access attempts and failures

Backup and Restore

- **All backups of encrypted clusters are encrypted** using the same CMK.

- Backups are not shareable unless key policies allow it.

IAM and Access Control

Fine-grained access is managed via:

- IAM policies for RDS and KMS

- Key policies on CMKs

- Resource-based permissions for snapshot sharing

Best Practice: Use separate CMKs for different workloads or environments (e.g., dev vs. prod) to enforce isolation.

Best Practices for KMS Key Management in Aurora

- **Use CMKs for regulated data** or multi-account environments.

- **Enable key rotation** (automatic or manual) to meet security baselines.

- **Label CMKs** clearly (e.g., `Aurora-Prod-Key`) and use AWS tags for classification.

- **Pre-authorize snapshot decryption** across accounts if building DR pipelines.

- **Use CloudTrail** to monitor and audit all encryption and key usage events.

- **Document and test key rotation procedures**— especially for production environments.

Summary

Amazon Aurora provides strong, flexible encryption at rest using AWS KMS, empowering organizations to meet a wide range of security and compliance requirements.

Feature	Default Key	Customer-Managed Key
Created By	AWS	You
Rotated By	AWS	Optional (by you)

Cross-account Sharing	No	Yes (if key is shared)
Cost	Free	$1/month per key
Access Control	Basic IAM	Full control with IAM + key policies
Visibility in Logs	Limited	Full (via CloudTrail)

When planning for snapshot portability, data isolation, or compliance audits, using CMKs offers significant advantages. However, AWS-managed keys are still a secure, low-friction default for many applications.

Chapter 23. Using AWS Secrets Manager with Aurora

Storing DB Credentials Securely

Managing database credentials securely is critical in any production-grade cloud application. Aurora integrates seamlessly with **AWS Secrets Manager**, a service that enables secure storage, fine-grained access control, and automatic rotation of secrets like database usernames and passwords.

Why Use Secrets Manager with Aurora?

Using Secrets Manager to manage Aurora credentials offers several advantages:

- **Improved security posture**: Secrets are encrypted at rest and in transit.

- **Centralized management**: All secrets can be stored and managed from a single console or API.

- **Automatic rotation**: Secrets Manager can rotate database credentials without application downtime.

- **Auditability**: Full integration with CloudTrail provides auditing of secret access.

- **Dynamic configuration**: Applications can fetch credentials at runtime, avoiding hardcoded secrets.

Supported Engine Versions

Secrets Manager works with:

- Aurora MySQL-compatible editions

- Aurora PostgreSQL-compatible editions

You must ensure that your engine version supports integration. For auto-rotation, only **single-master DB clusters** are supported—multi-writer Aurora MySQL clusters require manual handling.

Basic Workflow for Secure Credential Storage

1. **Store the secret**: Create a new secret in Secrets Manager with:

    - Username

    - Password

    - Engine type (Aurora MySQL or Aurora PostgreSQL)

    - DB cluster ARN

    - Hostname and port (optional)

2. **Grant access**: Assign an IAM policy to the application or Lambda function that allows access to the secret.

3. **Fetch at runtime**: Use AWS SDKs to securely retrieve the credentials.

Secret Structure Example (JSON)

```json
{

  "username": "app_user",

  "password": "p@ssw0rd!",

  "engine": "aurora-mysql",

  "host": "db-cluster.cluster-abc123.us-east-1.rds.amazonaws.com",

  "port": 3306,

  "dbInstanceIdentifier": "mydbinstance"

}
```

Using the AWS Console

When storing a secret:

- Choose **Other type of secret → Credentials for RDS database**

- Provide DB engine, user, and password

- Link the secret to an **Aurora cluster ARN**

- Optionally enable **automatic rotation** with a
  Lambda rotation function

Auto-Rotation

One of the most powerful features of Secrets Manager is
its ability to **rotate credentials automatically** on a defined
schedule (e.g., every 30 days) without requiring application
changes or manual intervention.

How Auto-Rotation Works

1. **Secrets Manager uses a Lambda function** to:

   - Create a new credential in the database.

   - Test the new credential.

   - Mark it as the active version of the secret.

   - Remove the old credentials if necessary.

2. The secret has **four stages** during rotation:

   - AWSCURRENT: The currently active version

   - AWSPENDING: The pending new version
     during rotation

   - AWSPREVIOUS: The last-used version
     (optional)

- ○ AWSCANCELLED: A failed or invalid version

Enabling Auto-Rotation

To enable rotation:

- Create or use an existing rotation Lambda function.

- Ensure the Lambda function has the correct IAM permissions.

- Enable rotation in the Secrets Manager console or via CLI.

Example CLI:

```
aws secretsmanager rotate-secret \

    --secret-id mydbsecret \

    --rotation-lambda-arn
arn:aws:lambda:us-east-
1:123456789012:function:SecretsManager
Rotation \

    --rotation-rules
AutomaticallyAfterDays=30
```

Built-In Rotation Support for Aurora

Secrets Manager provides **built-in rotation templates** for:

- `Aurora MySQL`

- `Aurora PostgreSQL`

When you enable rotation from the console for these engines, AWS automatically provisions a pre-built Lambda function and attaches it to your secret.

Zero-Downtime Rotation

- Applications should **retrieve credentials from Secrets Manager at runtime** (not hardcode them).

- If an app caches credentials, **rotation can break authentication**—avoid long-lived connections with static secrets.

Rotation Failures and Troubleshooting

- Use **CloudWatch Logs** to review the Lambda rotation logs.

- Use **CloudTrail** to trace secret access events.

- Common issues:

    - Lambda lacks permission to update secret or connect to DB.

- Rotation is blocked due to cluster unavailability.

- Application not configured to retrieve secrets dynamically.

Permissions and Integration Patterns

For secure and scalable operations, Secrets Manager must be integrated carefully with Aurora, IAM, and your application layer.

IAM Policy for Application Access

To allow an application (e.g., running on EC2, Lambda, or ECS) to access a secret, you must attach an IAM policy granting permission:

```
{

    "Version": "2012-10-17",

    "Statement": [

        {

            "Effect": "Allow",

            "Action": [
```

```
    "secretsmanager:GetSecretValue"

        ],

        "Resource":
"arn:aws:secretsmanager:us-east-
1:123456789012:secret:mydbsecret-
abc123"

            }

        ]

    }
```

Attach this policy to the IAM role used by your compute resource.

Secure Access from Aurora (Database Level)

Aurora does **not directly read secrets** from Secrets Manager. Instead, applications (or rotation Lambda functions) must:

- Retrieve the secret

- Use the CREATE USER or ALTER USER SQL commands to apply credentials

This indirect approach enforces least privilege and separation of duties.

Rotation Lambda Function Permissions

The rotation Lambda must be allowed to:

- Retrieve and update secrets in Secrets Manager

- Connect to the Aurora DB cluster

- Create, update, or delete DB users

Example IAM permissions for the Lambda:

- `secretsmanager:GetSecretValue`

- `secretsmanager:PutSecretValue`

- `secretsmanager:UpdateSecretVersionStage`

- `rds-data:*` (or limited RDS API calls)

Integration Patterns

There are several patterns for integrating Secrets Manager with Aurora-based applications:

1. Lambda/Serverless Applications

- Fetch secret at **cold start** or using SDK at runtime

- Cache the secret in memory for short-lived execution

- Use the retrieved credentials in database connection string

2. ECS/EKS/EC2-Based Services

- Use IAM roles for service accounts or EC2 instance roles

- Inject secret into **environment variables** or config files at container/task startup

- Optionally use **sidecar containers** or **init containers** for secret fetching

3. Aurora PostgreSQL and IAM Authentication (Advanced)

- Combine Secrets Manager with **IAM database authentication**

- Instead of storing static credentials, issue short-lived tokens via IAM

- Store DB metadata (e.g., hostname, port) in Secrets Manager, and use IAM tokens for auth

---

Best Practices

1. **Rotate secrets regularly**: Set rotation interval based on security requirements (e.g., every 30–60 days).

2. **Use fine-grained IAM**: Limit access to secrets to only the roles/services that need them.

3. **Audit access**: Enable **CloudTrail** for Secrets Manager and monitor who accesses and modifies secrets.

4. **Don't hardcode credentials**: Always retrieve secrets from Secrets Manager using SDKs or automation.

5. **Secure the rotation function**:

   ○ Restrict the execution role

   ○ Validate secrets before finalizing rotation

6. **Use tagging and naming conventions** for secrets to track purpose, environment, or ownership.

Limitations and Considerations

- **Cluster Availability**: During rotation, the rotation function must connect to the Aurora cluster. If the cluster is unavailable, rotation fails.

- **Multi-Writer Clusters**: Aurora MySQL multi-writer clusters **do not support** automatic secret rotation.

- **Latency**: Retrieving secrets at runtime introduces minimal but measurable latency—consider caching securely in short bursts.

- **Encryption Dependencies**: Secrets are encrypted using **AWS KMS**; ensure you manage key policies carefully.

Summary

Integrating **AWS Secrets Manager** with Amazon Aurora allows you to manage database credentials securely, reduce operational risk, and automate credential rotation without impacting applications.

Key takeaways:

- Secrets Manager helps avoid hardcoded credentials and centralized secret sprawl.

- Auto-rotation via Lambda is seamless and minimizes human error.

- IAM plays a central role in controlling access to secrets and ensuring secure integrations.

- Integration patterns vary depending on application architecture (serverless, containerized, or traditional compute).

By adopting Secrets Manager, you not only **enhance security and compliance** but also **streamline operational workflows** in a modern Aurora environment.

Chapter 24. Fine-Grained Access Control with Roles and Policies

Amazon Aurora offers multiple layers of access control that allow organizations to define **fine-grained, least-privilege permissions**—essential for operating secure, multi-tenant, and collaborative environments. With support for **database-level roles**, **resource-based policies**, and **AWS IAM integration**, Aurora enables secure delegation and auditing of access.

In this chapter, we explore how to implement and manage **fine-grained access control** using built-in features, AWS services, and best practices for large, multi-team environments.

Database-Level Permissions

Database-level permissions define what a user or role can do **within the database engine itself**, such as running queries, creating tables, or modifying schemas. These permissions are **engine-specific** and controlled by SQL-based GRANT/REVOKE statements or role hierarchies.

Aurora MySQL-Compatible Edition

Aurora MySQL uses the traditional **MySQL GRANT system** for managing access:

Users are defined using:

```
CREATE USER 'dev_user'@'%' IDENTIFIED
BY 'securepass';
```

-

Permissions are granted on specific objects:

```
GRANT SELECT, INSERT ON dbname.* TO
'dev_user'@'%';
```

-
- Privileges can be scoped to:

    - **Global level**: GRANT ALL ON *.*

    - **Database level**: GRANT ALL ON mydb.*

    - **Table level**: GRANT SELECT ON
      mydb.table1

MySQL also supports **role-based privileges**
(MySQL 8.0+):

```
CREATE ROLE analyst;

GRANT SELECT ON mydb.* TO analyst;

GRANT analyst TO 'report_user'@'%';
```

-

Aurora PostgreSQL-Compatible Edition

Aurora PostgreSQL supports **a rich role-based access model** with finer granularity than MySQL.

Roles can inherit permissions:

```
CREATE ROLE readonly;

GRANT CONNECT ON DATABASE mydb TO
readonly;

GRANT USAGE ON SCHEMA public TO
readonly;

GRANT SELECT ON ALL TABLES IN SCHEMA
public TO readonly;
```

-

    You can use **default privileges** to automatically apply permissions to future objects:

```
ALTER DEFAULT PRIVILEGES IN SCHEMA
public

GRANT SELECT ON TABLES TO readonly;
```

-
- PostgreSQL also supports **group roles, role inheritance, login roles**, and **NOINHERIT** for

tightly controlled delegation.

Key Concepts

- **Roles vs Users**:

    - PostgreSQL: Users are roles with login privilege.

    - MySQL: Roles are a newer concept and not as flexible as in PostgreSQL.

- **Connection Authentication**:

    - Handled separately via **IAM authentication**, SSL certs, or native password-based login.

Best Practices

- Use **roles instead of assigning privileges to individual users**.

- Separate **administrative roles** (e.g., `dba_admin`) from **application roles** (e.g., `web_reader`).

- Apply **least privilege principles**—only grant the permissions required for the task.

- Revoke privileges explicitly when users change teams or projects.

Resource-Based Access (Tags, ARNs)

Beyond database-level permissions, Amazon Aurora supports **resource-level control** using **AWS IAM policies**, **resource tags**, and **Amazon Resource Names (ARNs)**. This integration allows central access management via AWS Identity and Access Management (IAM) and Resource Access Manager (RAM).

IAM Policies for Aurora

AWS IAM policies allow you to control **who can create, modify, delete, or connect to Aurora clusters or instances**.

Example IAM policy to allow rds:Connect on a specific DB cluster:

```
{

    "Version": "2012-10-17",

    "Statement": [

        {

            "Effect": "Allow",

            "Action": "rds-db:connect",
```

```
      "Resource": "arn:aws:rds-db:us-
west-2:123456789012:dbuser:db-
ABCDEFGHIJKLMNOP/dbadmin"

    }

  ]

}
```

Resource Tag-Based Control

Aurora resources—clusters, instances, snapshots—can be tagged and access to them can be **granted or denied based on tags**.

Example Use Case:

- Tag clusters by environment: `Environment=Dev`, `Environment=Prod`

Apply IAM conditions:

```
"Condition": {

  "StringEquals": {

    "aws:ResourceTag/Environment":
"Dev"

  }
```

}

•

Benefits of tag-based access:

- Dynamic access control based on project, team, environment.

- Reduces hardcoding of ARNs or IDs.

- Supports automation through consistent tagging strategies.

ARN Granularity

Aurora supports granular ARNs for:

- DB Clusters: `arn:aws:rds:region:account-id:cluster:cluster-name`

- DB Instances: `arn:aws:rds:region:account-id:db:instance-name`

- IAM Database Users: `arn:aws:rds-db:region:account-id:dbuser:dbi-resource-id/db-username`

You can use these to:

- Restrict access to a specific instance or role.

- Define **fine-grained permissions for different services (e.g., Lambda, Redshift, Glue)** accessing Aurora.

IAM Authentication for DB Access

Aurora supports **IAM-based database authentication**, where users connect using **temporary AWS credentials** instead of passwords.

Setup Flow:

1. Enable IAM authentication on the DB cluster.

2. Create IAM roles/policies granting `rds-db:connect`.

3. Generate an authentication token using AWS CLI or SDK.

4. Use the token as the password for database login.

Advantages:

- No password rotation needed.

- Access is logged via CloudTrail.

- Fine-grained session control and revocation.

Best Practices for Multi-Team Setups

Large-scale environments often have multiple teams working on different parts of a system. Aurora provides mechanisms to **isolate, delegate, and audit access** effectively.

1. Role-Based Access Segregation

- Create **team-specific roles**:

    - `analytics_reader`

    - `webapp_writer`

    - `ml_engineer`

    Grant only necessary permissions:

    ```
    GRANT SELECT ON schema.analytics TO
    analytics_reader;
    ```

-

2. Use Resource Tags for Team Ownership

Tag Aurora resources with team identifiers:

```
"aws:ResourceTag/OwnerTeam": "ML"
```

IAM policies can then restrict access:

```
"Condition": {

  "StringEquals": {

    "aws:ResourceTag/OwnerTeam":
"Analytics"

  }

}
```

3. Implement Schema-Level Isolation (PostgreSQL)

Create a **dedicated schema per team**:

```
CREATE SCHEMA dev_team;

GRANT USAGE ON SCHEMA dev_team TO
dev_team_role;
```

-
- Prevent cross-team interference by:

  ○ Revoke default privileges.

  ○ Explicitly deny object creation outside
    assigned schema.

4. Delegate DB Access with IAM Roles

- Use **IAM roles for federated access** via AWS SSO, Cognito, or third-party IdPs.

- Each team can assume their own IAM role with scoped `rds-db:connect` permissions.

5. Monitor and Audit Access

- Enable **AWS CloudTrail** to track IAM and RDS API calls.

- Use **Performance Insights** to monitor who is running heavy queries.

- Log **connection attempts** using Aurora's enhanced logging.

6. Minimize Privileged Users

- Restrict SUPER, RDS_SUPERUSER, or `pg_monitor` roles to DBAs.

- Avoid using root/postgres in application-level connections.

7. Automate Policy Enforcement

- Use **Service Control Policies (SCPs)** in AWS Organizations.

- Enforce tagging and naming conventions via **AWS Config Rules** or custom Lambda audits.

- Use tools like **Terraform or AWS CloudFormation** to enforce consistent access controls.

Summary: Capability Comparison

Feature	Aurora MySQL	Aurora PostgreSQL
Role-Based Access	Basic (MySQL roles)	Advanced (Inheritance, NOINHERIT)
IAM Authentication	Supported	Supported
Tag-Based Access Control	Yes (via IAM)	Yes (via IAM)
Schema-Level Isolation	Not native	Native support
Resource-Level ARNs	Full support	Full support
Default Privileges	Limited	Fully supported

Final Thoughts

Fine-grained access control in Aurora provides powerful mechanisms to manage **who can do what** across a variety of contexts—whether it's within the database, across AWS services, or across organizational teams.

By leveraging a combination of **IAM, resource tagging, SQL roles, and schema-level controls**, you can create

secure, scalable access policies that enable agility without sacrificing governance.

> 💡 **Tip:** Use **least privilege + tag-based policies + role-based permissions** for a scalable, secure, and auditable access control model across teams and environments.

Part V: Performance and Monitoring

Chapter 25. Using Performance Insights

Amazon Aurora includes a powerful feature called **Performance Insights (PI)** that enables deep monitoring and performance tuning of your Aurora databases. Performance Insights helps you visualize and analyze **database load**, identify **slow or inefficient queries**, and diagnose **bottlenecks**—all through an interactive dashboard with fine-grained metrics.

This chapter provides a practical guide to using Performance Insights in Amazon Aurora, covering how to enable and configure the feature, navigate the dashboard, and interpret time-series data and load visualizations to make informed decisions for performance tuning.

Enabling and Configuring Performance Insights

Performance Insights is **available for both Aurora MySQL and Aurora PostgreSQL**. It can be enabled during DB cluster creation or enabled/disabled later via the console, CLI, or RDS API.

How to Enable Performance Insights

You can enable PI during DB cluster creation:

1. Open the **Amazon RDS console**.

2. Choose **Create database**.

3. In the **Database features** section, under **Database Insights**, select **Enable Performance Insights**.

4. Set the **retention period** (default is 7 days; up to 2 years available for a fee).

5. Choose an **AWS KMS key** for encrypting PI data, or use the default key.

To enable PI on an **existing DB cluster**:

1. Navigate to **Databases** in the RDS console.

2. Select your DB cluster.

3. Choose **Modify**.

4. In **Performance Insights**, check **Enable Performance Insights**.

5. Save changes—**no downtime or reboot required**.

CLI Example

```
aws rds modify-db-cluster \

  --db-cluster-identifier my-aurora-
cluster \
```

```
--enable-performance-insights \

--performance-insights-retention-
period 731 \

--apply-immediately
```

Key Configuration Options

- **Retention Period**: 7 days (free), 1–24 months (paid tier)

- **AWS KMS Key**: Optional; used to encrypt PI data at rest

- **Instance Type Support**:

    - **Not supported** on `db.t2`, `db.t3`, `db.t4g.micro`, or `db.t4g.small`

    - Fully supported on `db.r5`, `db.r6g`, `db.m6g`, and larger

Overview of the Dashboard

Once Performance Insights is enabled, you can access it from the **RDS console** by selecting your Aurora cluster and clicking **Performance Insights**.

Main Components of the Dashboard

The PI dashboard is composed of several interactive visual elements:

1. **Database Load Chart**

   ○ Primary chart showing **Average Active Sessions (AAS)** over time.

   ○ Represents how many sessions were actively running or waiting.

   ○ Color-coded by **wait state**, **SQL**, **host**, or **user**.

2. **Top Dimensions**

   ○ Below the load chart, see top SQL queries, users, hosts, or wait events contributing to DB load.

3. **Time Range Selector**

   ○ Choose predefined intervals (e.g., last 1 hour, 24 hours) or custom ranges.

   ○ Zoom in to correlate spikes in load with specific events or queries.

4. **Filter Controls**

   ○ Filter by SQL statement, host, user, or wait event.

- Helps isolate performance problems to specific workloads or sessions.

5. **Max vCPU Line**

- Horizontal line in load chart indicating maximum available CPU capacity.

- If AAS consistently exceeds this line, your instance is **CPU-bound**.

Example Use Case

A sudden spike in AAS shows on the chart. By filtering to the top SQL statements, you discover a query with a full table scan and high wait time. You can drill down to the **execution plan** and optimize the SQL or add an index.

Time-Series and Load Visualizations

Understanding the time-series visualizations in Performance Insights is critical for diagnosing issues and tuning performance effectively.

Understanding Database Load (DB Load)

- DB Load is measured in **Average Active Sessions (AAS)**.

- Represents the number of sessions that were **active** (on CPU or waiting) at a point in time.

- Each **colored band** in the chart shows the proportion of load due to a specific SQL statement, wait event, or user.

Types of Wait States

Every session is in one of two states:

- **Running (CPU)**: Actively executing on the CPU.

- **Waiting**: Blocked, possibly on I/O, locks, buffer pool access, etc.

Common wait event types include:

- **IO-related** (e.g., `io/table/sql/handler`)

- **Lock contention** (e.g., `lock/metadata/sql/mdl`)

- **Buffer pool access**

- **Replication delay**

AAS Calculation

AAS is calculated as:

pg

```
AAS = Total active session time /
Total time interval
```

For example, if you had 10 seconds of total active session time over a 5-second interval:

```
AAS = 10 / 5 = 2.0
```

This means on average, 2 sessions were active at all times during that interval.

Load Breakdown by Dimension

You can slice the DB load by multiple dimensions:

- **SQL Statement**: See top queries by load.

- **User**: Identify users generating most load.

- **Host**: Find noisy application servers.

- **Wait Event**: Diagnose bottlenecks in resource access.

Visual Cues to Performance Issues

- **AAS consistently above Max vCPU**: Indicates instance is under-provisioned or inefficient queries.

- **Spikes with heavy Wait states**: Signals locking, I/O, or memory contention.

- **Single SQL dominating load**: Indicates a performance issue in that query.

Visual Tips

- Use **"Top SQL"** to identify problematic queries.

- Compare AAS during **normal vs. degraded performance**.

- Combine PI with **CloudWatch metrics** for storage I/O, memory, and network stats.

Advanced Features and Insights

Proactive Recommendations (Paid Tier)

For Aurora MySQL/PostgreSQL (excluding Serverless v2), PI can provide:

- **Automatic detection** of performance anomalies

- **Suggested optimizations** for SQL statements

- **Highlighting of schema changes or plan regressions**

Integration with CloudTrail

All PI-related API calls can be logged with **AWS CloudTrail** for auditing and change tracking.

API Access to PI Metrics

You can programmatically access PI metrics via:

- `GetResourceMetrics` API

- Useful for custom dashboards or third-party monitoring integrations

Example:

```
aws pi get-resource-metrics \

  --service-type RDS \

  --identifier db-XXXXXXXX \

  --metric-queries file://metrics.json \

  --start-time 2024-03-28T00:00:00Z \

  --end-time 2024-03-28T01:00:00Z
```

Best Practices for Using Performance Insights

1. **Enable PI early in development** for baseline tracking.

2. **Correlate spikes** with application deployments or traffic surges.

3. **Set custom retention** for long-term trending and auditing.

4. **Tag critical SQL** for tracking known patterns in the dashboard.

5. **Monitor Max vCPU regularly** and scale up instance class as needed.

6. **Automate alerts** using CloudWatch thresholds on PI metrics.

Summary

Performance Insights transforms Aurora from a black box into a **transparent, actionable system**. With intuitive dashboards, time-series visualizations, and load breakdowns, you can optimize your databases like a pro.

To recap:

- **Enable PI** easily during or after cluster creation.

- Use the **dashboard** to visualize session-level load and bottlenecks.

- Understand **wait events**, top SQL, and AAS trends.

- Integrate with **CloudTrail**, **API**, and **CloudWatch** for complete observability.

In production environments, Performance Insights is **indispensable** for proactive tuning, cost control, and maintaining SLA-grade performance.

Chapter 26. Understanding DB Load: AAS and Wait Events

Introduction

Performance tuning in Amazon Aurora requires insight into what your database is doing at any given time. Rather than relying on raw CPU or memory usage alone, Aurora provides a high-level abstraction called **Database Load (DB Load)** via **Performance Insights**. The centerpiece of DB Load analysis is the **Average Active Sessions (AAS)** metric, which, along with **wait events** and **dimension slicing**, helps pinpoint inefficiencies and bottlenecks in workload execution.

This chapter explores how to analyze DB Load using AAS, understand session state transitions, and slice performance data by critical dimensions such as wait events, SQL statements, users, and hosts to diagnose and resolve database performance issues in Aurora clusters.

Active Sessions and Bottlenecks

What is an Active Session?

An **active session** in Aurora refers to any connection to the database that is either:

- **Running on CPU**, actively executing queries, or

- **Waiting** for a resource (e.g., locks, I/O, buffer pool access)

Inactive or idle sessions (those waiting for user input or sleeping) are excluded from DB Load measurements.

Understanding Bottlenecks

Bottlenecks occur when active sessions are waiting excessively for the same resource, slowing down overall throughput. Common indicators of bottlenecks include:

- Long-running queries with excessive locking

- High CPU usage due to poorly optimized queries

- Frequent disk I/O or contention in buffer/cache layers

- Network saturation when calling external systems

In Aurora, bottlenecks manifest as spikes in DB Load, and their root causes can be explored through **wait events** and other performance dimensions.

Key Bottleneck Signals

- **DB Load exceeding Max vCPU line**: Indicates CPU-bound workload

- **Spikes in AAS with WAIT states**: Points to blocked or stalled queries

- **Consistent high AAS for a specific SQL**: Signals inefficient query patterns

Average Active Sessions (AAS) Explained

Definition of AAS

AAS (Average Active Sessions) is the core metric in Aurora's Performance Insights. It measures the number of **simultaneously active sessions** over a specific time interval.

- Active = Executing or waiting

- Sampled every second

- Expressed as a time-weighted average over your selected time window

AAS Calculation

Aurora computes AAS by aggregating session samples per second, across all active connections.

Formula:

pg

```
AAS = Total Active Session Time /
Elapsed Time
```

Example:

Second	Active Sessions
1	2
2	0

3	4
4	0
5	4

```
Total Sessions = 2 + 0 + 4 + 0 + 4 =
10

Elapsed Time = 5 seconds

AAS = 10 / 5 = 2
```

Interpreting AAS

AAS Range	Interpretation
0–1	Low workload
1–n (below vCPU count)	Healthy load distribution
> vCPU count	Potential CPU bottleneck or query queueing

Use AAS to:

- Establish performance baselines

- Compare load across time intervals

- Identify performance regressions

Session State Analysis

Session States in Aurora

Performance Insights categorizes session state as:

- **CPU**: The session is actively consuming CPU (running queries)

- **Wait**: The session is blocked, waiting on a resource

Each session sampled is labeled with one of these states at that instant.

Wait States: Deep Dive

Wait states are further categorized into **wait events** (detailed below), and represent various reasons for delays:

- Lock contention

- Disk I/O

- Memory buffer waits

- Replication lags

- Network delays

Example: Diagnosing Query Queues

A consistent pattern of high AAS with CPU as the primary state suggests under-provisioned compute. Conversely, high WAIT sessions hint at inefficiencies such as:

- Missing indexes

- Application-level contention

- Suboptimal query plans

Wait Events: Identifying Performance Barriers

What Are Wait Events?

A **wait event** is a type of delay that causes a session to wait before continuing query execution. Each time a session is sampled in a WAIT state, Performance Insights records the reason.

Common categories include:

- **IO-related**: Waiting on disk read/write

- **Lock-related**: Waiting for table/row locks

- **Buffer/cache**: Waiting for memory buffers

- **Replication**: Waiting for replica sync or lag

- **Other**: User-defined events or external calls

Engine-Specific Events

Aurora's supported engines expose different wait events:

- **Aurora MySQL**: Leverages MySQL's Performance Schema

  - Examples: `wait/io/table/sql/handler`, `wait/synch/mutex/sql/LOCK_table`

- **Aurora PostgreSQL**: Leverages PostgreSQL's statistics collector

  - Examples: `LWLock`, `IO:DataFileRead`, `Lock:Relation`

Tuning with Wait Events

A wait event that appears consistently or accounts for a significant portion of DB Load points to a performance bottleneck.

Approach:

1. Identify top wait events (via Performance Insights)

2. Examine associated SQL statements

3. Tune schema, queries, or connection pooling as needed

Real-World Scenarios

- `buffer busy waits`: Indicates contention in buffer pool—consider increasing buffer pool size

- `log file sync`: Points to frequent commits—batch transactions or adjust fsync settings

- `Lock:Tuple`: Suggests row-level locking—analyze transaction isolation levels

---

DBLoad Dimension Slicing

What Are Dimensions?

Dimensions let you slice DB Load by attributes to pinpoint sources of performance issues.

Supported dimensions:

- **SQL**: Statement-level breakdown of load

- **User**: Authenticated DB user executing the queries

- **Host**: Application server or source host

- **Wait Event**: Resource delay type

- **Client Application**: If tagged using application_name or custom variables

Why Dimension Slicing Matters

Using dimensions helps isolate the **who**, **what**, and **where** of performance issues:

- Identify top resource-consuming queries

- Detect inefficient users or app components

- Locate problematic nodes in a distributed system

Top SQL Identification

Performance Insights surfaces **top SQL queries** by cumulative DB Load.

- Each SQL digest is normalized (e.g., parameterized queries)

- Full execution stats are provided:

    - Execution count

    - Average latency

    - Rows returned

    - Wait time distribution

Tips:

- Drill into the SQL execution plan

- Use EXPLAIN ANALYZE (PostgreSQL) or EXPLAIN FORMAT=JSON (MySQL) to identify inefficiencies

Example Slice: Wait Event by SQL

This approach answers the question:

Which queries are contributing most to lock waits?

Steps:

1. Use Performance Insights

2. Filter by Wait Event = `Lock:Tuple`

3. Sort by SQL digest with highest cumulative wait time

Visualizing and Interpreting DB Load

Performance Insights Dashboard

Aurora Performance Insights provides an interactive dashboard to visualize:

- DB Load over time (AAS)

- Breakdown by state (CPU vs. WAIT)

- Dimensions (SQL, user, host)

- Comparison with Max vCPU line

Features:

- Adjustable time windows

- Hover for per-second detail

- Zoom to spike intervals

Max vCPU Line

The **Max vCPU line** represents the DB instance's capacity to handle concurrent CPU threads.

- For example, `db.r6g.large` has 2 vCPUs, so 2 sessions can run simultaneously

- If DB Load (AAS) exceeds this line:

    - Queues form

    - Query latency increases

    - Throughput suffers

Resolution:

- Scale instance size

- Optimize queries

- Use read replicas for scale-out

Best Practices for DB Load Analysis

1. Baseline and Trend Analysis

- Establish baselines using AAS and wait event patterns

- Analyze periodic spikes and seasonality

- Tag deployments and schema changes to correlate with performance changes

2. Query Performance Optimization

- Regularly review top SQLs

- Use indexing strategies based on workload

- Avoid SELECT *; fetch only required columns

- Normalize or denormalize judiciously depending on query complexity

3. Resource Provisioning

- Ensure sufficient vCPU for baseline load

- Use Aurora Serverless v2 for variable workloads

- Add Aurora Replicas to distribute read load

4. Monitoring and Alerting

- Set alarms on:

    - AAS > Max vCPU

    - Wait events with rising trend

- Use Amazon EventBridge to trigger notifications or remediation actions

5. Use Query Hints and Planner Tools

- PostgreSQL: Use `pg_hint_plan` to override planner behavior

- MySQL: Use optimizer hints like `STRAIGHT_JOIN`, `USE INDEX`

Advanced Techniques

Correlating DB Load with Application Metrics

- Integrate Aurora with X-Ray or CloudWatch Logs

- Correlate DB spikes with application latency or API failures

- Use `application_name` tags in PostgreSQL for fine-grained attribution

Stored Procedure Monitoring

- Aurora captures execution metrics for stored procedures

- Monitor AAS spikes when procedures are called

- Refactor long procedures into smaller units for visibility

Parallel Query and DB Load

- Aurora PostgreSQL supports **parallel query execution**

- Watch for higher AAS from multiple workers per query

- Tune using `max_parallel_workers_per_gather` and planner cost parameters

Summary Table: AAS vs. Wait States vs. Actions

Symptom	State	Likely Cause	Recommended Action
High AAS, high CPU	CPU	Under-provisioned instance	Scale up instance or optimize SQL
High AAS, high Wait	WAIT	Resource contention (locks, I/O)	Tune schema, index, and queries
Low AAS, high latency	Mixed	App-side bottleneck	Analyze app-layer response times
AAS spikes post-deployment	Mixed	Regression or unoptimized schema	Rollback or optimize

Conclusion

Average Active Sessions and wait events provide a powerful lens into the runtime behavior of Aurora clusters. Instead of merely reacting to CPU or disk metrics, DB Load and its associated dimensions enable **root cause analysis at the query and session level**.

By combining real-time visualization with structured performance metadata, Aurora equips DBAs, developers, and architects with the insights they need to maintain performance, minimize cost, and deliver reliable experiences to users.

With a thoughtful approach to monitoring and continuous analysis of DB Load patterns, you can turn Aurora into a high-performing, self-optimizing database layer for your cloud-native applications.

Chapter 27. Top SQL Analysis and Execution Plans

Analyzing the most resource-intensive queries—often referred to as **Top SQL**—is a cornerstone of performance tuning in Amazon Aurora. Aurora integrates with **Performance Insights**, **EXPLAIN/EXPLAIN ANALYZE**, and other diagnostic tools to help identify bottlenecks and optimize query performance. This chapter delves into **query ranking**, **filtering techniques**, **execution plan inspection**, and **optimization strategies**, giving you actionable insights into how to improve performance in both Aurora MySQL and PostgreSQL environments.

Overview of Top SQL Analysis

Top SQL refers to queries that have the **greatest impact on your database load**. In Aurora, this is typically measured by metrics such as:

- **Average Active Sessions (AAS)**

- **Execution time**

- **Wait events (e.g., I/O, locks, CPU)**

- **Rows examined or returned**

- **Buffer or memory usage**

Aurora surfaces this data via:

- **Performance Insights Dashboard**

- **Aurora PostgreSQL built-in functions**

- **MySQL performance schema**

- **CloudWatch metrics**

Understanding and addressing Top SQL is critical for:

- Minimizing application latency

- Reducing resource contention

- Improving database scalability

Query Ranking and Filtering

Performance Insights: Ranking by DB Load

In the **Performance Insights Dashboard**, queries are automatically ranked by their contribution to **DBLoad**, which is measured in **Average Active Sessions (AAS)**.

Ranking dimensions include:

- SQL digest (normalized query text)

- Wait events

- User

- Host

- Database

Filtering options:

- **Time frame**: Narrow focus to specific spikes or patterns

- **SQL ID**: Drill into specific queries

- **User or host**: Isolate application sources

- **Wait states**: Filter by CPU-bound or I/O-bound queries

Top SQL view example:

- Top 5 queries sorted by AAS

- For each query:

  - Total execution count

  - Average latency

  - Top wait events

  - CPU usage

  - Links to view execution plan

PostgreSQL-Specific Query Analysis

Use PostgreSQL's **pg_stat_statements** to gather execution statistics:

```
SELECT query, calls, total_time,
mean_time, rows

FROM pg_stat_statements

ORDER BY total_time DESC

LIMIT 5;
```

MySQL-Specific Query Analysis

Use Performance Schema and digest tables:

```
SELECT digest_text, COUNT_STAR,
SUM_TIMER_WAIT

FROM
performance_schema.events_statements_s
ummary_by_digest

ORDER BY SUM_TIMER_WAIT DESC

LIMIT 5;
```

Viewing Execution Plans

Understanding a query's execution plan is essential for optimization. Aurora supports native mechanisms for viewing and interpreting plans.

EXPLAIN and EXPLAIN ANALYZE

These tools describe the **query planner's strategy** for executing a query.

Aurora PostgreSQL

```
EXPLAIN ANALYZE

SELECT * FROM orders WHERE customer_id
= 123;
```

Provides:

- Execution order

- Index usage

- Estimated vs actual rows

- I/O and CPU cost

- Timing for each step

Aurora MySQL

```
EXPLAIN FORMAT=JSON

SELECT * FROM orders WHERE customer_id
= 123;
```

Provides:

- Access methods (e.g., index scan, full table scan)

- Join types

- Filter pushdowns

- Estimated cost

Performance Insights Integration

You can link directly from a Top SQL entry in Performance Insights to its corresponding **execution plan** in the console. This helps correlate query behavior with its runtime structure.

Optimization Strategies

Once you've identified slow or resource-heavy queries, there are several methods to improve performance. These fall into three main categories: **Indexing**, **Query Rewriting**, and **Resource Management**.

1. Indexing Strategy

Add indexes on filter/join columns:

```
CREATE INDEX idx_customer_id ON
orders(customer_id);
```

-
- Use **covering indexes** to avoid accessing the table:

  - Combine SELECT columns into the index definition.

- Monitor with `pg_stat_user_indexes` or `SHOW INDEXES`.

Trade-offs:

- Indexes increase write latency and storage.

- Over-indexing can hurt performance — balance is key.

2. Query Rewriting

- Eliminate **SELECT *** — use only required columns.

- Break complex joins into smaller subqueries if necessary.

- Replace correlated subqueries with joins.

- Avoid unnecessary sorting or window functions.

Example:

```
-- Inefficient

SELECT * FROM orders WHERE customer_id
IN (SELECT id FROM customers);


-- Improved

SELECT o.* FROM orders o JOIN
customers c ON o.customer_id = c.id;
```

3. Caching and Materialization

- Use **materialized views** for expensive aggregations.

- Implement **result caching** at the application or database level.

- In PostgreSQL: consider `pg_stat_statements_reset()` to clear tracking after a caching change.

4. Aurora-Specific Optimizations

- **Aurora Parallel Query (APQ)**:

  - Enables parallel execution of full-table scans.

  - Great for large analytical queries.

  - Only available in Aurora MySQL 5.6+ and PostgreSQL 11+ with compatible storage.

- **Aurora Read Replicas**:

  - Offload read-heavy queries to replicas via reader endpoints.

- **Custom endpoints**:

  - Route analytical queries to specific replicas, reducing contention.

5. Parameter Tuning

- PostgreSQL:

- o `work_mem`, `effective_cache_size`, `random_page_cost`

- MySQL:

  - o `query_cache_size`, `innodb_buffer_pool_size`, `join_buffer_size`

Use **DB parameter groups** to tune these values cluster-wide.

Monitoring and Automation

CloudWatch Metrics

Monitor:

- CPU utilization

- Disk I/O

- DB connections

- Throughput (read/write)

Scheduled Analysis

- Automate query analysis using scripts or third-party tools (e.g., pgBadger, Percona Toolkit).

- Integrate with **Amazon CloudWatch Logs** for long-term tracking.

Best Practices for Top SQL Optimization

1. **Monitor continuously** using Performance Insights.

2. **Identify trends**: Look for queries that spike during certain workloads.

3. **Use query fingerprints**: Normalize queries to find repeating patterns.

4. **Validate every change**: Always test performance tuning in staging.

5. **Avoid over-tuning**: Not all slow queries need optimization — focus on those with the highest impact.

6. **Keep statistics up to date**:

   - PostgreSQL: ANALYZE

   - MySQL: ANALYZE TABLE

7. **Use connection pooling** (e.g., PgBouncer or ProxySQL) to reduce contention from inefficient queries.

Real-World Example

Scenario: A BI dashboard is loading slowly

Top SQL shows:

```
SELECT region, SUM(sales) FROM
transactions GROUP BY region;
```

-
- Execution plan shows full table scan, 10M rows.

- Optimization:

    - Created index on region

    - Created materialized view

    - Routed BI queries to a custom endpoint with high-memory replica

    - Reduced dashboard load time by 85%

Summary

Aurora's Top SQL analysis tools provide a robust framework for identifying and addressing inefficient queries. By combining query metrics, execution plan analysis, and strategic optimization, you can significantly enhance your database performance and resource efficiency.

Technique	Tools Used	Benefits
Query ranking	Performance Insights, pg_stat	Identify top contributors to load
Execution plan review	EXPLAIN, EXPLAIN ANALYZE	Understand query behavior
Optimization	Indexing, rewriting, parameter tuning	Reduce latency, improve scaling

Pro Tip: Focus on **queries with high wait time per execution** — these often yield the best ROI when optimized.

Chapter 28. Monitoring Replica Lag and vCPU Load

Monitoring replica lag and vCPU saturation is essential for maintaining a high-performing, resilient Amazon Aurora cluster. These metrics directly impact read consistency, write throughput, and application responsiveness. In this chapter, you'll learn how to measure, interpret, and act upon replica lag and vCPU load using Aurora-native insights, CloudWatch, and dashboarding strategies.

Replica Lag Metrics

Replica lag represents the time delay between data being committed on the **writer (primary)** instance and being visible to **read replicas**. In Amazon Aurora, this lag is typically low due to the high-performance distributed storage engine, but it can spike during heavy loads, replication issues, or network delays.

Key Concepts

- **Aurora Replicas** use **asynchronous replication**

- Replica lag is measured in **milliseconds**

- Aurora replicates **log records**, not physical data blocks, improving efficiency

Core Metrics

Metric Name	Source	Description

`AuroraReplicaLag`	Amazon CloudWatch	Time (ms) by which a replica lags behind the writer
`ReplicaLagMinimum, Maximum`	CloudWatch (aggregates)	Shows min/max replica lag across all replicas
`aurora_replica_status()`	Aurora SQL function	Detailed LSN and lag insight per replica
`visibility_lag_in_msec`	Aurora global clusters	Lag between primary and global secondary regions

SQL-Based Lag Insights

Use the built-in function `aurora_replica_status()` for in-depth replication insights:

```
SELECT server_id, session_id,
replica_lag_in_msec

FROM aurora_replica_status();
```

Example Output:

server_id	session_id	replica_lag_in_msec
db-aurora-writer	MASTER_SESSION_ID	NULL
db-aurora-reader1	88cc6c8b-5b3e-4a90-9f3d-e48b47ea2d56	9
db-aurora-reader2	a4e24f5c-f27a-4f56-8d69-51e9acb9fdee	11

Aurora Global Databases

In Aurora Global Database deployments, lag can occur between Regions. Use:

```
SELECT * FROM
aurora_global_db_instance_status();
```

For example:

aws_region	server_id	visibility_lag_in_msec
eu-west-1	db-instance-primary	NULL
us-east-1	db-instance-secondary	45

Max vCPU Line and Saturation

Aurora Performance Insights includes a **Max vCPU line**, a critical indicator of when your database is becoming CPU-bound.

What is the Max vCPU Line?

- Represents the number of virtual CPUs available to the Aurora DB instance

- Used as a reference line in Performance Insights' DB load chart

- If **Average Active Sessions (AAS)** consistently exceeds Max vCPU, the DB is saturated

DB Load vs. Max vCPU

- **DB Load**: Aggregate of session activity (either CPU or waits)

- **Max vCPU**: Hardware limit; crossing this means sessions queue for CPU

CPU Saturation Symptoms

- Increase in `CPU wait` events

- Spikes in **query latency** or **timeouts**

- High `Average Active Sessions` above vCPU count

Interpretation Guidelines

AAS vs Max vCPU	Interpretation	Recommended Action
AAS < Max vCPU	Healthy	No action needed
AAS ≈ Max vCPU	CPU nearing saturation	Monitor closely, investigate top queries
AAS > Max vCPU	CPU bottleneck	Consider scaling up or tuning queries

Sample Chart Analysis

If your instance has 8 vCPUs:

- DB Load stays below 8: Normal

- DB Load exceeds 8 with high CPU wait events: Performance degradation

- Top SQL shows high execution times: Likely culprit for overload

SQL View: Top Waits and CPU Contributors

Use Performance Insights or run:

```
SELECT * FROM
performance_schema.events_statements_s
ummary_by_digest

ORDER BY AVG_TIMER_WAIT DESC

LIMIT 5;
```

Monitoring Dashboard Setup

To monitor replica lag and vCPU load effectively, set up automated, real-time dashboards with Amazon CloudWatch and integrate with Performance Insights and RDS events.

CloudWatch Metrics to Monitor

Metric Name	Namespace	Dimensions
AuroraReplicaLag	AWS/RDS	DBClusterIdentifier
CPUUtilization	AWS/RDS	DBInstanceIdentifier
DatabaseConnections	AWS/RDS	DBInstanceIdentifier
FreeableMemory	AWS/RDS	DBInstanceIdentifier

DBLoad	AWS/RDS	Engine, Region

Sample CloudWatch Dashboard Widgets

1. Replica Lag Chart (Multi-Line)

```
{

  "metrics": [

    [ "AWS/RDS", "AuroraReplicaLag",
"DBInstanceIdentifier", "reader-1" ],

    [ ".", "AuroraReplicaLag",
"DBInstanceIdentifier", "reader-2" ]

  ],

  "stat": "Average",

  "period": 60,

  "title": "Aurora Replica Lag"

}
```

2. CPU Utilization vs. Threshold

```
{

  "metrics": [

    [ "AWS/RDS", "CPUUtilization",
"DBInstanceIdentifier", "writer" ]

  ],

  "view": "timeSeries",

  "stat": "Maximum",

  "title": "Writer CPU Usage"

}
```

3. **Alarm on High Replica Lag**

- Create CloudWatch alarm:

  - Metric: AuroraReplicaLag

  - Threshold: > 1000 ms

  - Action: Notify via SNS or trigger Lambda

4. **Performance Insights Dashboard**

Use the RDS Console for:

- Top SQL statements

- Wait events (e.g., CPU, IO, locks)

- Max vCPU line overlay

- Time-based filtering

Enabling Performance Insights (CloudFormation)

```
PerformanceInsightsEnabled: true

PerformanceInsightsRetentionPeriod: 7

EnableCloudwatchLogsExports:

    - slowquery

    - error
```

Integrating with Grafana or QuickSight

For advanced visualization:

- Use **Amazon Managed Grafana** with CloudWatch data source

- Use **Aurora Performance Insights API** to feed into external dashboards

- Use **QuickSight** for business-focused visualizations on replica lag trends

---

Best Practices for Monitoring and Alerts

- Set thresholds:

    - Replica lag > 1000 ms → warn

    - AAS > Max vCPU → critical

- Combine lag and CPU insights to **prioritize tuning** or **scaling**

- Alert on:

    - `ReplicaLagInMilliseconds > 500`

    - `CPUUtilization > 80%` for > 5 minutes

- Correlate logs with metrics:

    - Enable **slow query log**

    - Export to CloudWatch for centralized alerting

Real-world Scenarios and Recommendations

Scenario 1: Unexpected Latency During Peak Hours

Symptoms:

- DB Load exceeds Max vCPU

- Top waits: CPU, buffer latch

Resolution:

- Optimize slow SQLs using query plans

- Consider moving to a larger instance (e.g., r6g.xlarge → r6g.2xlarge)

Scenario 2: Lag Spikes in One Replica

Symptoms:

- Only one replica shows >2000ms lag

- Other replicas are healthy

Resolution:

- Verify if replica is under I/O or network pressure

- Restart or replace affected replica

- Avoid routing reads to that replica (custom endpoint filtering)

Summary

Monitoring replica lag and vCPU saturation helps ensure that your Aurora cluster stays responsive, scalable, and resilient. Combine **Aurora-native metrics**, **Performance Insights**, and **CloudWatch dashboards** to build observability into your architecture.

Key Takeaways:

- Always track `AuroraReplicaLag` across all replicas

- Compare `DB Load` to Max vCPU to detect CPU saturation

- Use `aurora_replica_status()` for replica health at the SQL level

- Set up CloudWatch dashboards and alarms to automate detection and response

- Enable and use **Performance Insights** to dig into root causes

Chapter 29. Using CloudWatch and Custom Metrics

Monitoring Amazon Aurora is critical for maintaining database health, identifying performance issues, and proactively responding to anomalies. Amazon Aurora integrates natively with **Amazon CloudWatch**, providing a rich set of metrics, logs, and alarm features. In addition, **custom metrics** and **CloudWatch dashboards** offer enhanced observability for developers, database administrators, and operations teams.

This chapter covers:

- **Aurora CloudWatch integration**: How Aurora emits metrics and logs to CloudWatch.

- **Alarm configuration**: Creating actionable alerts for thresholds and anomalies.

- **Custom dashboards**: Using Metrics Explorer and Dashboards for visual monitoring.

Aurora CloudWatch Integration

Amazon Aurora automatically sends a wide array of performance and health metrics to Amazon CloudWatch. These metrics help track everything from CPU and memory utilization to query performance and replication lag.

What is Monitored by Default?

When you create an Aurora DB cluster, CloudWatch begins collecting:

- **DB-level metrics** (e.g., CPUUtilization, FreeableMemory)

- **Cluster-level metrics** (e.g., VolumeWriteIOPS, DBClusterConnections)

- **Enhanced Monitoring** (if enabled, provides OS-level metrics)

- **Performance Insights data** (in a separate service but integrated)

- **Event notifications** (e.g., failovers, instance restarts)

Key Aurora Metrics in CloudWatch

Here are common metrics emitted by Aurora to CloudWatch:

Instance-level metrics (per DB instance):

- CPUUtilization: CPU load percentage

- FreeableMemory: Available memory in bytes

- ReadIOPS / WriteIOPS: Read and write operations per second

- DiskQueueDepth: Number of I/O operations waiting

- DatabaseConnections: Number of database client connections

Cluster-level metrics:

- VolumeReadIOPS / VolumeWriteIOPS: Cluster volume I/O operations

- AuroraReplicaLag: Replica lag for Aurora Replicas

- Deadlocks: Number of deadlocks detected

- EngineUptime: Time the engine has been active

Storage metrics:

- BackupStorageUsed: Total backup storage consumption

- VolumeBytesUsed: Total size of DB volume

🔍 *Tip:* Use CloudWatch namespaces AWS/RDS and AWS/Aurora to filter Aurora metrics specifically.

How Metrics Are Aggregated

Aurora metrics are published at **1-minute granularity** by default. You can filter them by:

- DB instance

- DB cluster

- DB engine

- Region

CloudWatch offers:

- **Sum, Average, Min, Max** aggregations

- **Percentile metrics** (e.g., p90, p95) for identifying outliers

---

Alarm Configuration

To detect anomalies or critical events in your Aurora environment, you can set up **CloudWatch Alarms** that monitor metric thresholds, anomalies, or composite conditions.

Creating Metric Alarms

You can set alarms on any supported CloudWatch metric:

1. Go to **CloudWatch > Alarms > Create Alarm**

2. Choose a metric (e.g., `CPUUtilization` from Aurora instance)

3. Define:

   - **Threshold** (e.g., `> 80%`)

   - **Evaluation period** (e.g., `3 out of 5 minutes`)

   - **Comparison type**: Greater, Less, Equal

4. Choose **notification target**:

   - **Amazon SNS** topic (email, SMS, Lambda, etc.)

   - **Auto Scaling action**

   - **AWS Systems Manager Automation**

Example: CPU Utilization Alert

```
Alarm Name: Aurora-HighCPU

Metric: CPUUtilization

Threshold: > 80%

Period: 1 minute
```

```
Evaluation: 3 datapoints within 5
minutes

Notification: Send to DevOps SNS topic
```

Alarm Actions

CloudWatch alarms can trigger:

- Email/SMS alerts via **SNS**

- **Lambda functions** for automated recovery

- **EC2 or Aurora scaling actions**

- **Incident response systems** (e.g., PagerDuty)

Composite Alarms

Create alarms that **combine multiple conditions** using Boolean logic.

Example:

```
IF (CPUUtilization > 80%) AND
(FreeableMemory < 100MB)

THEN Trigger Alarm
```

This is useful for reducing noise from false positives.

Anomaly Detection

CloudWatch offers **machine learning-based anomaly detection**:

- Detects out-of-pattern behavior based on historical data

- No need to specify fixed thresholds

  Available via console or CLI:

```
aws cloudwatch put-anomaly-detector \

  --metric-name CPUUtilization \

  --namespace AWS/RDS \

  --statistic Average \

  --dimensions
Name=DBInstanceIdentifier,Value=mydb-instance
```

-

Custom Dashboards with Metrics Explorer

CloudWatch Dashboards are customizable visual interfaces where you can monitor real-time Aurora metrics and alarms across multiple dimensions.

Creating a Dashboard

1. Go to **CloudWatch > Dashboards**

2. Click **Create dashboard**

3. Name your dashboard (e.g., `Aurora-DevOps-Dashboard`)

4. Add widgets:

   - **Line, Stacked Area, Number, Text**

   - Choose metrics from:

     - Aurora DB instance

     - Aurora DB cluster

     - Custom namespace

Example Dashboard Widgets

- **CPU & Memory**:

  - CPUUtilization (Line graph)

  - FreeableMemory (Gauge or Number)

- **Query I/O**:

  - VolumeReadIOPS / VolumeWriteIOPS

- **Replica Lag**:

  - AuroraReplicaLag per instance

- **Connection Health**:

  - DatabaseConnections over time

- **Custom Logs/Errors**:

  - Deadlocks or query errors from enhanced monitoring

⚒ *Tip:* You can add alarms to dashboards for visibility during incident response.

Using Metrics Explorer

CloudWatch **Metrics Explorer** allows ad-hoc exploration and discovery of Aurora metrics:

1. Navigate to **CloudWatch > All metrics > Metrics Explorer**

2. Choose dimension filters:

   - DB Cluster Identifier

   - DB Engine

o   Availability Zone

3. Add and save queries like:

   o   Top 5 DB instances by WriteIOPS

   o   Average Replica Lag by Cluster

   o   Memory usage over time across all clusters

This is ideal for **troubleshooting** and **capacity planning**.

Sharing Dashboards

- Dashboards can be:

   o   **Shared publicly** with read-only links

   o   **Embedded** in operational consoles

   o   **Integrated with AWS Systems Manager OpsCenter**

Custom Aurora Metrics

While Aurora emits a rich set of native metrics, you can enhance observability with **custom metrics**.

Publishing Custom Metrics

Use the `PutMetricData` API to send application-level metrics from EC2, Lambda, or your app:

```
aws cloudwatch put-metric-data \

  --namespace "Custom/AuroraApp" \

  --metric-name "QueryTimeouts" \

  --value 3 \

  --dimensions "DBCluster=dev-cluster"
```

Use Cases

- Track custom query counts

- Log application-side timeout rates

- Push connection pool sizes

- Monitor end-to-end transaction times

Cost Considerations

- First 10 custom metrics: Free (under basic CloudWatch)

- Pricing scales with volume and granularity

- Reduce cost by:

- Aggregating metrics before sending

- Using `StorageResolution=60` for standard granularity

Integrating with Aurora Logs

Combine CloudWatch metrics with:

- **RDS Enhanced Monitoring Logs**

- **Performance Insights**

- **Aurora MySQL/PostgreSQL logs** sent to CloudWatch Logs

This creates a unified observability view across layers.

Best Practices

Here are best practices for setting up and using CloudWatch with Aurora:

- **Tag and label dashboards** by environment (`Dev`, `Staging`, `Prod`)

- **Group alarms logically** (e.g., by DB Cluster, application module)

- Use **composite alarms** to reduce alert fatigue

- **Test alarm conditions** regularly with simulated load

- Use **anomaly detection** for CPU and IOPS to catch hidden issues

- **Automate response** with Lambda or SSM automation

- **Log alarm history** into a central notification channel (e.g., Slack, email, ticketing)

Summary: Building a Monitoring Strategy

To build a comprehensive monitoring solution with Aurora:

Component	Tool	Purpose
Metrics	CloudWatch	Real-time metrics on performance
Logs	CloudWatch Logs	Engine errors, slow queries
Alerts	CloudWatch Alarms	Notify on critical thresholds
Dashboards	Metrics Explorer	Visualize multi-cluster environments
Custom Data	PutMetricData	Track business-specific KPIs
Insights	Performance Insights	Deep analysis of query behavior

Part VI: Operational Management

Chapter 30. Backup and Restore Options

Backup and restore are critical aspects of database administration and disaster recovery planning. In Amazon Aurora, a variety of backup and restore options are available to help ensure data durability, support point-in-time recovery, and enable seamless data sharing across AWS accounts and regions. This chapter will cover the key backup and restore options available in Aurora, including automated backups and snapshots, manual backups, and snapshot sharing. By the end of this chapter, you will understand how to configure these options, the benefits they offer, and the best practices to follow for robust data protection.

Overview

Amazon Aurora provides a comprehensive suite of backup solutions designed to address different use cases:

- **Automated Backups and Snapshots**: Aurora can automatically back up your entire database cluster, including all databases in the cluster. These backups are stored in Amazon S3 and provide continuous, incremental backups that support point-in-time recovery (PITR).

- **Manual Backups**: In addition to automated backups, you can manually create snapshots at

364

any time. Manual snapshots are retained until you explicitly delete them, giving you more control over backup retention policies.

- **Snapshot Sharing**: Aurora snapshots can be shared across AWS accounts and even across regions, which is particularly useful for migrations, compliance audits, and collaboration among teams.

This chapter is organized into three main sections: automated backups and snapshots, manual backups, and snapshot sharing. Each section includes detailed explanations, configuration steps, examples, and best practices.

Automated Backups and Snapshots

Automated backups and snapshots in Aurora are designed to provide continuous protection of your data with minimal operational overhead. This section explains how these backups work, how to configure them, and how to leverage them for recovery.

What Are Automated Backups?

- **Definition**: Automated backups in Aurora automatically capture the entire state of your database cluster at regular intervals. They include both full and incremental backups, allowing you to restore your database to any point within a defined retention period.

- **Storage**: Backups are stored in Amazon S3, ensuring high durability and availability. The incremental nature of these backups minimizes storage overhead.

- **Point-in-Time Recovery (PITR)**: With automated backups, you can restore your DB cluster to any specific point in time within the backup retention period. This is crucial for recovery from accidental data loss or corruption.

How Automated Backups Work

1. **Continuous Backup Process**:

   - Aurora continuously backs up your data by capturing the transaction logs and database snapshots.

   - When a change occurs, Aurora logs the change and later stores this information as part of the backup process.

2. **Incremental Backups**:

   - After the initial full backup, subsequent backups capture only the changes (deltas) made since the previous backup.

   - This approach optimizes storage utilization and reduces backup time.

3. **Retention Period**:

- By default, Aurora retains automated backups for a period of seven days, but you can configure this retention period up to 35 days.

- The retention period defines how far back in time you can perform a point-in-time recovery.

Configuring Automated Backups

To configure automated backups, follow these steps:

1. **During DB Cluster Creation**:

   - In the RDS console, when creating an Aurora DB cluster, you can set the backup retention period.

   - Specify a retention period that meets your recovery objectives. For example, if you need to restore data up to two weeks old, set the retention period accordingly.

2. **Modifying an Existing DB Cluster**:

   - If your cluster is already running, you can modify the backup retention period via the RDS console, AWS CLI, or API.

Example CLI command:

```
aws rds modify-db-cluster \

  --db-cluster-identifier my-cluster \

  --backup-retention-period 14 \

  --apply-immediately
```

- ○
- ○ This command sets the retention period to 14 days.

3. **Backup Window**:

   - ○ Aurora allows you to specify a preferred backup window during which automated backups are performed.

   - ○ Setting a backup window ensures that backups occur during off-peak hours, minimizing performance impacts on your applications.

Automated Snapshots

- **Snapshot Creation**: Automated snapshots are created by Aurora as part of the backup process. They capture the current state of your DB cluster and serve as the basis for point-in-time recovery.

- **Restoration Process**:

- To restore an automated backup, you specify the desired point in time, and Aurora reconstructs your DB cluster using the available snapshots and transaction logs.

- The restoration process may involve applying incremental changes to bring your DB cluster up to the desired state.

- **Usage Considerations**:

  - Automated backups are managed by Aurora and are deleted once the retention period expires.

  - Ensure that your backup retention period aligns with your compliance and recovery requirements.

Benefits of Automated Backups and Snapshots

- **Operational Simplicity**: Automated backups run in the background, reducing the administrative burden of manual backup scheduling.

- **Point-in-Time Recovery**: Ability to restore your DB cluster to any point within the retention period minimizes data loss risks.

- **Cost Efficiency**: Incremental backups and efficient storage usage in Amazon S3 help control backup costs.

- **High Durability and Availability**: Backups stored in Amazon S3 benefit from S3's high durability (99.999999999% durability) and availability.

Use Cases

- **Disaster Recovery**: In the event of a system failure or data corruption, automated backups enable you to quickly restore your DB cluster.

- **Data Auditing**: Organizations can leverage point-in-time recovery to review historical data states for auditing or compliance purposes.

- **Development and Testing**: Developers can restore a backup to a test environment to reproduce issues or test new features without impacting production data.

Manual Backups

While automated backups provide continuous protection, manual backups give you the flexibility to capture the state of your DB cluster at a specific moment. This section explains how to create, manage, and restore manual backups.

What Are Manual Backups?

- **Definition**: Manual backups, or manual snapshots, are initiated by a database administrator. Unlike automated backups, manual snapshots are retained until you explicitly delete them.

- **Persistence**: Manual snapshots do not expire automatically. They remain available for as long as needed, making them ideal for long-term retention or regulatory compliance.

Creating a Manual Snapshot

There are several ways to create a manual snapshot:

1. **Using the AWS Management Console**:

   - Navigate to the RDS console and select your Aurora DB cluster.

   - Choose the option to create a snapshot.

   - Provide a descriptive name for the snapshot to help identify its purpose or the state of the data at the time of capture.

2. **Using the AWS CLI**:

   Example command:

```
aws rds create-db-cluster-snapshot \
   --db-cluster-identifier my-cluster \
   --db-cluster-snapshot-identifier my-cluster-snapshot-2025-03-30
```

- ○
- ○ This command creates a snapshot named `my-cluster-snapshot-2025-03-30` for the specified DB cluster.

3. **Using the API**:

   - ○ Aurora's API supports snapshot creation, which can be integrated into automated workflows or backup scripts.

   - ○ API calls allow you to trigger snapshot creation programmatically, ensuring that critical points in your application workflow are captured.

Managing Manual Snapshots

- **Retention**: Manual snapshots persist until you delete them. This makes them ideal for preserving backups beyond the automated backup retention period.

- **Cost Considerations**:

  - ○ Although manual snapshots incur storage costs, they allow you to manage retention explicitly. You can delete older snapshots that are no longer required.

- **Organization and Tagging**:

- Use consistent naming conventions and tagging strategies to organize snapshots.

- Tags can include information such as the snapshot purpose (e.g., pre-upgrade, post-migration) or the retention period.

- **Security**:

  - Snapshots can be encrypted using the same encryption key as the source DB cluster.

  - Ensure that access to snapshots is restricted via AWS IAM policies.

Restoring from a Manual Snapshot

Restoring from a manual snapshot is similar to restoring from an automated backup:

1. **Initiate the Restore Process**:

   - In the RDS console, select the manual snapshot you wish to restore.

   - Choose the "Restore DB Cluster" option.

2. **Specify Configuration Parameters**:

   - Configure the new DB cluster settings such as instance class, VPC, and security groups.

○   Optionally, rename the DB cluster to avoid
       conflicts with the existing production
       environment.

3. **Launch the New DB Cluster**:

   ○   Once restored, the new DB cluster can be
       used for testing, development, or as a
       replacement in a disaster recovery scenario.

Advantages of Manual Snapshots

- **Control**: You determine when a snapshot is taken
  and how long it is retained.

- **Compliance**: Manual snapshots are useful for
  meeting regulatory requirements that mandate data
  retention beyond the automated backup period.

- **Testing and Rollback**: Before making major
  changes (such as schema migrations or software
  upgrades), you can create a manual snapshot to
  serve as a rollback point.

Best Practices for Manual Backups

- **Schedule Regular Snapshots**: In addition to
  automated backups, schedule manual snapshots
  before major changes or on a periodic basis.

- **Monitor Storage Costs**: Periodically review and
  delete outdated snapshots to manage costs.

- **Automate Where Possible**: Leverage AWS Lambda or other automation tools to trigger manual snapshots during critical events (e.g., before a deployment).

- **Document and Tag**: Maintain detailed documentation and use tagging to record the purpose and context of each snapshot.

Snapshot Sharing

Snapshot sharing enables you to share manual snapshots with other AWS accounts or even across regions. This feature is invaluable for collaboration, migrations, and compliance audits.

What Is Snapshot Sharing?

- **Definition**: Snapshot sharing allows you to grant access to your Aurora manual snapshots to other AWS accounts. Shared snapshots can be used by the recipient to restore a DB cluster.

- **Public vs. Private Sharing**:

    - **Private Sharing**: You can share a snapshot with specific AWS account IDs.

    - **Public Sharing**: Although less common due to security considerations, you can mark a snapshot as public if needed.

- **Cross-Region Sharing**: Snapshot sharing is not limited to a single region. You can copy a shared snapshot to another region, enabling multi-region disaster recovery and migration strategies.

How to Share a Snapshot

1. **Identify the Snapshot**:

    ○ Choose the manual snapshot that you wish to share from the RDS console or via the AWS CLI.

2. **Modify Snapshot Attributes**:

    ○ In the RDS console, select the snapshot and choose "Share Snapshot."

    ○ Specify the AWS account IDs that should have access to the snapshot.

    ○ For public sharing, select the appropriate option; however, exercise caution and follow security best practices.

3. **Using the AWS CLI**:

    Example command to share a snapshot with a specific account:

```
aws rds modify-db-cluster-snapshot-
attribute \
```

```
--db-cluster-snapshot-identifier my-
cluster-snapshot-2025-03-30 \

--attribute-name restore \

--values-to-add 987654321098
```

- ○
  - ○ This command grants the AWS account
    with ID 987654321098 permission to
    restore the snapshot.

Security Considerations

- **Encryption**: Ensure that snapshots are encrypted
  before sharing. Recipients must have access to the
  encryption key or a key in their account that is
  equivalent.

- **Access Controls**: Use IAM policies to strictly
  control which accounts and roles can access
  shared snapshots.

- **Audit and Monitor**: Regularly audit shared
  snapshots using AWS CloudTrail and other
  monitoring tools to track who has accessed your
  snapshots.

Use Cases for Snapshot Sharing

- **Migration**: When moving your database from one
  AWS account to another, snapshot sharing

simplifies the migration process.

- **Collaboration**: Multiple teams or partners can collaborate on the same dataset without duplicating the backup process.

- **Compliance and Auditing**: Provide auditors with access to snapshots for regulatory compliance purposes.

- **Disaster Recovery Across Regions**: By sharing and copying snapshots to other regions, you can set up a multi-region backup strategy to further enhance resilience.

Copying Shared Snapshots Across Regions

In addition to sharing within a single region, you might need to copy a snapshot to another region for disaster recovery or migration. The process is as follows:

1. **Initiate the Copy Operation**:

   ○ In the RDS console or using the AWS CLI, initiate the snapshot copy.

Example CLI command:

```
aws rds copy-db-cluster-snapshot \
  --source-db-cluster-snapshot-
identifier arn:aws:rds:us-east-
```

```
1:123456789012:cluster-snapshot:my-
cluster-snapshot-2025-03-30 \

  --target-db-cluster-snapshot-
identifier my-cluster-snapshot-copy \

  --source-region us-east-1 \

  --region us-west-2
```

- ○
  - ○ This command copies the snapshot from the source region (us-east-1) to the target region (us-west-2).

2. **Verify the Copy**:

   - ○ Once the copy is complete, verify that the snapshot is available in the target region and is properly configured.

3. **Restore from the Copied Snapshot**:

   - ○ You can now restore a new DB cluster in the target region from the copied snapshot, facilitating regional failover or data migration.

Best Practices for Snapshot Sharing

- **Use Least Privilege**: Only share snapshots with accounts that require access.

- **Review Shared Snapshots Regularly**: Periodically audit shared snapshots and remove access if it is no longer required.

- **Document Sharing Decisions**: Maintain records of which snapshots have been shared, with whom, and for what purpose.

- **Automate Copying for DR**: Integrate snapshot copy operations into your disaster recovery plan to ensure recent snapshots are always available in secondary regions.

Best Practices and Real-World Applications

Implementing a robust backup and restore strategy in Aurora is not just about configuring the features—it's about integrating them into your overall operational and disaster recovery strategy. Here are some best practices:

- **Establish a Regular Backup Schedule**: Even with automated backups, consider scheduling manual snapshots before major changes.

- **Combine Automated and Manual Backups**: Use automated backups for daily point-in-time recovery and manual snapshots for long-term retention.

- **Monitor Backup Health**: Set up CloudWatch alarms to monitor backup completion and storage usage.

- **Test Your Restore Process**: Regularly perform test restores from both automated and manual backups to verify that your recovery procedures are effective.

- **Secure Your Backups**: Use encryption and strict IAM policies to protect backup data from unauthorized access.

- **Integrate with CI/CD**: Automate snapshot creation as part of your deployment process to capture stable points before major updates.

- **Documentation and Training**: Ensure that your team is familiar with both manual and automated backup processes and knows how to execute restores under pressure.

Conclusion

Amazon Aurora offers a comprehensive backup and restore solution that is flexible enough to meet a wide range of operational and compliance requirements. With automated backups providing continuous, incremental protection and manual snapshots allowing precise control over backup timing and retention, you can tailor your data protection strategy to the needs of your organization.

Snapshot sharing further enhances your ability to collaborate, migrate, and set up disaster recovery solutions across AWS accounts and regions. By understanding the differences between these backup methods and following best practices, you can ensure that your data is both secure and readily recoverable in any situation.

Whether you are planning for daily operational resilience, preparing for regulatory audits, or setting up a multi-region disaster recovery strategy, Amazon Aurora's backup and restore options provide the necessary tools to protect your data and maintain high availability.

> **Tip**: Regularly review your backup configurations and retention policies in light of your evolving business needs and compliance requirements. Test your restore procedures at least annually to ensure that your recovery time objectives (RTOs) and recovery point objectives (RPOs) are achievable in a real-world scenario.

By integrating these strategies into your overall database management plan, you not only safeguard your data but also build confidence in your ability to quickly recover from unexpected failures, ensuring business continuity and minimizing downtime.

Final Thoughts

Effective backup and restore processes are the backbone of a resilient database environment. Amazon Aurora's built-in capabilities simplify the complex task of managing backups while providing the flexibility needed for diverse use cases—from automated, continuous protection to manual, controlled snapshots and cross-account sharing.

By following the guidelines outlined in this chapter, you will be well-equipped to design and implement a backup strategy that meets both your operational needs and regulatory obligations. Whether it's recovering from a minor data corruption incident or a major system failure, the combination of automated backups, manual snapshots, and snapshot sharing ensures that your data is never at risk.

Chapter 31. Point-in-Time Recovery and Backtrack

When managing relational databases in production environments, the ability to recover from mistakes such as accidental data deletion or corruption is essential. Amazon Aurora provides two powerful mechanisms to address these situations: **Point-in-Time Recovery (PITR) and Backtrack**. While both features are designed to restore data to a previous state, they differ in granularity, speed, and how they impact the database cluster. This chapter explores their configurations, use cases, limits, and practical steps to perform a recovery.

Backtrack Configuration

Backtrack is a feature available exclusively for **Amazon Aurora MySQL-Compatible Edition** (version 2.0 and higher). It enables you to **roll back your database to a prior point in time without requiring a full restore** from backup.

Key Concepts

- **Operational Rewind**: Backtrack rewinds the DB cluster to a previous state while retaining its current endpoints, connections, and metadata.

- **Granular Reversal**: Supports recovery to a granularity of **seconds**, without recreating the DB cluster.

- **Faster than PITR**: Enables faster recovery from user errors such as accidental table drops or incorrect updates.

Enabling Backtrack

1. **At Cluster Creation**

   - Backtrack must be enabled during cluster creation via the AWS Console, CLI, or CloudFormation.

   - You must specify a **backtrack window** (in seconds), e.g., 1 hour = 3600 seconds.

2. **Backtrack Settings**

   - BacktrackWindow: Specifies how far back (in seconds) you can rewind. Maximum is **72 hours (259,200 seconds)**.

   - EnableBacktrack: Boolean flag to enable the feature.

   - You can increase or decrease the backtrack window after creation.

3. **Parameter Group Requirements**

   - Ensure that the **DB cluster parameter group** is compatible with backtrack.

- Some engine parameters related to logging must be enabled (e.g., binary logging).

4. **Monitoring and Cost**

   - Backtrack data is stored separately, and cost is based on the size and duration of the backtrack window.

   - Use CloudWatch metrics like `BacktrackChangeRecordsCreationRate` to monitor usage.

Example: Enable Backtrack via AWS CLI

```
aws rds create-db-cluster \

  --db-cluster-identifier my-cluster \

  --engine aurora-mysql \

  --engine-version 2.10.0 \

  --enable-backtrack \

  --backtrack-window 3600
```

Use Cases and Limits

Use Cases

Backtrack and PITR each excel in different scenarios. Understanding when to use each is critical for recovery planning.

Backtrack Use Cases

- **Accidental Data Manipulation**

    - Deleted or updated rows unintentionally? Backtrack the cluster to a safe point just before the query.

- **Application Errors**

    - Bug in deployment caused data corruption? Roll back the database to before deployment.

- **Development and Testing**

    - Reset a cluster to the same state multiple times during test iterations.

PITR Use Cases

- **Full Cluster Recovery**

    - Restore the entire DB cluster to a known point after a failure or destructive event.

- **Geographic Restoration**

- Restore data to a new cluster in a different region or environment.

- **Partial Restoration**

  - PITR enables selective snapshot-based restores, potentially isolating damaged data.

Backtrack Limitations

- **Engine Limitation**: Available **only for Aurora MySQL** (not supported for Aurora PostgreSQL).

- **Max Window**: Up to 72 hours of backtrack window can be retained.

- **Storage Overhead**: Additional I/O and storage for maintaining change records.

- **Unsupported Features**:

  - Aurora Serverless

  - Global Databases

  - Backtrack is **not a substitute for backups**; backups must still be configured for durable recovery.

- **DDL Operations**: Major schema changes (e.g., ALTER TABLE) cannot be undone with backtrack.

PITR Limitations

- **Restore Creates a New Cluster**: PITR doesn't rewind the existing cluster; it creates a **new DB cluster**.

- **Longer Recovery Time**: Recovery may take minutes or longer depending on data volume.

- **Point Accuracy**: PITR can restore to a point in time with **second-level granularity**, but not every millisecond.

Point-in-Time Recovery (PITR) Walkthrough

Aurora's **Point-in-Time Recovery** enables you to restore a DB cluster to any second within your backup retention window, which can be up to **35 days**.

Step-by-Step: PITR in Aurora

Step 1: Ensure Automated Backups Are Enabled

- PITR relies on **automated backups**, which are enabled by default when creating an Aurora cluster.

- Retention can be configured from **1 to 35 days**.

- Enabling backups also allows transaction logs to be used for point-in-time restore.

Step 2: Identify the Recovery Point

- You can restore to any point within your retention period.

- Use the AWS Console, CLI, or SDK to specify the **timestamp**.

- Use CloudWatch logs or RDS events to identify the appropriate time.

Step 3: Restore Using AWS Console

1. Navigate to the **Amazon RDS Console**.

2. Select **Databases** > your Aurora cluster.

3. Choose **Actions** > **Restore to point in time**.

4. Select the timestamp or use the default (latest restorable time).

5. Enter a new DB cluster identifier (this will be a **new cluster**).

6. Configure instance class, VPC, and security settings.

Step 4: Confirm Recovery

- The restore operation provisions a new cluster and replays changes from the snapshot to your specified point.

- The new cluster will become available in a few minutes.

Step 5: Redirect Application or Perform Validation

- Connect your application to the newly restored cluster.

- Validate data integrity and application behavior.

- Optionally, promote the restored cluster and delete the old one after verification.

CLI Example: PITR Restore

```
aws rds restore-db-cluster-to-point-
in-time \

  --source-db-cluster-identifier my-
original-cluster \

  --target-db-cluster-identifier my-
cluster-restored \

  --restore-to-time 2025-03-
30T15:20:00Z
```

Validation Queries (Post-Restore)

List tables and verify row counts

```
SHOW TABLES;

SELECT COUNT(*) FROM critical_table;
```

-

Check log events or errors

```
SELECT * FROM mysql.error_log WHERE
log_time > '2025-03-30 15:00:00';
```

-

Summary

Amazon Aurora offers robust recovery features tailored to different use cases:

Feature	Backtrack	Point-in-Time Recovery (PITR)
Aurora Edition	Aurora MySQL only	Both Aurora MySQL and PostgreSQL
Operation Type	In-place rewind	Creates new cluster
Recovery Time	Seconds to minutes	Minutes
Granularity	Seconds	Seconds
Max History	72 hours	35 days

Use Case	Rapid rollback for dev/test or mistakes	Disaster recovery, long-term restore
Limitations	No schema changes, no Serverless	Slower, new endpoint required

Both PITR and Backtrack are valuable tools in your recovery toolbox. Use **Backtrack** for fast, in-place reversals and **PITR** for more flexible or long-range data recovery.

Chapter 32. Maintenance Windows and Patching

Ongoing maintenance and patching are essential for keeping Amazon Aurora databases secure, performant, and compliant with best practices. While Amazon Aurora is a fully managed service, it allows users to **control the timing and frequency** of maintenance operations through well-defined mechanisms such as **maintenance windows**.

This chapter explores:

- How to choose and configure maintenance windows

- How Aurora applies updates, patches, and security fixes

- Strategies and tools for validating database performance and functionality post-maintenance

Proper planning of maintenance windows and validation workflows ensures minimal disruption to business-critical applications while taking advantage of AWS's managed updates.

Choosing Maintenance Windows

What Is a Maintenance Window?

A **maintenance window** in Aurora defines a recurring time frame when AWS is permitted to perform non-immediate, scheduled changes on your database cluster. These operations include:

- Minor version upgrades

- Security patches

- Operating system (OS) updates

- Underlying hardware maintenance

- Performance Insights or monitoring agent upgrades

Aurora does **not** apply changes arbitrarily outside this window unless:

- It's an **immediate security patch**

- You trigger a **manual update**

Default Behavior

By default:

- Aurora selects a random weekly maintenance window during cluster creation.

- The selected window is typically a 30-minute to 1-hour block within a 7-day recurring schedule.

- AWS only uses this window **if an update is pending**.

Guidelines for Selecting an Optimal Window

To minimize risk and downtime, choose a maintenance window that:

- **Falls during off-peak hours** for your application (based on region or user patterns)

- **Avoids critical processing periods**, such as payroll, batch ETL, or BI report generations

- **Allows sufficient monitoring time post-maintenance** (e.g., early in business hours for observability)

- **Aligns with business SLAs and DR plans**

Example: For a North America retail site, ideal windows might be:

- Weekdays: 1:00 AM–3:00 AM Central Time

- Weekends: Early Saturday morning (lowest traffic)

Configuring Maintenance Windows

Console Steps:

1. Go to **Amazon RDS Console > Databases**

2. Select your Aurora cluster or instance.

3. Choose **Modify.**

4. Under **Maintenance**, set a new **Preferred Maintenance Window**.

CLI Example:

```
aws rds modify-db-cluster \

  --db-cluster-identifier my-cluster \

  --preferred-maintenance-window
Sun:05:00-Sun:06:00 \

  --apply-immediately
```

Format:

- ddd:hh:mm-ddd:hh:mm (UTC time)

- Example: Sun:05:00-Sun:06:00 = 5–6 AM UTC on Sundays

Tip: You can assign different windows to **DB instances and clusters**. However, Aurora performs maintenance at the **cluster level**, so it's best to align them.

Applying Updates

Types of Updates in Aurora

Aurora receives three main classes of updates:

1. **Engine Version Updates**

   o Minor version patches (e.g., Aurora MySQL 8.0.26 → 8.0.28)

   o Performance enhancements and bug fixes

   o Sometimes mandatory for compliance or feature parity

2. **Operating System (OS) Updates**

   o Patches for kernel, system libraries, and OS security vulnerabilities

   o Transparent to applications but may require instance reboot

3. **Feature Agent Updates**

   o Updates for **Performance Insights**, enhanced monitoring agents, and RDS Proxy components

   o Typically applied without downtime

How Aurora Applies Updates

- Aurora queues updates during the **preferred maintenance window**.

- Updates **may trigger a reboot**, which causes a **brief failover** to another instance.

- In **Aurora clusters with replicas**, the reboot may be **non-disruptive** if the application uses reader endpoints or RDS Proxy.

- Aurora **does not auto-apply major version upgrades**.

Update Mechanisms:

- **In-place**: Apply directly to existing DB instances.

- **Blue/Green deployment**: For zero-downtime patching (ZDP) and risk-free testing.

Triggering Immediate Updates

You can choose to **apply updates immediately** (outside the window) using:

- Console (check "Apply immediately")

- AWS CLI with `--apply-immediately`

Example:

```
aws rds modify-db-instance \
```

```
--db-instance-identifier my-instance
\

--engine-version 13.9 \

--apply-immediately
```

Caution: Immediate application may cause downtime—
use with care in production.

Monitoring Update Status

You can track update status via:

- **RDS Console > Maintenance Tab**:

  - View pending maintenance and history.

- **CloudWatch Events or EventBridge**:

  - Subscribe to RDS-EVENT-0019 (pending maintenance)

  - Automate notifications or scripts via Lambda

CLI Example:

```
aws rds describe-pending-maintenance-
actions \
```

```
--resource-identifier
arn:aws:rds:region:account:cluster:my-
cluster
```

•

Typical Maintenance Event Codes

Event Code	Description
RDS-EVENT-0019	Maintenance scheduled
RDS-EVENT-0020	Maintenance started
RDS-EVENT-0021	Maintenance completed
RDS-EVENT-0079	OS patch applied
RDS-EVENT-1003	Instance rebooted due to patch

Post-Maintenance Validation

Why It's Critical

Even though Aurora is designed for high reliability, validating the system post-maintenance ensures:

- Business continuity

- Application compatibility

- Performance stability

- Early detection of regressions

Validation Checklist

1. **Connectivity Check**

    o Ensure your application can connect using updated endpoints.

    o Check that security groups and DNS resolutions remain intact.

2. **Performance Metrics**

    o Use **Performance Insights** to compare:

        ▪ CPU Utilization

        ▪ Wait events

        ▪ Active sessions

    o Watch for anomalies or spikes.

3. **Query Behavior**

    o Re-run a sample of critical transactions or read queries.

    o Validate latency and throughput benchmarks.

4. **Application Health**

    o Monitor application dashboards or alerts.

- Use AWS CloudWatch Synthetics or custom probes to verify SLA endpoints.

5. **Data Consistency**

    - Run checksum validations for recent inserts/updates.

    - Use business-level validations (e.g., row counts, invoice totals).

6. **Log Inspection**

    - Review logs (error logs, slow query logs).

    - Ensure no unexpected warnings or errors post-reboot.

7. **Replication and Read Replica Health**

    - Confirm replication lag is minimal.

    Run:

```
SELECT * FROM
mysql.rds_replica_status;
```

    -
8. **OS-Level Health (Optional for Enhanced Monitoring)**

- Check memory, I/O, and disk metrics at the OS layer.

- Use CloudWatch Enhanced Monitoring or CloudWatch Agent metrics.

Automating Validation

Consider automating validations using:

- **Lambda + EventBridge** (trigger checks after RDS maintenance events)

- **AWS Systems Manager Runbooks**

- **CI/CD Pipelines** (e.g., CodePipeline + custom health checks)

- **Amazon Inspector** (for compliance and vulnerability scans)

Advanced Strategies for Managing Maintenance

1. Zero-Downtime Patching (ZDP)

Aurora supports ZDP through:

- **Blue/Green deployments**: Apply patch to Green environment, test, then switch over.

- **Reader instance promotion**: For clusters with high read scale-out, promote patched reader to writer.

2. Cloning for Patch Validation

Use **Aurora cloning** to test updates in a staging cluster:

- Clone production to dev/test environment.

- Apply pending update and validate behavior.

- Helps avoid risk in regulated or high-SLA environments.

3. Custom Maintenance Playbooks

Create internal SOPs (Standard Operating Procedures) that include:

- Maintenance schedule approval workflows

- Expected changes and impact summary

- Rollback or failover plans

- Communication templates (to business stakeholders)

4. DR and Backups Before Maintenance

Always:

- Create a **manual snapshot** before applying major updates.

- Validate backup retention policies (especially before OS-level changes).

CLI Example:

```
aws rds create-db-cluster-snapshot \

  --db-cluster-snapshot-identifier
pre-maintenance-snap \

  --db-cluster-identifier my-cluster
```

Best Practices

- **Align maintenance windows with business availability** and monitoring coverage.

- **Avoid conflicting operations** (ETL, bulk loads) during scheduled windows.

- **Test patching strategies in staging** using clones or Blue/Green.

- **Enable Enhanced Monitoring** and **Performance Insights** for deeper observability.

- **Notify stakeholders** about upcoming changes using automated workflows.

- **Document everything**—post-mortems, success stories, or rollback cases.

Summary

Amazon Aurora provides a robust and flexible framework for managing updates through maintenance windows. When planned and validated correctly, patching becomes a smooth, low-risk operation that enhances your system's security and performance.

Area	Key Insight
Maintenance Windows	Define recurring timeframes for safe updates
Update Types	Include engine patches, OS fixes, and feature agents
Post-Validation	Critical to confirm system and app health
Automation	Use EventBridge, Lambda, and CloudWatch
Downtime Risk	Minimized with clustering and failover; can be zero with Blue/Green

By thoughtfully configuring maintenance windows, applying updates strategically, and validating your environment post-change, you can fully leverage Aurora's managed service model while maintaining full operational control and peace of mind.

Chapter 33. Aurora Failover and Recovery Scenarios

Manual Failover

Amazon Aurora is built with **high availability (HA)** in mind, utilizing a distributed storage layer, automatic replication across Availability Zones (AZs), and rapid failover mechanisms. While Aurora is designed to handle failover **automatically**, administrators may still need to perform **manual failover** under specific scenarios such as:

- Proactive disaster recovery testing

- Maintenance or upgrade planning

- Application readiness testing

- Investigating replication behavior or tuning cluster topology

What Is Manual Failover?

Manual failover in Aurora involves promoting a read replica (Aurora Replica) to become the new primary (writer) instance, typically in the same cluster and AZ or across AZs if configured.

When to Perform Manual Failover

- To simulate and prepare for a real failure

- To test the resiliency of applications and database connections

- To reduce the **time to recovery (TTR)** in case of unexpected outages

- Before performing updates or changes on the primary instance

How Manual Failover Works in Aurora

Aurora supports failover using the **RDS console, AWS CLI**, or **RDS API**. During failover:

1. The current primary is demoted.

2. A replica is promoted to primary.

3. Connections to the cluster endpoint are redirected to the new primary.

If the writer fails or is forcibly demoted, Aurora chooses the **most up-to-date and healthy** replica, usually with the lowest replica lag and matching instance class.

Manual Failover via Console

1. Go to **Amazon RDS Console**.

2. Select your Aurora DB cluster.

3. Click on the **"Actions"** dropdown and choose **"Failover"**.

4. Confirm the failover prompt.

You can optionally choose a specific replica to promote.

Manual Failover via AWS CLI

```
aws rds failover-db-cluster \

    --db-cluster-identifier my-aurora-
cluster
```

To specify a target replica:

```
aws rds failover-db-cluster \

    --db-cluster-identifier my-aurora-
cluster \

    --target-db-instance-identifier
replica-instance-1
```

What Happens During Failover?

- Connections to the writer are momentarily dropped.

- DNS endpoint (`<cluster-name>.cluster-XXXX.rds.amazonaws.com`) points to the new primary.

- Writer promotion and reader role change complete usually within **30 seconds to 2 minutes**.

Best Practices

- Use **custom endpoints** to avoid hardcoding writer instance names.

- Build applications to **retry transient failures** gracefully.

- Monitor **replica lag** to ensure a promoted replica has consistent data.

- Schedule **maintenance windows** to minimize impact when testing failover.

Failover Testing Procedures

Testing failover is a crucial part of validating your high availability and disaster recovery strategy. Aurora allows non-disruptive testing of failover under controlled conditions.

Why Test Failover?

- Validate application behavior and reconnection logic.

- Confirm that monitoring and alerting systems detect failover.

- Ensure that latency and data consistency remain within acceptable limits.

- Evaluate the time required for automatic or manual failovers.

Types of Failover Tests

1. **Planned (Manual) Failover**

   - Initiated by an admin or automation script.

   - Simulates a controlled role switch between instances.

2. **Unplanned Failover Simulation**

   - Simulate instance failure by stopping, rebooting, or disconnecting an instance.

   - Mimics unexpected outage behavior.

3. **Multi-AZ Network Fault Simulation**

   - Use network ACLs or chaos testing tools to drop packets or simulate AZ failure.

Pre-Test Checklist

- Ensure at least one **Aurora Replica** exists in a separate AZ.

- Confirm **automatic failover** is enabled (default behavior).

- Test against the **cluster endpoint**, not instance endpoints.

- Monitor:

    - Replica lag

    - Connection errors

    - Time to recovery

    - Application metrics

Sample Test Plan

1. **Preparation**

    - Tag test instances.

    - Set up CloudWatch alarms.

    - Notify stakeholders.

2. **Execution**

- Run failover command or stop writer instance.

- Observe logs, application behavior, and monitoring dashboards.

3. **Validation**

- Confirm replica promotion.

- Validate data consistency.

- Test reconnection logic in applications.

4. **Post-Test**

- Restore original topology if needed.

- Document results and any anomalies.

Tools for Automation

- **AWS Fault Injection Simulator**

- **AWS Systems Manager Automation Documents**

- **Custom Lambda scripts or shell automation**

Application Considerations

- Use connection pooling with retry logic (e.g., `pgbouncer`, `ProxySQL`, `RDS Proxy`).

- Allow for DNS TTL to propagate—use **low TTLs** or connection managers to mitigate.

- Ensure applications use **read/write split logic** properly with reader and writer endpoints.

Recovery from Corruption or Crash

Although Aurora is highly resilient, events like **application bugs, schema errors, or corrupt data ingestion** can compromise database integrity. Aurora provides multiple mechanisms to **recover quickly and safely**.

Types of Failure or Corruption

- Accidental DROP TABLE, DELETE or UPDATE without WHERE

- Application logic errors corrupting data

- Hardware or infrastructure-level failure

- Operating system crash or kernel panic (handled automatically in most cases)

- Aurora storage segment inconsistency (rare but possible)

Aurora Recovery Mechanisms

1. **Crash Recovery (Automatic)**

○ Aurora uses **distributed write-ahead logs** and **redo logs**.

○ If a crash occurs, the Aurora engine replays logs from the storage layer to bring the DB back to a consistent state.

○ This process is typically completed within **30–60 seconds**, even for large clusters.

2. **Backtrack (Aurora MySQL Only)**

○ Roll back a cluster to a previous point in time **without restoring from a snapshot**.

○ Useful for undoing destructive queries, schema changes, or application errors.

○ Granular to the **second**.

○ Limitations:

■ Not available for Aurora PostgreSQL.

■ Must be enabled at cluster creation.

■ Retains log history only for configured duration.

3. **Restore from Snapshot**

- Create a new cluster from a snapshot to recover lost or corrupted data.

- Manual or automated snapshots can be used.

- Slower than backtrack but works across both Aurora engines.

4. **Point-in-Time Recovery (PITR)**

- Restore to any second within the **retention window** (up to 35 days).

- Creates a new cluster with data as it existed at the specified time.

- Useful for recovering from logical corruption or user error.

Recovery Scenarios

Scenario	Recovery Option	Notes
DROP TABLE by mistake	Backtrack (MySQL) or PITR	Backtrack is faster
Corrupted data ingestion	PITR	Ensure ingestion point is known
Schema corruption	Snapshot restore or backtrack	Use testing to validate schema before applying
System crash	Automatic crash recovery	Transparent to users
Replication issue	Rebuild replica	Aurora allows re-creating replicas easily

Example: PITR via CLI

```
aws rds restore-db-cluster-to-point-
in-time \

  --db-cluster-identifier restored-
cluster \

  --source-db-cluster-identifier
myprodcluster \

  --restore-to-time 2025-03-
25T15:45:00Z \

  --engine aurora-mysql
```

Automatic Crash Recovery Process

1. Aurora detects the crash.

2. Distributed storage provides durable redo logs.

3. Logs are replayed on instance restart.

4. In-memory structures are rebuilt.

5. Connection endpoints are restored.

Monitoring Recovery

- Use **CloudWatch metrics**:

  - `DatabaseConnections`

  - `ReplicaLag`

  - `FreeableMemory`

  - `VolumeWriteIOPS`

- **Performance Insights** can help identify the source of slow recovery.

Best Practices for Failover and Recovery

- **Always have at least one Aurora Replica** in another AZ for fast failover.

- **Use backtrack or PITR** if you need rollback capabilities.

- Perform **regular snapshot backups**, especially before schema changes.

- Test failovers **monthly** to validate readiness.

- Enable **CloudWatch alarms** for lag, failover events, and storage health.

- **Tag resources** involved in failover and recovery for clear ownership.

- Use **Aurora Global Database** for cross-region disaster recovery.

Summary

Aurora provides powerful and flexible mechanisms to support high availability and recovery from failure, including:

- **Manual failover** to promote replicas

- **Testing tools and procedures** for disaster preparedness

- **Rapid crash recovery** leveraging Aurora's distributed log system

- **Backtrack and point-in-time restore** for logical recovery

By understanding and routinely exercising these mechanisms, you ensure that your Aurora deployments are **resilient, recoverable, and ready** to support mission-critical workloads under any condition.

Chapter 34. Cost Optimization and Instance Selection

Amazon Aurora delivers commercial-grade database performance at a fraction of the cost of traditional databases. However, to truly **optimize costs**, you need to understand Aurora's **pricing model**, the trade-offs between **On-Demand and Reserved Instances**, and how to **architect for fluctuating workloads**.

This chapter guides you through optimizing your Aurora deployments to maximize value while minimizing cost, with actionable strategies for both Aurora MySQL and Aurora PostgreSQL.

Aurora Cost Model

Aurora pricing is based on **four primary components**, which apply across both provisioned and serverless deployments:

1. **Compute**: Based on instance size and class (for provisioned) or Aurora Capacity Units (for Serverless).

2. **Storage**: Billed per GB-month for storage used.

3. **I/O Operations**: Measured per million requests, unless using I/O-Optimized storage.

4. **Additional Features**: Charges for backups, snapshots, data transfer, Performance Insights,

and global replication.

Aurora Provisioned Clusters

For **provisioned clusters**, you pay for:

- **Instance uptime** (per hour)

- **Storage** used (in GB)

- **I/O operations**, unless using Aurora I/O-Optimized

Pricing Model:

Component	Standard	Aurora I/O-Optimized
Compute	Per hour	Per hour
Storage	$0.10/GB	$0.10/GB
I/O Requests	$0.20/million	Included
Backups/Snapshots	$0.021/GB	$0.021/GB

Aurora Serverless v2

Aurora Serverless v2 charges are **usage-based**:

- **Compute**: Per-second billing in **0.5 Aurora Capacity Units (ACUs)** increments.

- **No charge when paused (v1 only), but v2 does not pause,** so cost reflects low idle usage.

- **Storage** and **I/O** are billed separately, just like provisioned clusters (unless I/O-Optimized is used).

Aurora Serverless v2 is ideal when workloads are **variable**, and high concurrency or scalability is required without full provisioning.

Reserved Instances vs On-Demand

Aurora supports **Reserved Instances (RIs)** for **provisioned clusters only**—not for Serverless clusters.

On-Demand Instances

- **Flexible, pay-as-you-go**

- Billed per second (with a 10-minute minimum)

- Best suited for:

    - Development and test environments

    - Short-lived or unpredictable workloads

Reserved Instances

- **Commit to 1- or 3-year terms**

- Offers up to **65% savings** over On-Demand

- Purchase options:

    - **No Upfront**

    - **Partial Upfront**

- All Upfront

Recommendation: Use RIs for production workloads with predictable usage and uptime >70%.

Reserved Instance Scope

- Applies to the instance class (e.g., `db.r6g.large`)

- Does **not cover storage or I/O costs**

- Choose between:

  - **Region scope**: Applies to any matching instance in the Region

  - **AZ scope**: Tied to a specific Availability Zone

Cost Example

Instance Type	On-Demand (hourly)	Reserved (1yr, no upfront)	Savings
db.r6g.large	$0.119	~$0.075	~37%
db.r6g.4xlarge	$0.952	~$0.603	~36%

For heavy workloads, this can amount to **tens of thousands in annual savings**.

Optimizing for Idle/Peak Workloads

Many real-world workloads are **burst-oriented**—e.g., traffic surges during business hours or periodic analytics jobs. Aurora offers multiple options to optimize for these patterns.

1. Use Aurora Serverless v2 for Variable Workloads

Aurora Serverless v2 is ideal when workloads fluctuate dramatically:

- Scales seamlessly between **0.5 and 128 ACUs**

- No manual intervention required

- Billed only for what you use

- Eliminates the need to over-provision

Example Use Case: A ticketing platform sees spikes during event sales. Instead of provisioning for the peak, use Serverless v2 to autoscale during traffic surges and scale down during idle hours.

2. Implement Read Scaling with Aurora Replicas

Reduce primary instance costs by offloading read workloads:

- Add **Aurora Replicas** in the same or cross-Region.

- Use **reader endpoints** to load-balance traffic.

- Replicas are cheaper than duplicating compute for write-heavy tasks.

Best Practice: Use **Auto Scaling for Aurora Replicas**:

```
aws rds register-db-instance-
automated-backups
```

Set minimum and maximum replica counts, and scale based on metrics like CPU or active connections.

3. Use I/O-Optimized Storage for High-I/O Workloads

If your workload has:

- 25 million I/O requests per month **per TB of storage**, OR

- **Spiky I/O patterns** with unpredictable demand

→ I/O-Optimized can significantly reduce cost.

Benefits:

- No per-I/O charges

- Predictable billing

- Up to 40% cheaper for I/O-intensive workloads

4. Schedule Stop/Start for Dev/Test Clusters

Aurora supports **automated stopping** of idle clusters:

- Can save up to **70% in dev/test environments**

- Use **Lambda or EventBridge rules** to schedule stop/start

- Use scripts like:

```
aws rds stop-db-cluster --db-cluster-
identifier dev-cluster

aws rds start-db-cluster --db-cluster-
identifier dev-cluster
```

5. Leverage Aurora Global Database Strategically

Global Databases allow read scaling across regions. However, they're **not cheap**.

Optimization Tip:

- Use **asynchronous replication** only where absolutely needed.

- Consider **partial replication** or **read-only replicas** in edge Regions.

Additional Cost Optimization Tips

Use Performance Insights and CloudWatch

- Identify expensive queries or periods of low utilization.

- Tune queries to reduce CPU and I/O footprint.

Enable Auto Minor Version Upgrades

- Keeps your cluster up-to-date without downtime.

- New versions may include **performance improvements** that reduce compute usage.

Choose Right Instance Classes

Aurora supports several instance families:

Instance Class	Best For	Notes
db.t3 / db.t4g	Burstable, cost-effective	Great for dev/test, limited prod use
db.r6g	Memory optimized	Ideal for OLAP, in-memory datasets
db.m6g	Balanced compute/memory	General-purpose workloads
db.x2g	High-memory	Enterprise-grade analytics, ML

Use **Graviton2-based instances (*.g)** for up to **20% better price-performance**.

Monitor Backup Storage Costs

- Automated backups are retained for 7–35 days (configurable).

- **Snapshots** are billed separately and persist until deleted.

- Use **lifecycle policies** to auto-delete old snapshots.

Summary: Strategies by Workload Type

Workload Type	Optimization Strategy
Dev/Test	Use T3/T4g or Serverless v1/v2 with pause enabled
Web Applications	Aurora Serverless v2 with autoscaling
High-Concurrency APIs	Serverless v2 or provisioned + RDS Proxy
Analytics/BI	Read replicas + I/O-Optimized + db.r6g or x2g instances
Enterprise Databases	Reserved Instances + Graviton2 + Aurora Global

---

Final Thoughts

Cost optimization in Aurora is not just about cutting expenses—it's about **aligning architecture with workload demand**. With Aurora's flexible deployment models, burstable instances, serverless options, and autoscaling features, you can build cost-efficient, highly-performant systems without sacrificing reliability.

💡 **Tip:** Use a layered strategy: start with Serverless v2 for flexibility, introduce RIs for stable workloads, and leverage I/O-Optimized for heavy throughput. Combine monitoring tools with automation for continuous cost governance.

Part VII: Developer Experience

Chapter 35. Connecting Aurora to Applications

Connecting your applications to Amazon Aurora is fundamental to leveraging the power of this fully managed relational database engine. Aurora supports standard **MySQL** and **PostgreSQL** wire protocols, allowing you to use familiar **JDBC/ODBC drivers**, language-specific libraries, and connection pooling frameworks to integrate seamlessly with your applications.

In this chapter, we'll explore how to connect to Aurora using various tools and languages, including configuration guidance for JDBC/ODBC drivers, code examples in Python, Node.js, and Java, and best practices for connection pooling to maximize efficiency and scalability.

Using JDBC/ODBC Drivers

Aurora is **wire-compatible** with MySQL and PostgreSQL, meaning it can be accessed using the same drivers and libraries you would use for those databases.

JDBC (Java Database Connectivity)

- Use the **standard MySQL or PostgreSQL JDBC driver** for Aurora.

- Connection string formats are:

Aurora MySQL:

```
jdbc:mysql://<cluster-
endpoint>:3306/<database>
```

Aurora PostgreSQL:

```
jdbc:postgresql://<cluster-
endpoint>:5432/<database>
```

- The JDBC driver should match your Aurora version:

    ○ Aurora MySQL: Use **MySQL Connector/J** (v8+)

    ○ Aurora PostgreSQL: Use **PostgreSQL JDBC Driver** (v42+)

ODBC (Open Database Connectivity)

ODBC drivers are commonly used for BI tools like Tableau, Power BI, and Excel.

- Download drivers from:

    ○ MySQL ODBC Connector

    ○   <u>PostgreSQL ODBC Driver</u>

- Sample ODBC DSN for Aurora:

```
[MyAuroraDSN]

Driver=MySQL ODBC 8.0 ANSI Driver

Server=mydb-cluster.cluster-
xxxxxxxxxx.us-west-2.rds.amazonaws.com

Database=mydb

UID=myuser

PWD=mypassword

Port=3306
```

Aurora Endpoints

- **Cluster endpoint**: Directs to the **writer** instance for write operations.

- **Reader endpoint**: Load balances across Aurora **replica** instances for read scaling.

- **Custom endpoint**: Targets a subset of instances (for multi-tenant or specific roles).

Python, Node.js, Java Examples

To help developers get started quickly, here are real-world connection examples using popular languages.

Python Example (using `psycopg2` for PostgreSQL or `mysql-connector-python` for MySQL)

Aurora PostgreSQL:

```python
import psycopg2


conn = psycopg2.connect(
    host='mydb-cluster.cluster-
xxxxxxxxxx.us-west-
2.rds.amazonaws.com',
    port=5432,
    database='mydb',
    user='myuser',
    password='mypassword',
    sslmode='require'
```

```
)

cur = conn.cursor()

cur.execute("SELECT version();")

print(cur.fetchone())

cur.close()

conn.close()
```

Aurora MySQL:

```
import mysql.connector

conn = mysql.connector.connect(
    host='mydb-cluster.cluster-
xxxxxxxxxx.us-west-
2.rds.amazonaws.com',
    port=3306,
    user='myuser',
    password='mypassword',
```

```
    database='mydb',

    ssl_disabled=False

)


cursor = conn.cursor()

cursor.execute("SELECT VERSION();")

print(cursor.fetchone())

cursor.close()

conn.close()
```

Node.js Example (using pg for PostgreSQL or mysql2 for MySQL)

Aurora PostgreSQL:

```
const { Client } = require('pg');


const client = new Client({
```

```
  host: 'mydb-cluster.cluster-
xxxxxxxxxx.us-west-
2.rds.amazonaws.com',

  port: 5432,

  user: 'myuser',

  password: 'mypassword',

  database: 'mydb',

  ssl: {

    rejectUnauthorized: false

  }

});


client.connect()

  .then(() => client.query('SELECT
version();'))

  .then(res => {

    console.log(res.rows[0]);

    return client.end();

  })
```

```
    .catch(err =>
console.error('Connection error',
err.stack));
```

Aurora MySQL:

```
const mysql = require('mysql2');


const connection =
mysql.createConnection({
  host: 'mydb-cluster.cluster-
xxxxxxxxxx.us-west-
2.rds.amazonaws.com',

  user: 'myuser',

  password: 'mypassword',

  database: 'mydb',

  port: 3306,

  ssl: true
});
```

```
connection.connect((err) => {

  if (err) throw err;

  console.log("Connected!");

  connection.query("SELECT VERSION()",
(err, results) => {

    if (err) throw err;

    console.log(results[0]);

    connection.end();

  });

});
```

Java Example (JDBC with MySQL/PostgreSQL)

Aurora MySQL (JDBC):

```
import java.sql.*;


public class AuroraMySQLExample {
```

```java
    public static void main(String[]
args) throws Exception {

        String url =
"jdbc:mysql://mydb-cluster.cluster-
xxxxxxxxxx.us-west-
2.rds.amazonaws.com:3306/mydb";

        String user = "myuser";

        String password =
"mypassword";


        Connection conn =
DriverManager.getConnection(url, user,
password);

        Statement stmt =
conn.createStatement();

        ResultSet rs =
stmt.executeQuery("SELECT
VERSION();");


        while (rs.next()) {


System.out.println(rs.getString(1));
```

```
            }


        rs.close();

        stmt.close();

        conn.close();

    }

}
```

Aurora PostgreSQL (JDBC):

```
import java.sql.*;


public class AuroraPostgresExample {

    public static void main(String[]
args) throws Exception {

        String url =
"jdbc:postgresql://mydb-
cluster.cluster-xxxxxxxxxx.us-west-
2.rds.amazonaws.com:5432/mydb";
```

```java
        String user = "myuser";

        String password =
"mypassword";


        Connection conn =
DriverManager.getConnection(url, user,
password);

        Statement stmt =
conn.createStatement();

        ResultSet rs =
stmt.executeQuery("SELECT
version();");


        while (rs.next()) {

System.out.println(rs.getString(1));

        }


        rs.close();

        stmt.close();
```

```
                    conn.close();

            }

    }
```

Connection Pooling Tips

Managing database connections efficiently is crucial for application performance, especially under high concurrency or burst traffic.

Why Use Connection Pools?

- Opening and closing DB connections is expensive.

- Aurora has **limits on max_connections**; inefficient use can lead to saturation.

- Pooling improves **latency, resource efficiency**, and **throughput**.

Common Connection Pooling Libraries

Language	Library
Java	HikariCP, C3P0
Python	SQLAlchemy Pool, Django ORM, psycopg2 pool
Node.js	pg-pool, generic-pool, mysql2 pool

Best Practices

1. **Use Amazon RDS Proxy** for managed connection pooling (recommended for Aurora).

   - Reduces connection overhead

   - Handles failover gracefully

   - Scales with Aurora clusters

2. **Tune max pool size** based on:

   - Application concurrency

   - Aurora `max_connections` value (varies by instance size)

   - Balance between reuse and overhead

3. **Use idle timeouts** to close unused connections.

   - Prevents exhaustion of connection limits

   - Helps with efficient scaling in serverless environments

4. **Avoid pooling inside serverless compute** (e.g., AWS Lambda)

   - Use **RDS Proxy** instead for persistent connections

   Example: HikariCP (Java)

```
HikariConfig config = new
HikariConfig();

config.setJdbcUrl("jdbc:mysql://mydb-
cluster.cluster-
xxxxxxxxxx.rds.amazonaws.com:3306/mydb
");

config.setUsername("myuser");

config.setPassword("mypassword");

config.setMaximumPoolSize(20); // Tune
based on workload


HikariDataSource dataSource = new
HikariDataSource(config);


try (Connection conn =
dataSource.getConnection()) {

    // use connection

}
```

Summary

Connecting your applications to Amazon Aurora is straightforward using standard JDBC/ODBC drivers and widely supported libraries in modern programming languages. For scalable and efficient performance:

- Use **standard MySQL or PostgreSQL drivers** for compatibility.

- Choose the **appropriate endpoint** (writer, reader, or custom).

- Apply **connection pooling** via libraries or **Amazon RDS Proxy**.

- Match pool configurations with your **Aurora instance's capacity** and **application concurrency**.

With these practices, your application can achieve **low-latency**, **high-throughput**, and **resilient** communication with Aurora databases.

Chapter 36. Using the RDS Data API

Introduction

The **Amazon RDS Data API** is a powerful service interface that allows applications to access Aurora Serverless (and some provisioned) clusters over HTTP without maintaining persistent database connections. It enables **stateless, secure, and scalable access** to Aurora databases using familiar AWS SDKs and CLI commands—making it ideal for **serverless applications, microservices, and containerized workloads** that operate in short-lived or asynchronous environments.

In this chapter, we'll explore how the RDS Data API works, demonstrate its stateless query model, walk through examples using SDKs and the AWS CLI, and discuss how it integrates seamlessly with AWS Lambda and microservice architectures.

Overview of the RDS Data API

What Is the RDS Data API?

The **RDS Data API** is a web-based interface that allows you to:

- Run SQL statements against Aurora databases over HTTPS

- Use **IAM-based authentication** instead of username/password

- Avoid managing persistent database connections

- Submit statements synchronously or asynchronously

- Handle result sets using JSON-friendly formats

The Data API is currently available for:

- **Aurora Serverless v1 (PostgreSQL and MySQL)**

- **Aurora provisioned clusters** (in limited cases, if enabled)

Use Case Highlights

- **Lambda functions** executing short-lived queries

- **Microservices** needing low-latency, secure DB access

- **Event-driven applications** or message-based architectures

- **Mobile and edge apps** interacting with Aurora securely via HTTPS

Stateless Query Execution

Connectionless Design

Traditional database clients maintain TCP connections, sessions, and resource state. In contrast, the RDS Data API uses a **stateless model**, where each API call:

- Authenticates using IAM

- Executes a single SQL statement (or a batch)

- Returns results or a statement ID for polling

This model suits applications where:

- Sessions can't be maintained (e.g., AWS Lambda)

- Resources must scale horizontally

- You want decoupled compute and data layers

Execution Flow

1. **StartSession (optional)**: Create a logical session for grouped execution

2. **ExecuteStatement** or **BatchExecuteStatement**: Run queries

3. **CommitTransaction** or **RollbackTransaction**: For multi-statement transactions

4. **DescribeStatement**: Get metadata

5. **GetStatementResult**: Retrieve result for async calls

6. **EndSession**: (Optional) Clean up logical session

Stateless Transaction Example

Although the API is stateless, it supports transactional operations:

```
1. BeginTransaction

2. ExecuteStatement (SQL INSERT)

3. ExecuteStatement (SQL UPDATE)

4. CommitTransaction
```

Each operation references the **transaction ID** and **resourceArn**, **secretArn**, and **database name**.

SDK and CLI Usage

Authentication and Setup

To use the RDS Data API, you need:

- An Aurora Serverless DB cluster with Data API **enabled**

- An **AWS Secrets Manager secret** containing DB credentials

- An IAM role or user with `rds-db:connect`, `secretsmanager:GetSecretValue`, and `rds-data:*` permissions

Required Parameters for API Calls

Parameter	Description
resourceArn	ARN of the Aurora cluster
secretArn	ARN of the Secrets Manager secret
sql	SQL statement to run
database	DB name
transactionId	For grouped transactions (optional)

AWS CLI Example: SELECT

```
aws rds-data execute-statement \

  --resource-arn arn:aws:rds:us-west-
2:123456789012:cluster:mydb \

  --secret-arn
arn:aws:secretsmanager:us-west-
2:123456789012:secret:MySecret-AbCdEf
\

  --database mydatabase \
```

```
  --sql "SELECT * FROM users WHERE
status = :status" \

  --parameters
'[{"name":"status","value":{"stringVal
ue":"active"}}]'
```

SDK Example: Python (boto3)

```python
import boto3


client = boto3.client('rds-data')


response = client.execute_statement(
    resourceArn='arn:aws:rds:us-west-
2:123456789012:cluster:mydb',


secretArn='arn:aws:secretsmanager:us-
west-2:123456789012:secret:MySecret',
    database='mydatabase',
    sql='SELECT * FROM orders WHERE
order_id = :orderId',
```

```python
    parameters=[

        {'name': 'orderId', 'value':
{'longValue': 101}}

    ]

)



print(response['records'])
```

Batch Execution

```json
{

  "sqlStatements": [

    "INSERT INTO users (name) VALUES
('Alice')",

    "INSERT INTO users (name) VALUES
('Bob')"

  ]

}
```

Use `batchExecuteStatement()` when running multiple DML statements.

Lambda and Microservice Integration

Why Use the Data API with Lambda?

Aurora Serverless and Lambda are both **serverless** by design. The RDS Data API acts as the glue between them by:

- Eliminating the need for VPCs and database drivers

- Allowing IAM-based secure access

- Enabling asynchronous interaction via API Gateway, Step Functions, or EventBridge

Lambda Integration Pattern

1. **Trigger** (e.g., API Gateway, SNS, EventBridge)

2. Lambda reads event and constructs SQL query

3. Calls RDS Data API with credentials from Secrets Manager

4. Processes results

5. Returns response to the event source

Example Lambda Code (Node.js)

```javascript
const AWS = require('aws-sdk');

const rdsData = new
AWS.RDSDataService();


exports.handler = async (event) => {

  const params = {

    resourceArn:
process.env.CLUSTER_ARN,

    secretArn: process.env.SECRET_ARN,

    database: 'mydatabase',

    sql: 'SELECT * FROM inventory
WHERE product_id = :pid',

    parameters: [

      {

        name: 'pid',

        value: { longValue:
parseInt(event.productId) }
```

```
      }

    ]

  };


  const result = await
rdsData.executeStatement(params).promi
se();

  return result.records;

};
```

Environment Variables:

- `CLUSTER_ARN`: ARN of the Aurora cluster

- `SECRET_ARN`: ARN of the database credentials

Serverless Microservices Pattern

- **RESTful endpoints via API Gateway**

- Stateless Lambda functions that use Data API

- Aurora Serverless DB handles variable workloads

Advantages:

- Cost-effective scaling

- Low operational overhead

- IAM-only access control

- Easy CI/CD integration via SAM or CDK

Performance, Limitations, and Considerations

Strengths

- **No persistent connection pooling** required

- IAM authentication improves security posture

- No driver dependencies in Lambda layers or containers

- Works **outside VPC** (no ENI needed)

- Handles short-lived workloads well (under 1 second)

Known Limitations

Limitation	Details
Engine support	Only Aurora Serverless v1 (and some provisioned)
Query complexity	No support for cursors or multiple result sets
Timeout	1-minute timeout per request

No native support for stored procedures	Use inline SQL instead
Result set size	Maximum 1000 rows per response
Data types	Not all PostgreSQL/MySQL types are supported

Workarounds

- Paginate large results manually using `LIMIT` and `OFFSET`

- For long-running analytics, use ETL pipelines instead of Data API

- For batch updates, use `batchExecuteStatement()`

Security Best Practices

- Use **IAM roles for Lambda** with scoped permissions to only the required resources

- Store DB credentials in **Secrets Manager**

- Use **parameterized queries** to prevent SQL injection

- Enable **audit logging** on the Aurora cluster to track access

- Limit access to the Data API via **VPC endpoints** or **resource-based policies**

Real-World Use Cases

Case 1: Event-Driven Inventory Update

- **Trigger**: SNS message for product restock

- **Action**: Lambda updates inventory quantity using `executeStatement`

- **Benefit**: No need to maintain persistent DB connections for each event

Case 2: API Gateway + Lambda + Aurora Backend

- **API Gateway** exposes REST endpoints

- **Lambda** handles business logic and DB queries

- **Aurora Serverless** processes SQL via Data API

- **Result**: Fully serverless microservice backend without provisioning compute

Case 3: Workflow via Step Functions

- State machine runs a series of queries using Lambda + RDS Data API

- Each step updates a customer record, logs audit, and checks balance

- All steps are stateless and auditable

Best Practices Summary

Area	Recommendation
Performance	Keep SQL statements short; use LIMITs
Transaction Mgmt	Use `BeginTransaction`/`CommitTransaction` wisely
IAM Security	Use least-privilege roles with scoped secret access
Secrets Rotation	Enable rotation for Secrets Manager credentials
Logging	Enable Aurora audit logging + CloudWatch Logs

Comparison Table: RDS Data API vs Traditional Access

Feature	RDS Data API	JDBC/ODBC Drivers
Connection state	Stateless	Persistent connection
Authentication	IAM + Secrets Manager	Username/password
Network configuration	No VPC required	VPC/private subnet required
Lambda-friendly	Yes	Requires custom layers
Transaction support	Yes (explicit)	Implicit
Result size limit	1000 rows	None
Suitable for long queries	No	Yes

Conclusion

The RDS Data API is a modern, secure, and developer-friendly way to interact with Amazon Aurora, especially in **serverless and distributed architectures**. By abstracting away the need for drivers and persistent connections, it enables flexible integrations with services like AWS Lambda, API Gateway, Step Functions, and more.

While the API has limitations compared to traditional database drivers, it excels in short-lived workloads and stateless environments. With proper use of parameters, IAM roles, and Secrets Manager, you can build secure, scalable, and cloud-native applications on top of Aurora with minimal overhead.

Chapter 37. Aurora PostgreSQL Functions and Extensions

Amazon Aurora PostgreSQL-Compatible Edition delivers a powerful combination of PostgreSQL's advanced capabilities with AWS's cloud-native enhancements. One of the key advantages of Aurora PostgreSQL is its support for **built-in Aurora functions, PostgreSQL's extensive system views**, and **popular extensions** like `PostGIS`, `pg_cron`, and others.

This chapter explores Aurora's unique PostgreSQL functions, how to monitor and manage performance using `pg_stat` views and **Cluster Cache Management (CCM)**, and how to integrate extensions to enhance your Aurora PostgreSQL workloads.

Built-in Aurora Functions

Aurora PostgreSQL includes several **custom AWS-developed functions** that go beyond the standard PostgreSQL functionality. These functions enable advanced observability, replication tracking, and diagnostic capabilities specifically designed for Aurora's distributed architecture.

Categories of Built-in Functions

Function Group	Description
`aurora_replica_status()`	Provides detailed replication lag and state across readers
`aurora_global_db_status()`	Shows durability and RPO lag in global clusters

aurora_global_db_instance_status()	Per-instance visibility and replication status in global databases
aurora_stat_*()	Access Aurora-specific metadata on wait events, files, cache, etc.
aurora_list_builtins()	Lists all built-in Aurora-specific functions
aurora_version()	Returns the current Aurora PostgreSQL version
aurora_ccm_status()	Provides metrics from the Cluster Cache Management system

Examples

1. List All Built-in Functions

```
SELECT * FROM aurora_list_builtins();
```

This displays function names, argument types, result types, and short descriptions.

2. Check Aurora Version

```
SELECT aurora_version();

-- Output: 'Aurora PostgreSQL-
Compatible Edition 13.9 (Aurora
3.4.0)'
```

3. Get Current Replica Lag

```
SELECT * FROM aurora_replica_status();
```

Returns detailed stats like:

- `replica_lag_in_msec`

- `feedback_epoch`

- `last_error_timestamp`

- `log_stream_speed_in_kib_per_second`

These are particularly useful for diagnosing replica synchronization issues.

---

pg_stat Views and Cluster Cache Management (CCM)

Aurora PostgreSQL retains full compatibility with PostgreSQL's rich set of statistics and monitoring views under the `pg_stat_*` family.

Key `pg_stat` Views

View	Purpose

pg_stat_activity	Shows current database connections and query states
pg_stat_replication	Tracks WAL sender and replication progress
pg_stat_statements	Tracks SQL execution frequency, time, rows, and more
pg_stat_user_indexes	Monitors index usage to optimize or prune indexes
pg_stat_bgwriter	Details background writer activity (checkpoints, buffers)
pg_stat_database_conflicts	Tracks query cancellations due to replication lag or conflicts

Enabling `pg_stat_statements`

This extension must be enabled to use the `pg_stat_statements` view:

```
CREATE EXTENSION IF NOT EXISTS
pg_stat_statements;
```

Set these parameters in the DB parameter group:

```
shared_preload_libraries =
'pg_stat_statements'

pg_stat_statements.track = all
```

Restart is required after changes.

Example: Top Slow Queries

```
SELECT query, total_time, calls,
mean_time

FROM pg_stat_statements

ORDER BY total_time DESC

LIMIT 5;
```

Cluster Cache Management (CCM)

CCM is a performance feature unique to Aurora PostgreSQL that **pre-warms the buffer cache on reader instances**, drastically reducing replica lag during failover or read redirection.

Key Concepts

- Works only when:

    - The writer and reader use **identical instance types**

    - A single **Tier-0 reader** is defined

- Uses **aurora_ccm_status()** to expose metrics

Enabling CCM

1. Create a custom DB cluster parameter group.

Set:

```
apg_ccm_enabled = 1
```

2.
3. Assign to your cluster and reboot.

Checking CCM Status

```
SELECT * FROM aurora_ccm_status();
```

Metrics include:

- `buffers_sent_last_minute`

- `buffers_found_last_scan`

- `warm_percent` (cache hit ratio during scans)

Sample query for warm percent:

```
SELECT

  buffers_sent_last_minute * 8/60 AS
warm_rate_kbps,

  100 * (1.0 - buffers_sent_last_scan
/ buffers_found_last_scan) AS
warm_percent

FROM aurora_ccm_status();
```

PostgreSQL Extensions in Aurora

Aurora PostgreSQL supports many popular PostgreSQL extensions to enrich analytics, scheduling, spatial querying, and more.

Commonly Used Extensions

Extension	Use Case
pg_cron	Schedule SQL queries like a cron job
PostGIS	Geospatial queries and spatial indexing

hll	HyperLogLog probabilistic data structures for cardinality estimation
pg_partman	Automated partition management
pglogical	Logical replication, often used for multi-version upgrades
uuid-ossp	Generate UUIDs
citext	Case-insensitive text type
pg_stat_statements	Collects query execution stats

PostGIS: Spatial Data Support

PostGIS enables Aurora PostgreSQL to act as a spatial database, allowing advanced geospatial queries using geometry types and indexes.

Installation

```
CREATE EXTENSION postgis;
```

Example: Find Nearby Locations

```
SELECT name

FROM cities

WHERE ST_DWithin(

  geography(loc),
```

```
  geography(ST_MakePoint(-71.060316,
48.432044)),

  5000  -- meters

);
```

Notes:

- Geospatial indexes (`GIST`) significantly speed up spatial queries.

- PostGIS is fully supported in Aurora PostgreSQL 10+.

---

pg_cron: SQL-Based Job Scheduler

Aurora PostgreSQL supports `pg_cron`, which enables time-based job scheduling directly inside the database.

Installation

```
CREATE EXTENSION pg_cron;
```

Example: Schedule a Daily Cleanup

```
SELECT cron.schedule(

  'daily_cleanup',

  '0 2 * * *',

  $$DELETE FROM session_logs WHERE
  created_at < now() - interval '30
  days'$$

);
```

Features:

- Supports standard cron expressions

- Executes in the database backend

- Logging available via `cron.job_run_details`

Permissions:

- The `rdsadmin` role handles job execution

- Requires `superuser` permissions or IAM-authenticated admin access

Managing Extensions in Aurora

Installation

You can install supported extensions using:

```
CREATE EXTENSION extension_name;
```

View Available Extensions

```
SELECT * FROM pg_available_extensions;
```

View Installed Extensions

```
SELECT * FROM pg_extension;
```

Important: Aurora supports only a curated set of extensions. Not all extensions from the PostgreSQL ecosystem are available due to security and performance reasons.

Best Practices

- **Enable pg_stat_statements early** in your performance lifecycle.

- Use **aurora_replica_status()** to continuously monitor replication lag.

- Apply **CCM** in high-availability setups with read replicas for faster failovers.

- Schedule maintenance jobs with **pg_cron** to offload periodic logic from the app layer.

- Use **PostGIS** only with spatial workloads and understand its impact on index maintenance.

- Test **extensions** in staging clusters before production use to avoid compatibility surprises.

Summary

Aurora PostgreSQL is not just a managed PostgreSQL— it's an enhanced platform with cloud-native features and deep observability through built-in functions, `pg_stat` views, and powerful extensions.

Feature	Benefits
Aurora Built-in Functions	Deep replication, cache, and cluster visibility
pg_stat Views	Transparent performance monitoring
PostGIS	Native geospatial query support
pg_cron	In-database job scheduling
CCM	Faster failover via buffer cache replication

Pro Tip: Combine `pg_stat_statements` + `aurora_replica_status()` for a 360° view of query health and cluster performance.

Chapter 38. Aurora MySQL Stored Procedures and Binlog Tools

Amazon Aurora MySQL provides a rich set of **custom stored procedures** and **binary log (binlog) management tools** that extend MySQL's native capabilities. These features are particularly useful for **replication scenarios**, **binlog-based integrations**, and **fine-tuned session control** in managed Aurora environments.

In this chapter, we explore Aurora MySQL stored procedures, focusing on:

- Custom RDS-provided procedures

- Tools for setting up external replication

- Enabling and managing binlog behavior

- Recovery, SSL handling, and troubleshooting

Custom Procedures

Aurora MySQL includes **RDS-specific stored procedures** that allow DBAs and developers to manage features like binary logging, external replication sources, and SSL materials—all within the database session.

Key Procedure Categories

1. **Session-level binlog controls**
   Control binary logging at a session level, useful for

replication filtering or selective logging.

2. **External replication configuration**
   Establish Aurora as a replica of an external MySQL-compatible source, or replicate from Aurora to an external target.

3. **SSL setup for encrypted replication**
   Import SSL certificates and configure secure channels for replication.

4. **Recovery and troubleshooting utilities**
   Manage replication state, handle IO errors, and manually advance log positions.

Session-Level Binlog Control

These procedures allow you to toggle binary logging for the **current session**.

```
mysql.rds_disable_session_binlog
```

- **Purpose:** Disable binary logging for the current session.

Syntax:

```
CALL
mysql.rds_disable_session_binlog();
```

-

- **Use case:** Useful during operations you do **not** want replicated, such as bulk loads or temp table manipulations.

`mysql.rds_enable_session_binlog`

- **Purpose:** Re-enable binlog after it's disabled in the session.

Syntax:

```
CALL
mysql.rds_enable_session_binlog();
```

-

`mysql.rds_set_session_binlog_format`

- **Purpose:** Set the binlog format (ROW, STATEMENT, or MIXED) for the session.

Syntax:

```
CALL
mysql.rds_set_session_binlog_format('R
OW');
```

-

Tip: Changing binlog format can help when debugging replication issues or tuning write performance.

Replication Procedures (e.g., `rds_set_external_master`, etc.)

Aurora MySQL supports **external replication** using binlogs. You can configure Aurora as a **replica of an external MySQL database** (or vice versa). The procedures listed below are essential for setting up and managing such replication.

Commonly Used Procedures for Replication

Procedure Name	Purpose
mysql.rds_set_external_master	Configure Aurora to replicate from an external master
mysql.rds_start_replication	Start replication process
mysql.rds_stop_replication	Stop replication
mysql.rds_skip_repl_error	Skip a replication error (e.g., duplicate key)
mysql.rds_reset_external_master	Clear current replication source configuration
mysql.rds_next_master_log	Advance binlog pointer to next log (for error 1236)
mysql.rds_import_binlog_ssl_material	Load SSL certs for secure replication
mysql.rds_set_master_auto_position	Enable GTID-based replication

Example: Configuring Aurora as a Replica

```
CALL mysql.rds_set_external_master (

    'external-mysql.mycorp.com',

    3306,

    'repl_user',

    'repl_password',

    'mysql-bin.000002',

    120,

    0

);
```

- **GTID-based replication?**
  If your external source supports GTID, use
  `mysql.rds_set_external_master_with_auto_position()` instead.

Starting Replication

```
CALL mysql.rds_start_replication;
```

To stop:

```
CALL mysql.rds_stop_replication;
```

Skipping Replication Errors

Sometimes replication halts due to data inconsistency. You can skip an error manually:

```
CALL mysql.rds_skip_repl_error;
```

Use this cautiously—it's better to understand **why** the error occurred.

Enabling Binlog and Recovery Options

Aurora MySQL provides additional procedures and configurations for controlling **binlog availability**, required for replication or point-in-time recovery.

Enabling Binlog (Cluster-Level)

Aurora does **not enable binary logging by default**. You must turn it on through a **DB cluster parameter group**:

1. Navigate to the **RDS Console** → Parameter Groups

2. Modify your DB cluster parameter group:

   - Set `binlog_format` = `ROW`

   - Set `binlog_row_image` = `FULL`

   - Set `log_bin` = 1

3. Apply and **reboot** the cluster for changes to take effect.

Key Binlog Parameters

Parameter	Description	Recommended Setting
`log_bin`	Enables binlog	1 (enabled)
`binlog_format`	Logging format	ROW
`sync_binlog`	Sync binlog to disk	1 (durability)
`expire_logs_days`	Log retention in days	Depends on use case

Recovery Using Binlogs

Aurora uses **continuous backups**, but binlogs are also useful when:

- You want to **replicate Aurora MySQL to external systems**

- You need **binlog-based CDC** (Change Data Capture)

- You require **logical backups** (e.g., using `mysqlbinlog`)

Advancing Past a Broken Binlog

If replication breaks with:

```
Last_IO_Error: Got fatal error 1236
from master...
```

Use:

```
CALL mysql.rds_next_master_log(12345);
```

This skips to the next binlog file index (12345 in the example), bypassing the corrupted or missing segment.

⚠ Warning: This can result in **data loss** if unreplicated transactions are skipped. Use only after careful review.

SSL-Based Replication Support

For **secure replication** across Regions or accounts, you may need SSL encryption.

Importing SSL Materials

Use `mysql.rds_import_binlog_ssl_material()` to load client certs and keys:

```
CALL
mysql.rds_import_binlog_ssl_material('
{

   "ssl_ca":"-----BEGIN CERTIFICATE----
-...END CERTIFICATE-----",

   "ssl_cert":"-----BEGIN CERTIFICATE--
---...END CERTIFICATE-----",

   "ssl_key":"-----BEGIN PRIVATE KEY---
--...END PRIVATE KEY-----"

}');
```

Setting SSL for External Source

```
CALL mysql.rds_set_binlog_source_ssl(

  ca_required => 1,

  verify_peer_cert => 1

);
```

This enforces peer certificate validation, ensuring the source server is legitimate.

Best Practices and Tips

- Always configure **GTID-based replication** when possible
  (`rds_set_external_master_with_auto_position`)

- **Never modify** `mysql.rds_` procedures—they are managed by AWS

  Monitor replication using:

  ```
  SHOW REPLICA STATUS\G
  ```

-

- Use **CloudWatch alarms** for replication lag, errors, or connection issues

- Store replication credentials securely (AWS Secrets Manager)

Troubleshooting Common Issues

Issue	Symptom	Fix
Binlog not enabled	`SHOW BINARY LOGS` returns empty	Check parameter group: `log_bin = 1`, reboot required
Replication error 1236	I/O Error, cannot find binlog file	Use `mysql.rds_next_master_log()` cautiously

485

Duplicate entry errors	Replication stops	Use `mysql.rds_skip_repl_error()` (understanding the root cause is ideal)
SSL handshake failed	Replication fails with SSL errors	Re-import SSL materials and validate certs

Summary

Amazon Aurora MySQL extends native MySQL functionality with a suite of powerful stored procedures for managing binary logs and replication. These tools allow:

- Fine-grained session-level binlog control

- External replication configuration (as source or replica)

- Encrypted replication using custom SSL materials

- Recovery workflows using log advancement and error skipping

By understanding and applying these stored procedures, you gain deep control over Aurora MySQL replication pipelines, CDC streams, and cross-system integrations.

Chapter 39. Performance Tuning and Parameter Groups

Amazon Aurora provides a robust performance tuning framework via **parameter groups**, real-time monitoring tools, and query-level diagnostics. By carefully adjusting database parameters, developers and database administrators can fine-tune query execution, resource utilization, and storage behavior across Aurora clusters and instances.

This chapter explores:

- The difference between **cluster-level** and **instance-level** parameter groups

- Important **query tuning parameters**

- How to **monitor and audit** configuration changes

These techniques are essential for optimizing production workloads, fine-tuning development environments, and ensuring consistent performance across deployments.

Cluster vs Instance Parameter Groups

Aurora DB configurations are controlled by **parameter groups**, which come in two types:

1. **DB Cluster Parameter Group**

2. **DB Instance Parameter Group**

Each serves a specific layer of configuration control within the Aurora architecture.

DB Cluster Parameter Groups

These affect **cluster-level settings**, shared across all DB instances in a cluster. They're used to control:

- Query cache behavior

- Storage engine settings

- Logging parameters

- Aurora-specific options (e.g., global database replication)

Applies to:

- All writer and reader instances in a cluster

- Aurora MySQL and Aurora PostgreSQL

Common parameters:

- `binlog_format` (MySQL)

- `aurora_enable_repl_bin_log` (MySQL)

488

- `log_statement` (PostgreSQL)

- `aurora_parallel_query` (PostgreSQL)

📝 *Example:* Enabling binary logging for replication across the entire cluster.

DB Instance Parameter Groups

These affect **individual instances** (writer or reader). They're used to configure:

- Memory allocation

- Workload size

- Query timeout thresholds

- Caching at the instance level

Applies to:

- One DB instance (can differ between writer and reader)

Common parameters:

- `innodb_buffer_pool_size` (MySQL)

- `work_mem`, `shared_buffers` (PostgreSQL)

- `max_connections`

Practical Differences

Feature	Cluster Parameter Group	Instance Parameter Group
Scope	Whole cluster	Single instance
Use case	Replication, logging	Memory, CPU tuning
Applies to	All instances	Writer or specific reader
Requires reboot for changes	Sometimes	Sometimes
Can have multiple versions applied	No	Yes

Applying Parameter Groups

You assign parameter groups during cluster or instance creation, or modify them later:

- Via AWS Console: **Modify DB Cluster** or **Modify DB Instance**

    CLI:

```
aws rds modify-db-cluster \

    --db-cluster-identifier my-cluster \

    --db-cluster-parameter-group-name
my-cluster-param-group
```

-

Changes may require a **reboot** or **maintenance window** application, depending on the parameter type.

Query Tuning Parameters

Performance issues often arise from inefficient queries, suboptimal memory allocation, or lack of indexing. Aurora provides several parameters to fine-tune query execution paths, memory usage, and concurrency.

Key Aurora MySQL Parameters

1. `query_cache_type` **and** `query_cache_size`

    o Controls MySQL's legacy query cache (disabled by default in Aurora)

2. `max_connections`

    o Sets the number of simultaneous connections

    o Adjust based on connection pooler behavior (e.g., RDS Proxy)

3. `innodb_buffer_pool_size`

    o Major performance factor

    o Should be set to 70–80% of instance RAM for read-heavy workloads

4. `innodb_log_file_size`

    o Larger log files reduce checkpointing
      frequency, improving write performance

5. `slow_query_log`, `long_query_time`,
   `log_queries_not_using_indexes`

    o Helps identify performance bottlenecks and
      missing indexes

6. `tmp_table_size` **and** `max_heap_table_size`

    o Increase to reduce disk-based temporary
      table creation

   💡 *Tip:* Use EXPLAIN to analyze query
   execution plans for problematic queries.

   Key Aurora PostgreSQL Parameters

1. `work_mem`

    o Memory for sorting and hash operations

    o Increase to improve performance on joins
      and aggregates

2. `shared_buffers`

    o Typically set to 25–40% of total memory

- Critical for caching data blocks

3. `effective_cache_size`

   - PostgreSQL uses this to estimate how much data is cached at OS level

4. `log_min_duration_statement`

   - Logs queries exceeding a duration threshold (in milliseconds)

5. `jit` **(Just-In-Time compilation)**

   - Enables JIT for query execution

   - Boosts performance for complex queries

6. `random_page_cost`

   - Helps optimizer choose index scans over sequential scans

   - Reduce to favor index usage on SSD-backed Aurora

Aurora-Specific Parameters

- `aurora_parallel_query` (PostgreSQL)

  - Enables parallel execution of analytical queries

- `aurora_enable_repl_bin_log` (MySQL)

  - Controls binary log replication (for external replicas)

- `aurora_statement_timeout` (MySQL & PostgreSQL)

  - Statement execution timeout at the Aurora layer

Performance Tuning Scenarios

Scenario	Tuning Strategy
Write-intensive workloads	Increase `innodb_log_file_size`, enable async_commit
Analytical queries	Enable `aurora_parallel_query`, increase `work_mem`
High memory pressure	Tune `shared_buffers`, `effective_cache_size`
Spiky connections	Use RDS Proxy or increase `max_connections`
Join-heavy queries	Increase `work_mem`, analyze indexes

Monitoring Config Changes

Monitoring parameter changes is essential for understanding performance trends and avoiding misconfiguration issues.

AWS Tools for Monitoring

1. **RDS Events**

- Tracks parameter group changes and applications

- Available in **CloudTrail** and RDS Console

2. **CloudTrail Logging**

   - Every change via API or CLI is logged:

     - `ModifyDBParameterGroup`

     - `ApplyPendingMaintenanceActi on`

3. **CloudWatch Metrics**

   - Use to detect performance deviations after changes

   - Correlate parameter changes with metrics like:

     - `CPUUtilization`

     - `ReadIOPS` / `WriteIOPS`

     - `DatabaseConnections`

4. **Performance Insights**

   - Review **query execution time** and **wait events**

o   Identify regressions after parameter updates

Viewing Pending vs Applied Settings

Use the CLI to check parameter status:

```
aws rds describe-db-parameters \

  --db-parameter-group-name my-group \

  --query
"Parameters[?ApplyType=='dynamic'].{Na
me:ParameterName,
Value:ParameterValue}"
```

In Console:

- View parameters as:

    o   **Static** (require reboot)

    o   **Dynamic** (take effect immediately)

Auditing Parameter Group History

- Use AWS Config to track resource configuration history

- Query historical states for compliance and debugging

- Sample config rule: Ensure production clusters don't exceed `max_connections` threshold

Applying Parameters Safely

- **Use staging environments** to test new parameter sets

- **Create parameter group snapshots** (manual clone) before change

- **Apply changes during low traffic** windows

- Monitor **replica lag** and **CPU spikes** after changes

Real-World Use Cases

Tuning a PostgreSQL cluster for analytics

- Increase `work_mem` to 64MB

- Enable `jit` for complex queries

- Enable `aurora_parallel_query`

- Monitor with Performance Insights for CPU-bound bottlenecks

Scaling a MySQL cluster for web traffic

- Increase `max_connections` to 2000

- Tune `innodb_buffer_pool_size` to 75% of memory

- Monitor `DatabaseConnections` and `CPUUtilization` via CloudWatch

- Log slow queries using `slow_query_log`

Managing parameter differences between writer and readers

- Use **different instance parameter groups**:

  - Writer: More aggressive caching

  - Reader: Optimized for analytical workloads

- Useful in Blue/Green and canary deployments

Best Practices for Parameter Tuning

- **Iterate and test** – Avoid applying untested parameter changes to production

- **Use IAM permissions** – Restrict who can modify parameter groups

- 🧊 **Version your parameter groups** – Clone and label groups per environment (e.g., `prod-v1`, `prod-v2`)

- 📊 **Benchmark workloads** – Use Aurora Benchmarks, pgbench, or sysbench

- 🖋 **Test failover and restart impact** – Some parameters impact failover behavior

---

Summary: Tuning Aurora with Precision

Performance tuning in Amazon Aurora is a balance between resource management, workload characteristics, and query behavior. Parameter groups offer a centralized and reproducible mechanism to configure your DB cluster and instances.

Category	Key Actions
Configuration Layer	Use the right parameter group type
Query Tuning	Adjust memory, caching, and execution parameters
Monitoring	Use RDS Events, CloudTrail, and CloudWatch
Change Management	Audit changes, test in staging, monitor impact

By thoughtfully adjusting Aurora's parameter landscape, you can dramatically enhance performance and ensure your clusters scale predictably with your workloads.

Chapter 40. Building Serverless Architectures with Aurora & Lambda

Introduction

Serverless architectures are redefining the way applications are designed, built, and operated. By eliminating the need to manage infrastructure, developers can focus entirely on writing code and delivering features. Amazon Aurora integrates deeply with **AWS Lambda**, enabling **event-driven architectures** that are reactive, scalable, and cost-effective.

This chapter explores how to build serverless solutions using Amazon Aurora and AWS Lambda. We will cover the core patterns of **event-driven processing**, how to configure **Lambda triggers with Aurora**, and examine practical **use cases** like audit logging, real-time alerts, and background job processing.

Event-Driven Processing

What Is Event-Driven Architecture?

Event-driven architecture (EDA) is a design paradigm where system components communicate by emitting and reacting to events. Rather than polling or scheduling tasks, event-driven systems respond in real time to changes in state or user actions.

In the context of Amazon Aurora:

- Events are **data changes** (e.g., inserts, updates, deletes).

- Reactions are **Lambda functions** that get invoked to perform an action (e.g., send an email, write to S3, post to a webhook).

Benefits of Event-Driven Architectures with Aurora

- **Scalability**: Serverless components scale automatically with demand.

- **Decoupling**: Business logic is separated from data logic.

- **Cost-efficiency**: You pay only when functions run.

- **Real-time responsiveness**: Systems respond immediately to database events.

Architectural Overview

An event-driven system using Aurora and Lambda typically includes:

- **Amazon Aurora** as the transactional data store.

- **Amazon RDS Proxy** (optional) to manage DB connections from Lambda.

- **AWS Lambda** for reactive, stateless compute.

- **Amazon EventBridge** or **Amazon S3** for event capture or chaining.

- **Amazon CloudWatch Logs** for observability and monitoring.

Lambda Triggers with Aurora

Lambda can be invoked in response to changes in Aurora databases. There are two main approaches for integrating Aurora with Lambda:

1. **Using Amazon Aurora Database Activity Streams (PostgreSQL only)**

2. **Using custom triggers via stored procedures and AWS SDK**

3. **Using scheduled polling with Aurora and Lambda (indirect pattern)**

1. Native Integration via Aurora Database Activity Streams (Aurora PostgreSQL)

For **Aurora PostgreSQL, Database Activity Streams (DAS)** can be enabled to send detailed activity logs to **Kinesis Data Streams**, which can then trigger a Lambda function.

How It Works

- Aurora streams database activities (e.g., SQL statements) to Kinesis.

- Kinesis delivers records to a subscribing Lambda.

- Lambda processes each record—for example, parsing INSERT statements into audit logs.

Setup Steps

1. **Enable Activity Streams**:

   o In RDS Console or via CLI/API.

   o Select your Aurora PostgreSQL DB cluster.

   o Configure target Kinesis Data Stream and encryption.

2. **Create Kinesis Stream**:

   o Name your stream, set number of shards based on throughput.

   o Ensure Aurora has write permissions.

3. **Create Lambda Consumer**:

   o Attach a trigger to the Kinesis stream.

   o Write business logic in Lambda function (e.g., send alert, write to S3).

4. **IAM Permissions**:

   ○ Aurora must have `kinesis:PutRecord`.

   ○ Lambda must have
     `kinesis:ReadRecords`.

Example Use Case

A new row inserted into a `payments` table can automatically trigger a Lambda that sends a Slack alert to the finance team or logs the transaction in an immutable store.

> ⚠ Note: Database Activity Streams is available only for **Aurora PostgreSQL** and incurs additional costs.

2. Custom Triggers Using Stored Procedures and AWS SDK

For **Aurora MySQL** or PostgreSQL (without DAS), you can implement custom logic by combining database triggers and Lambda invocation via SDK calls.

Pattern

- Use **AFTER INSERT/UPDATE/DELETE triggers** to call a stored procedure.

- The procedure inserts event metadata into an "events" table.

- A scheduled Lambda polls this table, processes new events, and clears them.

Implementation Steps

Create Events Table:

```
CREATE TABLE audit_events (

    id SERIAL PRIMARY KEY,

    event_type TEXT,

    event_payload JSONB,

    processed BOOLEAN DEFAULT FALSE,

    created_at TIMESTAMP DEFAULT now()

);
```

1.

Create Trigger Function (PostgreSQL example):

```
CREATE OR REPLACE FUNCTION log_event()

RETURNS trigger AS $$

BEGIN
```

```
  INSERT INTO audit_events
(event_type, event_payload)

  VALUES (TG_OP,
row_to_json(NEW)::jsonb);

  RETURN NEW;

END;

$$ LANGUAGE plpgsql;
```

2.

Attach Trigger:

```
CREATE TRIGGER trg_audit

AFTER INSERT ON orders

FOR EACH ROW EXECUTE FUNCTION
log_event();
```

3.
4. **Lambda Polling**:

   ○ Use AWS Lambda (scheduled with Amazon EventBridge) to poll `audit_events`.

   ○ Process unhandled events.

   ○ Update `processed = true` once done.

5. **RDS Proxy (Optional)**:

   o   Use RDS Proxy to manage connection
       pooling from Lambda to Aurora.

Pros and Cons

Feature	Pros	Cons
DAS	Real-time, native, no polling	Limited to Aurora PostgreSQL, additional cost
Custom Triggers	Works with MySQL/PostgreSQL, full control	Slightly delayed, requires polling, extra logic

Use Cases: Audit Logs, Alerts, Background Jobs

Aurora and Lambda can be combined to power a variety of
serverless patterns. Below are some common use cases
with design considerations and implementation tips.

Use Case 1: Audit Logging

Goal

Track all database changes (CRUD operations) in an
immutable audit trail.

Solution Design

- **Source**: Aurora PostgreSQL or MySQL

- **Trigger Mechanism**:

- PostgreSQL: DAS or triggers

- MySQL: triggers with polling

- **Lambda Logic**:

  - Write audit data to Amazon S3, DynamoDB, or an external audit service.

  - Optionally transform or enrich audit payloads.

- **Storage Options**:

  - **Amazon S3**: Scalable, durable log storage.

  - **Amazon DynamoDB**: Low-latency read/write for compliance dashboards.

Example Lambda Output

```
{

  "event_type": "INSERT",

  "table": "users",

  "data": {

    "user_id": 123,

    "name": "Jane Doe"
```

```
    },

    "timestamp": "2025-03-30T14:22:55Z"

}
```

Use Case 2: Real-Time Alerts

Goal

Notify operations or business teams immediately when critical events occur.

Example Scenarios

- High-value transaction processed

- Failed login attempt exceeds threshold

- System-level errors logged in a `logs` table

Solution Design

- **Aurora triggers** capture critical rows.

- **Lambda** checks business rules and thresholds.

- Sends:

    ○ **SNS** message for system alerts.

- ○ **Slack notification** to engineering.

- ○ **SES email** to compliance team.

Sample Output

```
{
  "alert_type":
"payment_threshold_exceeded",

  "amount": 10000,

  "currency": "USD",

  "user_id": 456,

  "time": "2025-03-30T15:02:10Z"
}
```

Use Case 3: Background Job Execution

Goal

Run asynchronous jobs in response to user actions or scheduled workflows.

Examples

- Resize uploaded images referenced in DB

- Recalculate analytics after data update

- Generate PDF invoices after order placement

Architecture

- Insert task metadata into a `jobs` table in Aurora.

- Use a Lambda function to poll for unprocessed jobs.

- Process the task and update status (`in_progress`, `complete`, `failed`).

Bonus Pattern: Chaining Lambdas

- Once a job is complete, trigger downstream Lambda (e.g., send user confirmation).

- Use Amazon EventBridge or SNS to decouple and sequence.

Best Practices

Security

- **Use IAM roles and least privilege**:

- Lambda should only access tables and services required.

- **Encrypt sensitive audit data** using KMS or at rest via Aurora encryption.

- **Audit and log Lambda invocations** using CloudTrail.

Performance and Reliability

- **Use RDS Proxy** to manage database connections.

- **Batch reads and writes** in Lambda to avoid timeouts.

- **Handle failures gracefully**: use retries and dead-letter queues.

Observability

- Enable **CloudWatch Logs and metrics** on Lambda.

- Use **CloudWatch Dashboards** to monitor latency and throughput.

- Log key events for audit trail traceability.

Cost Optimization

- Design Lambdas to run efficiently—under 1 second where possible.

- Schedule polling wisely to avoid excessive invocations.

- Consider batching and rate limiting for event streams.

Conclusion

By integrating Aurora and AWS Lambda, you can build powerful serverless solutions that respond to database events in real time. Whether it's capturing audit logs, sending alerts, or triggering downstream workflows, this architecture offers the agility, scalability, and cost-efficiency needed for modern applications.

With Aurora acting as the reliable data layer and Lambda providing the compute glue, your applications become more reactive, resilient, and loosely coupled. Combined with AWS services like EventBridge, Kinesis, SNS, and S3, the possibilities are endless.

> 💡 **Next Step**: Try building a prototype that logs all inserts on your `orders` table and pushes them to S3 via Lambda—then expand it into a real-time alerting pipeline.

Appendices

Appendices A. Glossary of Aurora Terminology

This glossary provides clear and concise definitions of key Amazon Aurora terms and concepts. It serves as a quick reference for architects, developers, DBAs, and engineers working with Aurora MySQL or Aurora PostgreSQL in the AWS Cloud. Understanding this terminology is essential for designing, configuring, and operating Aurora-based systems efficiently and securely.

Aurora-Specific Concepts

Amazon Aurora

A cloud-native relational database engine built for the AWS Cloud, offering MySQL- and PostgreSQL-compatible editions. Aurora combines the performance and availability of high-end commercial databases with the simplicity and cost-effectiveness of open source.

Aurora DB Cluster

A collection of DB instances that share a single cluster volume and can include one writer (primary) instance and multiple reader instances (Aurora Replicas). The cluster includes configuration, endpoints, and replication metadata.

Aurora Replica

A read-only DB instance within an Aurora cluster that shares the same storage volume as the writer. Up to 15 replicas are supported per cluster. Replicas can be promoted to writer roles during failover.

Aurora Global Database

A feature that enables cross-region replication with sub-second latency, designed for globally distributed applications. Aurora Global Database supports one primary AWS Region and up to five read-only secondary Regions.

Aurora Serverless

A deployment option where Aurora automatically adjusts compute capacity based on actual usage. Aurora Serverless v2 supports fine-grained scaling and is suitable for variable or infrequent workloads.

Aurora Machine Learning (Aurora ML)

An integration between Aurora and Amazon SageMaker that allows invoking ML models directly within SQL queries using simple syntax (e.g., `aws_comprehend()`), without application code changes.

Backtrack

A feature for Aurora MySQL that allows you to quickly move a database backward in time without creating a new cluster. Ideal for recovering from user errors like accidental deletions or schema changes.

Cluster Endpoint

A connection endpoint that always points to the current writer (primary) instance. Used for write operations.

Reader Endpoint

An endpoint that distributes connections across all available Aurora Replicas for horizontal read scaling.

Custom Endpoint

An endpoint that can be associated with a subset of DB instances in a cluster (e.g., specific replicas). Useful for workload isolation and routing.

Storage and Performance

Cluster Volume

The shared storage layer used by all instances in a DB cluster. Aurora's distributed and log-structured storage engine ensures durability and consistency.

Storage Auto-Scaling

Aurora automatically expands your cluster volume in 10 GB increments up to 128 TB as your data grows, without downtime.

Survivable Page Cache

A cache that persists across DB failovers and instance restarts, improving recovery times and read performance post-restart.

Performance Insights

An advanced database performance monitoring and tuning feature that provides real-time visibility into database load, wait events, and top SQL queries.

Query Plan Management (QPM)

A feature that allows you to manage and control query execution plans in Aurora PostgreSQL to avoid performance regressions after upgrades or schema changes.

Parallel Query

An Aurora feature that pushes parts of query processing down to the storage layer, enabling faster analytical queries on large datasets (Aurora MySQL only).

High Availability and Scaling

Multi-AZ Deployment

Aurora clusters replicate data across multiple Availability Zones (AZs) by default, enabling fast recovery and high availability.

Failover

The automatic process of promoting an Aurora Replica to be the new primary instance if the current writer fails. Typically completes within 30 seconds.

Auto Scaling

Dynamic adjustment of Aurora Replicas or compute capacity in Aurora Serverless v2 based on application load.

Blue/Green Deployment

A deployment strategy that lets you create separate environments (blue and green) for staging and production to reduce the risk of changes and enable fast rollbacks.

Security and Access Control

IAM Database Authentication

A feature that lets you connect to Aurora using AWS IAM credentials and tokens instead of native database passwords.

SSL/TLS

Encryption protocol used to secure client connections to Aurora DB instances. Enabled by default.

KMS (Key Management Service)

Used by Aurora to encrypt data at rest using customer-managed or AWS-managed encryption keys.

Database Activity Streams

A real-time stream of database activity that integrates with AWS security services such as Amazon Kinesis and AWS CloudTrail for compliance and audit logging.

Integration and APIs

RDS Proxy

A fully managed database proxy that enables connection pooling, automatic failover, and IAM-based authentication with Aurora.

Zero-ETL Integration

An Aurora feature that allows near-real-time replication of transactional data into Amazon Redshift for analytics, without managing extract-transform-load (ETL) jobs.

Data API

A RESTful API for executing SQL statements against Aurora Serverless clusters without managing persistent client connections.

Event Subscriptions

Allow you to receive notifications (via Amazon SNS) about specific changes or events related to Aurora clusters, such as failovers or backups.

Maintenance and Backup

Point-in-Time Recovery (PITR)

A recovery method that allows restoring an Aurora cluster to any second within the backup retention window (up to 35 days).

Snapshots

User-initiated backups of Aurora DB clusters that can be restored to create new clusters. Snapshots are stored in Amazon S3.

Retention Period

Defines how long automatic backups and PITR data are retained. Can be configured from 1 to 35 days.

Backtrack Window

Defines the maximum time (up to 72 hours) to which you can rewind a cluster using the Backtrack feature.

Monitoring and Diagnostics

CloudWatch Metrics

Aurora integrates with Amazon CloudWatch to provide instance- and cluster-level metrics for CPU, memory, IOPS, storage usage, replication lag, and more.

Enhanced Monitoring

Provides real-time operating system metrics at the host level, including CPU, RAM, and disk usage.

Aurora PostgreSQL Functions

Built-in SQL functions such as `aurora_global_db_instance_status()` and `aurora_replica_status()` provide replication and health information at the SQL layer.

Replication and Recovery

Replication Lag

The delay between when a transaction is committed on the writer and when it becomes visible to replicas. Aurora's shared storage replication minimizes this lag to milliseconds.

Durable LSN

The Log Sequence Number that has been safely persisted in Aurora's distributed storage engine. Used for tracking replication and recovery progress.

Global Write Forwarding

A Global Database feature that allows write forwarding from secondary regions to the primary region (Aurora MySQL only).

Miscellaneous Terms

DB Cluster Parameter Group

A container for engine configuration values that apply to all DB instances in an Aurora cluster.

DB Parameter Group

A container for engine configuration values that apply to a single DB instance.

Instance Class

Defines the hardware configuration (CPU, RAM, network) for an Aurora DB instance (e.g., `db.r6g.large`, `db.t4g.medium`).

Reserved Instance

A billing option offering discounted rates for long-term Aurora usage (1- or 3-year commitments).

VPC Security Group

Controls inbound and outbound network traffic to Aurora DB instances within a Virtual Private Cloud.

Appendices B. Sample Architecture Diagrams

This appendix provides reference architecture diagrams for common Amazon Aurora deployment patterns. These visual models help solution architects, DevOps engineers, and developers plan for scalability, high availability, disaster recovery, and integration with broader AWS services.

Each architecture is explained with its purpose, components, use cases, and recommended AWS services.

Legend (for visual association)

- ■ Aurora Cluster
- ▣ Replication
- ⊕ Global Deployment
- ▮ IAM/Secrets Manager
- \u{2699} Lambda/Event Processing
- ▤ Applications/Services
- \u{1F5A5} Monitoring (CloudWatch, etc.)

Architecture 1: Highly Available Aurora Cluster (Single Region)

Overview: Baseline Aurora cluster design for production workloads requiring high availability and failover within a single AWS Region.

Diagram Description:

- ■ Aurora DB Cluster
  - o One Writer

- - Two Aurora Replicas (read-only)
- 🖥 Client Applications
  - Connect via Cluster Endpoint (read/write)
  - Connect via Reader Endpoint (scale-out reads)
- VPC with Subnets across 3 AZs
- \u{1F5A5} CloudWatch, 🔒 Secrets Manager, optional RDS Proxy

Use Cases:

- OLTP systems
- Web and mobile apps with consistent uptime needs

Architecture 2: Aurora Global Database (Cross-Region)

Overview: Aurora Global Database replicates data across AWS Regions with sub-second latency.

Diagram Description:

- 🗄 Primary Cluster in Region A
  - One Writer, Multiple Replicas
- 🗄 Secondary Cluster in Region B
  - Read-only replicas
- 🔄 Storage-level async replication (<1s lag)
- Manual failover support for disaster recovery

Use Cases:

- Global SaaS
- Read-optimized global apps
- Cross-Region disaster recovery

Architecture 3: Blue/Green Deployment Workflow

Overview: Enables safe version upgrades and schema changes with minimal risk.

Diagram Description:

- ▨ Blue Environment: Production Aurora Cluster
- ▨ Green Environment: Cloned test Aurora Cluster
- Auto-managed replication before switchover
- RDS endpoint promotion upon cutover

Use Cases:

- CI/CD pipelines
- Version rollouts and rollback scenarios

✦ **Tip**: Use CloudFormation for environment cloning.

Architecture 4: Aurora with RDS Proxy and Lambda

Overview: Event-driven design for serverless compute and scalable DB access.

Diagram Description:

- ▨ Aurora DB Cluster (1 Writer + Readers)
- Amazon RDS Proxy
    - o Connection pooling
    - o IAM authentication
- \u{2699} Lambda Functions
    - o Triggers from API Gateway, SQS, EventBridge

- 🔒 Secrets Manager for credentials

Use Cases:

- Audit/event tracking
- Low-latency APIs
- Mitigating connection overload

Architecture 5: Aurora + Redshift Zero-ETL Integration

Overview: Enables real-time analytics by streaming Aurora data directly to Redshift.

Diagram Description:

- 🗄 Aurora Cluster (source)
- 🗄 Redshift Cluster (target)
- Zero-ETL pipeline using Aurora CDC
- BI tools or ML workloads on Redshift

Use Cases:

- Unified OLTP/OLAP
- Real-time dashboards
- Simplifying ETL pipelines

Architecture 6: Aurora Serverless v2 with Auto Scaling

Overview: Auto-scales Aurora compute using Aurora Capacity Units (ACUs).

Diagram Description:

- ▪ Aurora Serverless v2 Cluster
  - o Dynamic compute scaling
- Multi-AZ VPC deployment
- ▪ Client Applications
  - o Use same endpoints as provisioned clusters
- \u{1F5A5} CloudWatch for autoscaling alerts

Use Cases:

- Variable traffic apps
- Dev/test workloads
- Cost-optimized startups

Architecture 7: Aurora with Multi-Tenant Isolation

Overview: Supports SaaS use cases with tenant isolation models.

Diagram Variants:

1. **Logical Separation**
   - o Shared Aurora cluster
   - o Isolation via schema or RLS (Row-Level Security)
2. **Physical Separation**
   - o One Aurora cluster per tenant
   - o Provisioned via CloudFormation/CDK

Use Cases:

- B2B SaaS platforms
- Fintech with strict compliance
- Tiered SLA models

Architecture 8: Aurora with Cross-VPC and Cross-Account Access

Overview: Enables secure access across AWS accounts or VPCs.

Diagram Description:

- Aurora in VPC-A (Account A)
- App in VPC-B (Account B)
- Connectivity options:
    - VPC Peering (Route tables, SGs)
    - PrivateLink (Interface Endpoint)
- 🔒 IAM and resource policies to enforce security

Use Cases:

- Centralized DB services
- Shared services model
- 3rd-party integrations

Architecture 9: Aurora in Microservices Environment

Overview: Supports microservice-based apps (containerized or Lambda).

Diagram Description:

- ▦ Aurora Cluster
- Multiple ▦ Microservices (Order, Billing, Auth)
- RDS Proxy + Secrets Manager per service
- Optionally use App Mesh or Cloud Map

Use Cases:

- DDD apps on ECS/EKS
- Granular IAM control
- DevOps-first environments

Architecture 10: Aurora + AI/ML Inference (Aurora ML)

Overview: Embeds real-time predictions into queries.

Diagram Description:

- Aurora Cluster with Aurora ML
- Amazon SageMaker Model Endpoint
- SQL calling ml.predict(...)
- App consumes prediction results

Use Cases:

- Fraud scoring
- Smart recommendations
- Predictive search results

Architecture 11: Aurora MySQL Multi-Master

Overview: Active-active write capability in Aurora MySQL.

Diagram Description:

- Aurora Multi-Master Cluster (2 writers)
- Shared storage
- Conflict detection at storage layer

Use Cases:

- Write-heavy apps
- HA APIs with distributed state

⚠ Caveats:

- App must handle retries and idempotency
- Not supported in Aurora PostgreSQL

Architecture 12: CI/CD for Aurora with Infrastructure as Code

Overview: Automates Aurora provisioning and schema management.

Diagram Description:

- CI/CD Pipeline (CodePipeline, GitHub Actions, etc.)
- IaC templates (CDK, Terraform, CFN)
- Aurora Cluster + RDS Proxy
- Schema versioning via Liquibase or Flyway

Use Cases:

- Regulated deployments
- DevOps teams
- Staged production rollouts

Summary of Architectural Patterns

Pattern	Goal	Best For

HA Cluster	Resilience & scaling	Production OLTP apps
Global DB	Cross-region replication	DR, global read access
Blue/Green	Seamless updates	Version upgrades, patching
RDS Proxy + Lambda	Serverless & pooling	API, microservices
Aurora + Redshift	Analytics pipeline	Hybrid OLTP/OLAP
Serverless v2	Elastic scaling	Spiky workloads
Multi-Tenant	SaaS models	Logical or physical isolation
Cross-VPC/Account	Secure shared DB	Platform & partners

Appendices C. Troubleshooting and Error Codes

Amazon Aurora, while designed for high availability and operational resilience, may still encounter issues that require attention from administrators, developers, or support engineers. This appendix provides a detailed guide to **troubleshooting common Aurora issues**, interpreting **error messages and codes**, and applying **systematic approaches** to identify and resolve problems effectively.

Common Troubleshooting Categories

Aurora issues typically fall into several common categories:

1. **Connectivity and Authentication Failures**

2. **Performance Degradation**

3. **Storage and Replication Issues**

4. **Instance Availability or Failover Problems**

5. **Backup and Snapshot Failures**

6. **Query or Transaction Errors**

7. **Cluster Metadata or Configuration Inconsistencies**

8. **Security and Permission Denials**

Each category is addressed below with common symptoms, diagnostic steps, and recommended actions.

---

1. Connectivity and Authentication Failures

Symptoms

- "Unable to connect to database"

- "FATAL: password authentication failed"

- "Access denied for user"

- Application timeout or refusal to establish connection

Diagnostic Steps

- **Check the DB endpoint**:

    - Use the **cluster endpoint** for writers.

    - Use **reader endpoint** for read-only queries.

    - Validate DNS resolution via `nslookup`.

- **Check port access**:

    - Default ports: `3306` (MySQL), `5432` (PostgreSQL)

    - Use `telnet` or `nc` to verify connectivity.

- **Inspect security groups**:

    - Ensure correct inbound rules exist for your app's IP/CIDR.

- **VPC/Subnet configuration**:

    - Ensure the DB instance and client are in routable subnets.

- **IAM and password issues**:

    - For IAM DB authentication, validate token expiration and IAM role permissions.

    - For standard auth, confirm password validity in **Secrets Manager** or manual entry.

Common Fixes

- Restart application or connection pool.

- Update security group or NACL rules.

- Recheck secrets stored in Secrets Manager.

- Verify TLS requirements (e.g., enforce SSL connection settings).

---

2. Performance Degradation

Symptoms

- Slow query execution

- High CPU utilization

- Lock contention or query timeouts

- Frequent failovers under load

Diagnostic Tools

- **Performance Insights**:

  - View DB load (AAS), top SQLs, wait events.

- **CloudWatch Metrics**:

- `CPUUtilization`, `FreeableMemory`, `DatabaseConnections`, `VolumeRead/WriteIOPS`

- **Enhanced Monitoring**:

  - OS-level metrics per instance.

- **pg_stat_activity / INFORMATION_SCHEMA.PROCESSLIST**:

  - Shows currently running queries and locks.

Common Causes

- Inefficient queries (missing indexes, full-table scans)

- Lock contention on frequently updated tables

- Poor memory configuration (e.g., buffer pool size)

- High connection churn

- Overloaded instance class

Recommended Actions

- Tune queries using `EXPLAIN` and Performance Insights.

- Add or adjust indexes.

- Increase instance size or use Aurora Replicas for read offload.

- Use connection pooling (`pgbouncer`, `ProxySQL`).

- Consider RDS Proxy for session management.

---

3. Storage and Replication Issues

Symptoms

- Replica lag increasing

- Replica not catching up

- VolumeWriteIOPS spikes

- "Replica is not in sync with writer"

Diagnostic Tools

- **CloudWatch metrics**:

  - `ReplicaLag`, `VolumeWriteIOPS`, `AuroraReplicaLagMinimum/Maximum`

- **Aurora functions**:

  - `aurora_replica_status()` (PostgreSQL)

- SHOW SLAVE STATUS (MySQL)

- **Logs**:

    - Check error logs for replication errors or storage alerts.

Causes and Fixes

- **High write throughput**:

    - Consider scaling write workload or sharding.

- **Network blips across AZs**:

    - Verify network metrics and retry logic.

- **Read replicas overloaded**:

    - Add replicas or balance reads across nodes.

- **Error 1236 in MySQL replicas**:

    - Caused by invalid binlog position.

    - Use CALL mysql.rds_next_master_log(...) carefully.

---

4. Instance Availability and Failover Problems

Symptoms

- Instance becomes unavailable

- Failover takes longer than expected

- App does not reconnect after failover

Diagnostic Steps

- Check **event logs** in the RDS console.

- Use **CloudTrail** to track DB instance changes.

- Inspect **Aurora failover events**:

    o RDS-EVENT-0043: failover started

    o RDS-EVENT-0044: failover completed

Fixes and Prevention

- Ensure app uses **cluster endpoint**, not instance endpoint.

- Use **exponential backoff** and retries in client logic.

- Add **Aurora Replicas** in separate AZs.

- Ensure DNS caching is configured for low TTL.

---

5. Backup and Snapshot Failures

Symptoms

- Automated snapshot fails

- Manual snapshot creation error

- Point-in-time restore not possible

Error Codes and Meanings

- `SnapshotQuotaExceeded`: Too many snapshots

- `SnapshotNotFound`: Incorrect snapshot name or deletion

- `KMSAccessDenied`: Snapshot encrypted with inaccessible KMS key

Fixes

- Delete old manual snapshots.

- Validate snapshot ARN and encryption key.

- Reconfigure snapshot settings via lifecycle policies.

- Ensure correct KMS key policy for cross-account restores.

6. Query or Transaction Errors

Common Messages

- `ERROR 1205 (HY000): Lock wait timeout exceeded`

- `FATAL: deadlock detected`

- `Query killed due to replication lag`

- `Out of memory while executing query`

Troubleshooting Steps

- Use `SHOW ENGINE INNODB STATUS` (MySQL) or `pg_locks` (PostgreSQL)

- Monitor long-running queries and idle-in-transaction sessions.

- Enable **query logging** or **slow query logs**.

Fixes

- Tune transaction size and frequency.

- Reduce contention on hot rows.

- Limit `autocommit = off` scenarios.

7. Cluster Metadata or Configuration Inconsistencies

Symptoms

- Parameters not taking effect

- Aurora Serverless stuck in scaling loop

- Endpoint not updating properly

Resolution

- Ensure **parameter group** is applied at the cluster or instance level.

- Reboot DB instance after applying static parameters.

- For Serverless:

    - Validate min/max ACUs and scaling policies.

    - Check for VPC/subnet incompatibilities.

---

8. Security and Permission Denials

Symptoms

- `AccessDeniedException` when accessing Secrets Manager

- `rds:ModifyDBInstance` not permitted

- Database user lacks SUPER or `rds_superuser`

Actions

- Use **IAM Access Analyzer** to validate roles.

- Confirm roles assigned to **Lambda functions**, **EC2**, or **ECS** tasks.

- Modify database-level grants using GRANT statements.

- Confirm `rds_iam` plugin is enabled for IAM DB authentication.

Selected Aurora Error Codes and Their Meanings

Error Code	Engine	Description	Action
1236	Aurora MySQL	Binlog replication error (position mismatch)	Use `mysql.rds_next_master_log()`
57014	Aurora PostgreSQL	Query canceled (e.g., due to timeout or conflict)	Review timeout configs or locks

			Check password, IAM policy, or user grants
`1045`	Aurora MySQL	Access denied for user	Check password, IAM policy, or user grants
`42704`	Aurora PostgreSQL	Undefined object (e.g., function, schema)	Validate object name and context
`KMSAccessDenied`	Both	KMS key not accessible	Update KMS policy to include IAM principal
`SnapshotQuotaExceeded`	Both	Manual snapshot limit reached	Delete unused snapshots
`InsufficientDBInstanceCapacity`	Both	No available resources for scaling	Choose different instance class or AZ

Tools for Effective Troubleshooting

- **CloudWatch Logs and Metrics**

- **Aurora Performance Insights**

- **Enhanced Monitoring**

- **Database logs (error, general, slow query)**

- **Amazon RDS Events**

- **AWS Health Dashboard**

- **CloudTrail logs**

- **Aurora-specific SQL functions** (e.g., `aurora_stat`, `aurora_replica_status`)

Summary

Aurora provides a wealth of diagnostic and recovery tools that, when combined with a structured troubleshooting approach, make it possible to quickly resolve most issues without downtime or data loss.

Key takeaways:

- Always start with **event logs and CloudWatch metrics**.

- Use **SQL views and Aurora-specific functions** for deep diagnostics.

- Apply **least privilege IAM practices** and test failover and backup procedures regularly.

- Reference **Aurora engine error codes** for targeted fixes.

Appendices D. Developer Quick Start Guides

This appendix provides a set of **quick start guides** tailored for developers looking to get hands-on with Amazon Aurora. Whether you're building with **Aurora MySQL** or **Aurora PostgreSQL**, using **provisioned instances** or **Serverless**, or integrating with services like **Lambda**, **S3**, or **Redshift**, these guides will help you launch fast and follow best practices from the start.

Getting Started with Aurora MySQL

Step 1: Launch an Aurora MySQL Cluster

You can create an Aurora MySQL DB cluster via the AWS Console, AWS CLI, or AWS SDK.

Using AWS Console:

1. Go to the **Amazon RDS** service.

2. Click **Create Database**.

3. Choose **Amazon Aurora**.

4. Select **MySQL-compatible** and choose a version.

5. Select **Provisioned** or **Serverless v2**.

6. Configure:

- ○ DB cluster identifier

- ○ Master username/password

- ○ Instance size (e.g., `db.t3.medium`)

7. Enable **IAM DB authentication** (optional).

8. Click **Create Database**.

Using AWS CLI:

```
aws rds create-db-cluster \

    --db-cluster-identifier dev-mysql-
cluster \

    --engine aurora-mysql \

    --master-username admin \

    --master-user-password
MySecurePass123 \

    --engine-version
8.0.mysql_aurora.3.04.1 \

    --db-subnet-group-name default \

    --vpc-security-group-ids sg-
xxxxxxx
```

Step 2: Connect from a Local MySQL Client

```
mysql -h your-cluster-
endpoint.rds.amazonaws.com \

    -u admin -p
```

Step 3: Create Tables and Load Sample Data

```
CREATE DATABASE myapp;

USE myapp;


CREATE TABLE users (

    id INT AUTO_INCREMENT PRIMARY KEY,

    name VARCHAR(100),

    email VARCHAR(100) UNIQUE

);
```

Step 4: Enable Performance Insights

To analyze query load:

- Go to **RDS > Databases > [your cluster]**

- Choose **Modify**

- Enable **Performance Insights**

Getting Started with Aurora PostgreSQL

Step 1: Create an Aurora PostgreSQL Cluster

Using AWS Console:

1. Choose **Amazon Aurora**.

2. Select **PostgreSQL-compatible**.

3. Pick version (e.g., PostgreSQL 15.3).

4. Configure cluster as **Provisioned** or **Serverless v2**.

5. Set credentials and instance type.

Using AWS CLI:

```
aws rds create-db-cluster \

    --engine aurora-postgresql \
```

```
    --engine-version 15.3 \

    --db-cluster-identifier dev-pg-
cluster \

    --master-username admin \

    --master-user-password
MySecurePass123 \

    --vpc-security-group-ids sg-
xxxxxxx
```

Step 2: Connect with `psql`

```
psql \

  --host=your-cluster-
endpoint.rds.amazonaws.com \

  --port=5432 \

  --username=admin \

  --dbname=postgres
```

Step 3: Create Sample Schema

```
CREATE DATABASE devdb;

\c devdb


CREATE TABLE events (

  id SERIAL PRIMARY KEY,

  event_name TEXT,

  created_at TIMESTAMPTZ DEFAULT now()

);
```

Step 4: Enable Extensions

```
CREATE EXTENSION IF NOT EXISTS
pg_stat_statements;

CREATE EXTENSION IF NOT EXISTS
pgcrypto;
```

Quick Start: Aurora Serverless v2 with Lambda

Step 1: Launch Aurora Serverless v2 Cluster

- Choose **Serverless v2** during DB creation.

- Ensure it's in the same VPC and subnets as your Lambda function.

- Enable **Data API** if using Aurora PostgreSQL.

Step 2: Create a Lambda Function

```python
import boto3

import json


def lambda_handler(event, context):

    client = boto3.client('rds-data')


    response =
client.execute_statement(

resourceArn='arn:aws:rds:region:acct:cluster:mycluster',

secretArn='arn:aws:secretsmanager:region:acct:secret:mysecret',
```

```
        database='mydb',

        sql='SELECT * FROM users'

    )


    return {

        'statusCode': 200,

        'body':
json.dumps(response['records'])

    }
```

Step 3: Add IAM Permissions

Attach `AmazonRDSDataFullAccess` and `SecretsManagerReadWrite` to your Lambda role.

Quick Start: Integrating Aurora with Amazon S3

Aurora MySQL and PostgreSQL support data export to and import from S3.

Aurora MySQL – Export Table to S3

```
SELECT * INTO OUTFILE S3 's3://my-
bucket/data.csv'

FIELDS TERMINATED BY ',' LINES
TERMINATED BY '\n'

FROM users;
```

Requires setting up an **S3 integration role**
using `aws_iam_role` and configuring
`aurora_load_from_s3_role`.

Aurora PostgreSQL – Import from S3 via `aws_s3` Extension

```
SELECT aws_s3.table_import_from_s3(

    'events',

    '',

    '(FORMAT csv)',

    'my-bucket',

    'events.csv',

    'us-west-2'

);
```

Quick Start: Zero-ETL to Amazon Redshift

Step 1: Enable Zero-ETL

- Aurora must be **MySQL 3.04+** or **PostgreSQL 15.4+**.

- Enable **Zero-ETL integrations** in the cluster settings.

Step 2: Connect Aurora to Redshift

- In the RDS Console, choose **Zero-ETL integrations** > **Create integration**.

- Select Aurora as source and Redshift as target.

- Redshift will receive data changes continuously.

Step 3: Verify in Redshift

```
SELECT * FROM aurora_schema.users;
```

Redshift will auto-create mirrored schemas and tables for real-time analytics.

Quick Start: IAM Authentication for Secure DB Access

Step 1: Enable IAM Auth in Aurora Cluster

- Modify the cluster.

- Under **Database authentication**, enable **IAM database authentication**.

Step 2: Create IAM Policy

```
{

  "Effect": "Allow",

  "Action": "rds-db:connect",

  "Resource": "arn:aws:rds-db:us-west-
2:123456789012:dbuser:db-
XXXXXXX/dbuser"

}
```

Step 3: Connect Using Token

```
aws rds generate-db-auth-token \
```

```
--hostname your-
cluster.rds.amazonaws.com \

--port 3306 \

--region us-west-2 \

--username dbuser
```

Use the generated token as the password in your client.

Helpful CLI Commands for Developers

Task	Command
List DB clusters	`aws rds describe-db-clusters`
Start/stop a cluster	`aws rds start-db-cluster`, `stop-db-cluster`
Modify cluster settings	`aws rds modify-db-cluster`
Generate IAM auth token	`aws rds generate-db-auth-token`
Run query via Data API	`aws rds-data execute-statement`
Export snapshot to S3	`aws rds start-export-task`
Describe backups/snapshots	`aws rds describe-db-cluster-snapshots`

Developer Best Practices

- Use **parameter groups** to control engine settings like `max_connections`, `work_mem`, or `query_cache_size`.

- Enable **slow query logging** and integrate with CloudWatch Logs for performance tuning.

- Use **performance schema** (MySQL) or **pg_stat_statements** (PostgreSQL) for query-level diagnostics.

- Automate DB provisioning via **Terraform, AWS CDK, or CloudFormation**.

- Protect credentials with **AWS Secrets Manager** and rotate them regularly.

Appendices E. Real-World Aurora Case Studies

Understanding how Amazon Aurora is used in real-world scenarios can help organizations visualize how they might implement or optimize Aurora for their own workloads. This appendix provides a collection of real-world case studies across industries and use cases, illustrating the benefits, architectural patterns, challenges, and outcomes of adopting Aurora.

These examples span from high-throughput e-commerce platforms to real-time analytics engines and globally distributed SaaS applications, each showcasing how Aurora's features—such as high availability, scalability, serverless compute, and global database replication—can solve complex operational and business challenges.

Case Study 1: Global SaaS Provider Scaling with Aurora Global Database

Company Profile:

A multi-region SaaS provider offering real-time collaboration tools to enterprise customers across North America, Europe, and Asia.

Challenge:

- Users in different geographies experienced latency when accessing a single-region PostgreSQL database.

- Compliance required data residency and low-latency performance per region.

Aurora Implementation:

- Migrated to **Aurora PostgreSQL with Global Databases**.

- Primary writer in **us-east-1** with read replicas in **eu-west-1** and **ap-southeast-1**.

- Used `aurora_global_db_instance_status()` to monitor replication lag.

Results:

- Reduced average latency by **45%** for EU and APAC users.

- Maintained compliance with data locality laws.

- Achieved RPO < 1 second for disaster recovery and business continuity.

Key Aurora Features Used:

- Aurora Global Database

- Cluster endpoints for regional read scaling

- PostgreSQL-native analytics functions

- IAM database authentication for secure access

Case Study 2: E-commerce Platform Migrates to Aurora MySQL

Company Profile:

A top-50 online retailer with seasonal spikes and high transaction throughput during events like Black Friday and Cyber Monday.

Challenge:

- Legacy MySQL database on EC2 had scalability and failover limitations.

- Downtime during version upgrades was costly.

Aurora Implementation:

- Migrated to **Aurora MySQL** using **Database Migration Service (DMS)**.

- Leveraged **Aurora Replicas** for horizontal read scaling.

- Implemented **Blue/Green Deployments** for zero-downtime upgrades.

Results:

- 3x performance improvement on checkout operations.

- Upgraded minor versions with **zero downtime**.

- Achieved 99.99% availability SLA.

Key Aurora Features Used:

- Aurora MySQL with Multi-AZ setup

- Aurora Replicas for read scaling

- Blue/Green Deployments for safe rollouts

- Performance Insights for query tuning

Case Study 3: FinTech Startup Leveraging Aurora Serverless v2

Company Profile:

A fast-growing financial services startup with unpredictable, burst-heavy workloads.

Challenge:

- Traffic varied widely based on trading hours, requiring elastic scalability.

- Budget constraints made overprovisioning costly.

Aurora Implementation:

- Adopted **Aurora Serverless v2 (PostgreSQL)** for auto-scaling compute.

- Scaled from **2 ACUs to 64 ACUs** during high activity, back down at night.

- Implemented **RDS Proxy** to manage thousands of concurrent Lambda connections.

Results:

- Cut database compute costs by **40%** compared to provisioned capacity.

- Reduced cold-start issues by using **warm ACU pools**.

- Supported 10x user growth without scaling bottlenecks.

Key Aurora Features Used:

- Aurora Serverless v2

- RDS Proxy for connection pooling

- IAM-based authentication and Secrets Manager

- Fine-grained scaling with sub-second latency

Case Study 4: AI/ML Platform Integrating Aurora with SageMaker

Company Profile:

A data science platform offering automated ML pipelines for customers in healthcare and retail.

Challenge:

- Needed real-time inference and historical data queries in a unified system.

- Data engineers required SQL-based access to features used in ML models.

Aurora Implementation:

- Built feature store on **Aurora PostgreSQL** with materialized views and JSONB fields.

- Integrated with **Amazon SageMaker** for model training and inference.

- Used **Aurora ML** for in-database inference.

Results:

- Reduced feature engineering latency from 20 minutes to 2 minutes.

- Enabled real-time inference from Aurora via SageMaker endpoints.

- Improved model accuracy by 15% using historical feature enrichment.

Key Aurora Features Used:

- Aurora PostgreSQL with Aurora ML integration

- In-database JSON and GIS support

- Materialized views for pre-aggregated features

- PostgreSQL stored procedures for feature transformations

Case Study 5: Government Agency with Secure, Audited Deployment

Organization:

A national government agency delivering digital public services under strict security compliance (FedRAMP High, HIPAA).

Challenge:

- Required encrypted, audited, multi-zone deployment for mission-critical workloads.

- Needed to maintain long-term query logs and compliance trails.

Aurora Implementation:

- Deployed **Aurora PostgreSQL** in a **Multi-AZ** configuration.

- Enabled **Performance Insights with extended retention (24 months)**.

- Logged all API activity with **CloudTrail**, stored in encrypted S3.

- Enabled **pgAudit** to track access to sensitive tables.

Results:

- Met full FedRAMP compliance and passed annual audits.

- Reduced administrative overhead by 60% using Aurora's managed backups and upgrades.

- Enabled near-real-time monitoring of workload anomalies using CloudWatch and Performance Insights.

Key Aurora Features Used:

- Performance Insights with long-term retention

- Aurora Multi-AZ deployment

- Integration with CloudTrail, AWS KMS, and IAM

- PostgreSQL extensions for security and auditing (e.g., pgAudit, SSL)

Case Study 6: Media Company Migrating from Oracle to Aurora PostgreSQL

Company Profile:

A global media and streaming company seeking to modernize its data stack and reduce licensing costs.

Challenge:

- High TCO with Oracle databases; limited flexibility for CI/CD and microservices integration.

- Needed feature parity with PL/SQL and advanced indexing.

Aurora Implementation:

- Used **Aurora PostgreSQL** with compatibility extensions for Oracle-style stored procedures.

- Migrated using **AWS Schema Conversion Tool (SCT)** and **DMS**.

- Designed microservices to access data via **Aurora custom endpoints**.

Results:

- Reduced database licensing costs by **$1.2M/year**.

- Improved development velocity through PostgreSQL JSON and CTE support.

- Integrated with streaming analytics via **AWS Glue and Amazon Redshift**.

Key Aurora Features Used:

- Aurora PostgreSQL with PL/pgSQL

- AWS SCT + DMS for migration

- Custom endpoints for multi-tenant routing

- JSONB for semi-structured data

Summary: Key Themes Across Case Studies

Theme	Aurora Feature Highlighted
Global scale & compliance	Aurora Global Database, Multi-AZ, IAM auth, KMS encryption

Cost efficiency	Aurora Serverless v2, Graviton, RDS Proxy
Performance & observability	Performance Insights, CloudWatch, pg_stat_statements
Modern data architectures	Aurora ML, JSONB, materialized views, RDS Data API
Security & auditability	pgAudit, CloudTrail, IAM, KMS
Migration & modernization	AWS SCT, DMS, PostgreSQL compatibility

Appendices G. Amazon Aurora Cheat Sheet: Quick Reference Guide for Architects and Developers

✦ Aurora Cluster Types

Cluster Type	Description	Ideal Use Case
Single-Writer Cluster	One writer, multiple read replicas in a single Region	OLTP systems, web/mobile backends
Aurora Global Database	Primary writer in Region A, replicas in Region B+	Global apps, DR, low-latency reads
Aurora Serverless v2	Auto-scales compute with ACUs	Variable workloads, dev/test, cost-saving
Multi-Master (MySQL Only)	Multiple active writers with conflict resolution	Write-heavy, active-active HA systems

⚖ Key Metrics to Monitor (CloudWatch)

- **CPUUtilization**: Overall CPU usage per instance
- **AuroraReplicaLag**: Replication lag in seconds
- **DatabaseConnections**: Active DB sessions
- **FreeableMemory**: Memory left on the instance
- **Deadlocks**: Count of deadlocks over time

📄 RPO / RTO Quick Reference

Scenario	RPO	RTO

Same-Region Failover	~0 seconds	< 30 seconds
Global DB Cross-Region DR	~1 second	~1–2 minutes
Manual Restore from Snapshot	As old as backup	Several minutes

💻 Common CLI Commands (AWS CLI)

```
# Create a new Aurora cluster
aws rds create-db-cluster \
  --db-cluster-identifier my-cluster \
  --engine aurora-mysql \
  --master-username admin \
  --master-user-password secret123

# Failover to another instance
aws rds failover-db-cluster \
  --db-cluster-identifier my-cluster

# Modify serverless scaling config
aws rds modify-db-cluster \
  --db-cluster-identifier my-cluster \
  --serverless-v2-scaling-configuration
MinCapacity=2,MaxCapacity=16
```

✦ Aurora Best Practices

- Enable **Backtrack** for MySQL to undo user errors quickly.
- Use **RDS Proxy** for serverless and high-connection apps.
- Separate **read/write traffic** via reader and writer endpoints.

- Use **Performance Insights** to analyze slow queries.
- Apply **parameter groups** for tuning (e.g., `max_connections`, `innodb_buffer_pool_size`).
- Schedule **minor version upgrades** during low-traffic windows.

🛠 Common Use Cases

- **Transactional Apps**: eCommerce, finance, gaming
- **Global SaaS**: Aurora Global DB + CI/CD
- **Event-driven Systems**: Aurora + Lambda + EventBridge
- **Analytics**: Aurora + Redshift Zero-ETL
- **Multi-Tenant SaaS**: Logical or physical DB separation

🌐 Connection Strings

PostgreSQL

```
jdbc:postgresql://<cluster-endpoint>:5432/mydb
```

MySQL

```
jdbc:mysql://<cluster-endpoint>:3306/mydb
```

Use **Secrets Manager** to rotate credentials securely.

Appendices E: Useful Links and Further Reading

Below is a curated list of open-access resources to help you deepen your understanding of Amazon Aurora and related AWS technologies. These links are intended for further reading, architecture inspiration, troubleshooting, and keeping up-to-date with new features.

✦ Official AWS Documentation

- **Aurora MySQL:**
  https://docs.aws.amazon.com/AmazonRDS/latest/AuroraUserGuide/AuroraMySQL.html
- **Aurora PostgreSQL:**
  https://docs.aws.amazon.com/AmazonRDS/latest/AuroraUserGuide/AuroraPostgreSQL.html
- **Aurora Global Database:**
  https://docs.aws.amazon.com/AmazonRDS/latest/AuroraUserGuide/aurora-global-database.html
- **Aurora Serverless v2:**
  https://docs.aws.amazon.com/AmazonRDS/latest/AuroraUserGuide/aurora-serverless-v2.html
- **RDS Proxy:**
  https://docs.aws.amazon.com/AmazonRDS/latest/UserGuide/rds-proxy.html

---

▦ Architecture & Best Practices

- **Aurora Performance Insights:**
  https://docs.aws.amazon.com/AmazonRDS/latest/AuroraUserGuide/USER_PerfInsights.html

- **Aurora Multi-Master:**
  https://docs.aws.amazon.com/AmazonRDS/latest/AuroraUserGuide/aurora-multi-master.html
- **Aurora Backtrack:**
  https://docs.aws.amazon.com/AmazonRDS/latest/AuroraUserGuide/aurora-mysql-backtrack.html
- **Aurora with Redshift Zero-ETL:**
  https://docs.aws.amazon.com/redshift/latest/dg/aurora-zero-etl.html
- **Database Monitoring:**
  https://docs.aws.amazon.com/AmazonCloudWatch/latest/monitoring/rds-metricscollected.html

---

⚖ Security & IAM

- **IAM for RDS/Aurora:**
  https://docs.aws.amazon.com/AmazonRDS/latest/UserGuide/UsingWithRDS.IAM.html
- **Secrets Manager:**
  https://docs.aws.amazon.com/secretsmanager/latest/userguide/intro.html
- **Aurora Encryption at Rest:**
  https://docs.aws.amazon.com/AmazonRDS/latest/AuroraUserGuide/Overview.Encryption.html

---

✦ Developer Resources

- **AWS CLI for RDS:**
  https://docs.aws.amazon.com/cli/latest/reference/rds/index.html
- **Aurora Quick Start Templates:**
  https://aws.amazon.com/quickstart/architecture/aurora/

- **Aurora MySQL vs. PostgreSQL Comparison:**
  https://docs.aws.amazon.com/AmazonRDS/latest/AuroraUserGuide/CHAP_AuroraOverview.html

---

🧑‍💼 Blogs & Learning Paths

- **AWS Database Blog:**
  https://aws.amazon.com/blogs/database/
- **AWS Training (Databases):**
  https://www.aws.training/Details/Curriculum?id=20685
- **AWS re:Invent Videos:**
  https://www.youtube.com/c/AWSEvents/playlists